THE REPUBLIC IN PERIL: 1812

Roger H. Brown has taught at Dartmouth College and Harvard University and is now Professor of History at The American University. He is also the author of *The Struggle for the Indian Stream Territory*.

THE REPUBLIC
IN PERIL: 1812

ROGER H. BROWN

With a new Appendix

W · W · NORTON & COMPANY

New York · London

TO FREDERICK MERK

Books That Live
The Norton imprint on a book means that in the publisher's
estimation it is a book not for a single season but for the years.
W. W. Norton & Company, Inc.

W. W. Norton & Company, Inc., 500 Fifth Avenue, New York, N.Y. 10110
W. W. Norton & Company Ltd., 37 Great Russell Street, London WC1B 3NU

ISBN 0-393-00578-X

PRINTED IN THE UNITED STATES OF AMERICA

4567890

PREFACE

This book shows for the first time how republicanism and concern for the republican "experiment" led to the American decision to declare war on Great Britain in 1812. It does not attempt to be a full account of the diplomatic controversy that led to war nor of the political and parliamentary maneuvering that produced the final war declaration. Others have dealt extensively with the diplomatic history of the war, and it would require a broader task than I have set myself to do justice to the full congressional story. I have been primarily interested in the motives of members of the American Executive and Congress who stood for and against war.

It became apparent as this book neared completion that the preoccupation with republicanism that existed in 1812 was no isolated occurrence in the nation's early history. Cecelia Kenyon in a recent article has freshly suggested the importance of republicanism in the American Revolution, and other forthcoming studies promise further exploration of this important theme.* It is my belief that these studies will reinforce each other and cumulatively form a coherent pattern of new interpretation in the history of the Revolutionary and early national periods.

I have benefited greatly from the generous aid and assistance of others in the preparation of this book. A Social Science Research Council Dissertation Completion Fellowship helped to make possible a year without interruption at a crucial stage. The

* Cecelia Kenyon, "Republicanism and Radicalism in the American Revolution: an Old Fashioned Interpretation," *William and Mary Quarterly*, XIX (1962), 153–62. An example of new work in this area is Bernard Bailyn's introduction to *Pamphlets of the American Revolution, 1750–1776* to be published in the John Harvard Library series in 1964 by Harvard University Press.

Faculty Committee on Research, Dartmouth College, authorized funds for typing which Mrs. Jennie K. Wells performed with notable skill. The able editorial work of Miss Julie Gordon of the Columbia University Press aided greatly in the final revision of the manuscript. Alan Thompson of the Manuscript Division, Library of Congress, gave more generously of his time and labor than duty required. I have profited much from discussion with Louis Morton and Bernard Bailyn. Richard Buel, Jr., and Paul Goodman kindly permitted me to read unpublished versions of their own work in progress. The penetrating and constructive criticism of George Juergens, F. David Roberts, Eric L. McKitrick, and Edward R. Brown has greatly helped to strengthen this book. The wide knowledge and perceptive criticism of Harry N. Scheiber and Bradford Perkins has led to many important improvements. I have been fortunate indeed to have the aid and interest of such valued friends and colleagues.

I must pay special tribute to Frederick Merk of Harvard University for criticism and suggestions and for the inspiration of his encouragement and example. Others who have been his students will understand the nature of this debt.

The wives of scholars help them in many ways. Mine at various times aided in the task of research and composition. More important has been the sustaining influence of her belief in high standards in the teaching and writing of history.

ROGER H. BROWN

August, 1963
Lyme, New Hampshire

CONTENTS

THE REPUBLIC IN PERIL: 1812

(I)

WILL REPUBLICANISM
PREVAIL?

Ever since the seventeenth century when the Puritans reached
New England there have been Americans who have felt a strong
sense of world mission. "For wee must Consider that wee shall be
as a Citty upon a Hill. The eies of all people are uppon us,"
John Winthrop avowed as the ship *Arbella* approached the
shores of the future Bible commonwealth. A small but vocif-
erous group of continental expansionists in the mid-1840s appealed to Americans to extend their freedom over the hemi-
sphere for the benefit of neighboring peoples—it was their "manifest destiny." Abraham Lincoln, in the midst of the great crisis
of the Civil War, summoned countrymen at the Gettysburg bat-
tlefield to preserve democracy for the world, to resolve "that government of the people, by the people, for the people, shall not
perish from the earth." John F. Kennedy on assuming the presidency called upon the nation to bear the heavy burden of "a long
twilight struggle, year in and year out . . . against the common enemies of man: tyranny, poverty, disease and war itself." [1]
The awareness of a special American destiny to improve man's
condition is a fundamental part of the national heritage.

Never was a generation more deeply conscious of mission than
the men who won independence from Great Britain and founded
the American nation. Much more than a simple severance of
colonial bonds, a breaking of the imperial tie, in American eyes
the Revolution signified the beginning of a new political era,
the opening of an age that would exhibit to the world the tran-
scendent blessings of a republican form of government. The war

that won national independence seemed to usher in a new epoch, a *novus ordo saeclorum*, in the form of government it established at home and in its promise of a world republicanized. It was the rejection of all rule by an hereditary monarch and the adoption of government by regularly elected and accountable representatives that gave the Revolution its "revolutionary" quality. Americans often underestimated, if they perceived at all, the contemporary development of representative institutions within the hereditary governments of Great Britain and Europe. They considered their new form of government to be entirely unique and felt that it was their national purpose to spread the gospel of republicanism and redeem mankind.

Contemporaries defined republicanism as government by representatives responsible to the people. George Washington stated that a republican government was one "in which all power is derived from, and at stated periods, reverts to" the people. James Madison wrote that it was "a government which derives its powers directly or indirectly from the great body of the people, and is administered by persons holding their offices during pleasure, for a limited period, or during good behavior." Men thought of republican government as providing "equal liberty" to the citizen, as affording personal autonomy to the individual, an independence from superior political authority. Under hereditary monarchy or aristocracy the majority of citizens must obey, with no recourse to the ballot box, the will of the one or the few, a status that republicans considered dependent and unfree.[2]

The Revolutionary generation remained acutely conscious of the isolation of their enterprise. Not since Rome, so men believed, had there been in the world a successful and permanent republic of major size. They welcomed enthusiastically the revolutionary movement that spread through Europe during the 1780s and 1790s, leaving in its wake republics in France, the Low Countries, Switzerland, and Italy. But the downfall of the French republic and the ensuing subjugation of all others to the yoke of Napoleon Bonaparte left the United States the only remaining republic by the turn of the century. Men wondered whether there was some fatal weakness inherent in the republican form of government that accounted for its rare and fleeting occurrence. The failure of the republics of ancient and modern times to sustain themselves gave little assurance.

Indeed, the very quality that distinguished republican government from hereditary monarchy and aristocracy might well prove a crucial defect. Proponents of monarchy and aristocracy maintained that hereditary forms were more compatible with good government than representative forms. The majority of men, according to these advocates, were selfish, grasping, and ambitious—oblivious to the well-being and happiness of fellow citizens and insensitive to calls of national honor and independence. Hereditary governments had removed rulers from the pressures of an electorate and made it their own interest to promote good government; republics, on the other hand, were vulnerable to every selfish desire and whim that could paralyze responsible action or injure a minority interest. America was a broad land of diverse and often sharply conflicting economic, religious, class, and ethnic groups. Would her elected repre sentatives govern effectively according to criteria of good government, or would they bow to the selfish pressures of special interests? Did the American people possess the fixity of purpose and firmness of will to undertake and complete costly and arduous ventures in behalf of good government? Even as late as the 1830s the French traveler and political scientist Alexis de Tocqueville made the point: "It is difficult to say what degree of effort a democratic government may be capable of making on the occurrence of a national crisis. No great democratic republic has hitherto existed in the world." American advocates of republicanism hoped their countrymen possessed the necessary good sense and virtue. Theirs was an uncertain trust.[3]

The Revolutionary generation understood the importance of showing conclusively that republicanism could lead to greater human well-being and happiness than hereditary monarchy or aristocracy. They had to prove that republican government not only assured liberty but could be consistent with security of life and property and with protection of national honor and independence—in short, that it fulfilled all the purposes that any government must fulfill. If the governments of the American Confederation failed in these essential tasks, warned James Madison, a leading proponent of the republican faith, in 1783, "the great cause which we have engaged to vindicate, will be dishonored and betrayed; the last and fairest experiment in favor of the rights of human nature will be turned against them." Should republicanism prove to be incompatible with good government, it could not hope to win converts in lands still ruled by kings, princes, and aristocrats, nor could it retain the loyalty of citizens in the one country where it had already been established. To his fellow countrymen Madison's warning defined the task ahead. The future of America and of mankind depended on the success of the American project. Republicanism must prove itself by action and deeds as well as words. Therefore, they called it an experiment.[4]

Concern for the republican experiment directed the efforts of men who drafted the American Constitution at Philadelphia during the summer of 1787. State legislatures in the years since the Peace of 1783 had spurned congressional requests for financial assistance towards common national expenses. They had passed laws impeding the collection of debts by foreign creditors, imposed tariffs on commerce en route to other states, squabbled over rival land claims, undercut retaliatory commercial legislation aimed at Great Britain, and authorized inflationary amounts of paper money. In the fall of 1786 Shays's Rebellion, an agrarian protest movement in central and western Massachusetts, raised the specter of mob violence and confiscation and dramatized the feebleness of state and national authorities.[5] Here for all to see was the selfishness and small-mindedness that had traditionally been associated with republicanism and presumably accounted for its rare and fleeting appearance in history. In light of these new evidences of an historic tendency it was natural for men to anticipate that Americans might abandon their present republican system for presumably more efficient forms. Thus George

Washington in the summer of 1786 could write that prominent citizens had begun to discuss "a monarchical form of Government without horror," and Madison wrote Thomas Jefferson in March, 1787, that the evils of the Confederation had "tainted the faith of the most orthodox republicans." [6]

By 1787 a few men had indeed lost confidence in the practicality of a large American republic. William Bingham of Pennsylvania openly declared to Congress early that year that it would be advisable to divide "into several distinct confederacies," the country's "great extent & various interests, being incompatible with a single Government." Newspaper essays recommended division of the Union into three or four separate republics in which social and economic uniformity would make possible effective and satisfactory rule. Benjamin Tupper, a Massachusetts legislator who pressed for the hereditary form in 1787, advocated monarchy: "I cannot give up the Idea that Monarchy in our present situation is become absolutely necessary to save the States from sinking into the lowest abbiss of Misery." Even John Adams avowed in 1789, in a passing mood of pessimism, that "hereditary monarchy or aristocracy" were the "only institutions that can possibly preserve the laws and liberties of the people," and held that "America must resort to them as an asylum against discord, seditions and civil war, and that at no very distant period of time." But the real point was whether disillusion would spread through the population. John Marshall of Virginia, the future great chief justice and one not given to ill-considered judgments, deplored in January, 1787, how recent events had "cast a deep shade over that bright prospect which the revolution in America and the establishment of our free Governments had opened to the votaries of liberty throughout the globe" and warned that "we may live to see another revolution." Washington foresaw on the eve of the Convention that if reform failed to correct present evils a "conviction of the necessity of a change [to monarchy] will be dissiminated among all classes of the People." [7]

It was understandable, therefore, that a fortnight before the Constitutional Convention assembled in 1787 James Madison should have written: "The nearer the crisis approaches, the more I tremble for the issue." The seriousness of the moment was not lost on the delegates who shortly thereafter gathered at Philadelphia. They well understood the significance of the gathering and the implications of their task. Edmund Randolph of Virginia could thus avow that "the salvation of the Republic was at stake." Gouverneur Morris of Pennsylvania spoke for many when he declared before the assembly: "He came here as a Representative of America; he flattered himself he came here in some degree as a Representative of the whole human race; for the whole human race will be affected by the proceedings of this Convention." Elbridge Gerry of Massachusetts agreed that something must be done "or we shall disappoint not only America but the whole world." James Madison observed that the work of the Convention could very well "decide forever the fate of republican government." [8]

After adoption of the Constitution concern over the outcome of the republican experiment continued to guide American action. There was first of all the famous economic program of Alexander Hamilton. Hamilton at the Philadelphia Convention had "acknowledged himself not to think favorably of republican government," praised the British government of King, Lords, and Commons as "the best in the world," and "doubted much whether anything short of it would do in America." But no one campaigned more vigorously or tirelessly for the plan finally adopted, or worked more conscientiously to make the new system a success.[9] All his great early recommendations—funding and assumption of the Revolutionary War debt, the national bank, the common protective tariff, government subsidies to manufacturing, and the excise—pointed towards this goal. The new government must have what the Confederation lacked— the authority and power that comes from an ample purse. Hence the provisions to restore credit, provide an available fund of capital, and assure a steady revenue. He intended also to win the support of all Americans, rich and poor alike. Funding, assumption, and investment opportunities in the national bank and manufacturing enterprises would interest men of capital in the government. Appreciated public securities and available bank credit would augment capital and stimulate all forms of economic activity—trade, manufacturing, and agriculture—to the benefit of the working classes. His zeal for energetic counter-measures in the Whiskey and Fries Rebellions of 1794 and 1799 reveal a man who wanted the government to prove it could put down mob disorders. "The consideration of expense is of no moment compared with the advantages of energy," he advised in 1799.

Even so, to the very end, he remained doubtful as to the efficacy of republicanism. He professed attachment to "the republican theory" and wished "above all things to see the equality of political rights, exclusive of all hereditary distinction, firmly established by a practical demonstration of its being consistent with the order and happiness of society." Yet he was "far from being without doubts," deemed the success of republicanism "as yet a problem," and considered it "yet to be determined by experience whether [republicanism] be consistent with that stability and order in government which are essential to public strength and private security and happiness." The Jeffersonians charged him with plotting a restoration of monarchy. These charges he heatedly denied, and there is no reason to doubt his denials. Indeed, his bitter diatribes against the emergent Republican "faction" stemmed to a very great degree from conviction that irresponsible obstructionism would paralyze government operations and undermine its still doubtful authority. We may take as sincere his own political epitaph written in 1802: "Perhaps no man in the United States has sacrificed or done more for the present Constitution than myself; and contrary to all my anticipations of its fate, as you know from the very beginning, I am still laboring to prop the frail and worthless fabric." [10]

Concern for republicanism in the 1790s also furnished motivation for the formation of political parties. Hamilton's efforts to bolster the new constitutional structure provoked sharp reaction, and opponents gradually came to believe that the Secretary of the Treasury and his congressional supporters plotted a restoration of monarchy. Men who did not fully grasp Hamilton's purposes and perhaps recalled his statements at the Constitutional Convention believed that his program was aimed at remaking the American government on the British model. As Thomas Jefferson put it: Hamilton and his party sought to consolidate all power in the central government, establish means of controlling the legislature through executive corruption, and thus "prepare the way for a change from the present republican form of government to that of a monarchy, of which the English Constitution is to be the model." [11] Private correspondence attests to the sincerity of such expressions, for men do not consistently write political cant to family, friends, associates, and European correspondents.[12] To arouse public opinion against the "Anglican monarchical aristocratical party," to retire its members from public office, and to ensure future control of the government by loyal republicans, the organization of the Republican party was begun.[13]

The process of party formation, as Joseph Charles, Noble Cunningham, and William Chambers have made clear, was a gradual and complex one. But the chief impulse for organization came from a corrosive mutual distrust that developed out of controversy over domestic and foreign policy. Thus Hamilton and Jefferson, in differing over measures calculated to turn the newly established government into a viable, going concern, lost all confidence in each other's devotion to the welfare of the Republic. Hamilton saw in Jefferson the ambition, malice, and irresponsibility of the typical demagogue. Jefferson, on the other hand, perceived his great rival as deeply involved in conspiratorial efforts to restore monarchy to republican America. Scores of other members of the government became alienated in some such fashion from colleagues. No doubt personal ties, organizational initiative and skill, legacies of old political feuds, and reluctant commitment to divergent positions pulled men into rival camps. But the conflict between Republicans and Federalists is most clearly understood if, as Joseph Charles has emphasized, one regards it primarily as a conflict "between two shifting groups of men who, differing upon practical problems as they arose, came to suspect the views and purposes of those in the opposite camp and to regard their own pursuit of power and their determination to defeat their opponents as the supreme consideration." [14]

The socioeconomic bases of the Federalist-Republican division is still the subject of investigation. Recent studies suggest that the most successful and prominent mercantile, professional, farming, and landlord groups in commercial and tenanted areas of the country, heavily concentrated in the northeast but present also in the south, made up the Federalist leadership. The Republican party, on the other hand, drew its strength from rising business, professional, and farming groups in commercial areas, from tenant farmers, and from large, middling, and small planters and farmers in the south and west. To a considerable extent these men, like Jefferson, became alarmed over the Hamiltonian financial and manufacturing policies and viewed them as intended to subvert the Republic. Federalists, conversely, when charged with plotting to destroy liberty and the state, reacted with comparable suspicion and presumed their opponents to be unprincipled demagogues—driven by class hatred, sectional rivalry, personal jealousy, and cynical ambition.[15]

Republicans and Federalists did not lightly undertake party organization. Deeply mistrustful of parties, they were loath to encourage the very phenomena whose selfish and even treasonable obstructionism and plotting had proved the bane of other republics. Parties were dangerous, indeed immoral, that is, unless the threat was so great as absolutely to require organized countermeasures. So Jefferson told a Virginia Republican leader in 1796:

Were parties here divided merely by a greediness for office, as in England, to take a part with either would be unworthy of a reasonable or moral man, but where the principle of difference is as substantial and as strongly pronounced as between the republicans & the Monocrats of our country, I hold it as honorable to take a firm & decided part, and as immoral to pursue a middle line, as between the parties of Honest men, & Rogues, into which every country is divided.

Suspicion of this kind helps us to understand why members of Congress, many of them former comrades in the common cause of the American Revolution, by the mid-1790s would not speak to each other and even crossed a street to avoid meeting. It explains the bitterness of party contests in a Congress where, in the words of one observer, men were "as much divided and the parties in it as much embittered against each other as it is possible to conceive." They explain, as we shall see, the rigid party-line voting that persisted throughout the Federalist and Jeffersonian eras.[16]

Republicanism guided initial Jeffersonian policies after the Republican victory in the election of 1800. Never very far from Jefferson's mind at any time was the need to protect the Republic against destruction by its enemies. He gave full backing to plans to wipe out the national debt, that source of corruption and influence that Hamilton had so skillfully used to advance his "subversive" plans. His administration reduced the army and assigned it to posts and garrisons throughout the country; no standing force must ever again threaten the state as during the French invasion scare of 1798–99. A purge of presumed monarchists in public office got under way. Hamiltonians, Essex men, and Revolutionary Tories—Federalists who hid "under the mask of federalism hearts devoted to monarchy"—must be removed, the President declared. "The safety of the government absolutely required that its direction in its higher departments should be taken into friendly hands." [17]

It is true that following the election Jefferson had written optimistically to the famous scientist Joseph Priestley that the "order & good sense" displayed by the people in their recent recovery from delusion "augurs well for the duration of our Republic," and that he was "much better satisfied now of it's stability" than he had been previously. It is true that during his presidency he predicted that the whole mass of Federalists, except royalist leaders, would eventually join their fellow citizens, that the south was solidly Republican and the north was fast becoming so, and that the monarchists could never succeed in their effort to win public support.[18] Yet caution tempered optimism. He warned Governor Hall of Georgia against the possibility of the resurgence of the Federalist party. The Federalist leaders say "that man can not be trusted with his own government. We must do no act which shall replace them in the direction of the experiment." He asked the Secretary of the Treasury, Albert Gallatin, whether the directors and stockholders of state banking corporations could be won to the Republican party by shrewd distribution of federal funds among those banks exhibiting loyalty. "It is material to the safety of Republicanism to detach the mercantile interest from its enemies and incorporate them into the body of its friends." Perhaps it would be well to prosecute a few of the most slanderous Federalist newspapers in state courts, he suggested to Governor Thomas McKean of Pennsylvania. "Not a general prosecution, for that would look like persecution: but a selected one." It had been quite all right for Republican papers to denounce Federalism—they told truths. But Federalist lies must not continue to mislead citizens. The Bank of the United States, in Jefferson's eyes a Federalist stronghold, needed curbing. We should limit the power of this "hostile" institution he advised his Secretary of the Treasury in 1803. Suppose "a series of untoward events should occur, sufficient to bring into doubt the competency of a republican government to meet a crisis of great danger, or to unhinge the confidence of the people in the public functionaries." Could not the Bank, "penetrating by it's branches every part of the Union, acting by command & in phalanx," intervene at a critical moment and "upset the government? . . . Now, while we are strong, it is the greatest duty we owe to the safety of our Constitution, to bring the powerful enemy to a perfect subordination under it's authorities." [19]

Republicanism even influenced the Jeffersonian response to British and French action against American commerce. The truce of 1801 and the subsequent Peace of Amiens had brought to a temporary halt the long struggle between the two great European antagonists, Great Britain and France. In May, 1803, the powers resumed the conflict, and the Jefferson administration found itself facing renewed seizure of American ships and impressment of sailors on the high seas. It resolved to contest these seizures through diplomatic protest and commercial restrictions. Certainly both Jefferson and Secretary of State James Madison genuinely believed seizure and impressment to be in violation of fundamental national and moral principles. When the British and French governments prohibited vessels from trading with countries of their choice and seized sailors from American vessels, they infringed national independence, for the control of a nation's commerce and sailors on the high seas seemed an essential attribute of sovereignty. Impressment meant arbitrary deprivation of a man's liberty without a fair trial. The economic consequences of seizures were also too serious to ignore. A single condemned vessel and cargo might cost its owner as much as $60,000, and even if not condemned by admiralty courts, the delays, inconveniences, and court expenses were burdensome. Furthermore, both Virginians believed it their constitutional responsibility to protect maritime commerce. As Jefferson put it: "[T]he constitution permitting it's citizens to follow agriculture, commerce, navigation & every other lawful pursuit all these rights are equally under the protection of the nation whenever & wheresoever violated." [20]

Most important, to have abandoned commerce would have injured the republican cause, would have invited violent criticism of the Republican administration and the government. This point becomes evident in private correspondence among Republican leaders. Elbridge Gerry, a leader of the party in Massachusetts and future governor and vice-president, advised Secretary of State Madison early in 1806 that firm and decisive measures were needed to protect commerce. Already delay had produced "chagrin, on the part of friends to Government, & sneers from the disaffected." Should Congress fail to act decisively, he wrote again, "in that case, I fear, that the Government & nation at

home & abroad will fall into disrepute." The Virginia leader
James Monroe, on diplomatic service in London in 1806, delivered a similar warning. He had just returned to England from
Madrid, he wrote the President, where he had been unsuccessful
in negotiations with Spain over commercial spoiliations claims
and a boundary treaty setting the limits of Louisiana. Learning
of a rash of recent seizures of vessels in the reexport trade he had
entered a strong protest with the British government—it had
been ignored. His letter was, as he said, "not only private but
in confidence only to you and Mr. Madison." We must apply "a
suitable pressure" that is both "unequivocal & decisive" on Britain or Spain. All Europe doubted our firmness, and if no decisive
measure were taken, he would not be surprised "to see them all
unite at the end of this war in a system agnst us, carried to the
greatest extent." But if we show firmness "we may succeed in
what is right with any of them. . . . I know the course is
hasardous, but hasard is on both sides, & in all doubtful cases a
bold and manly council ought to be preferr'd. It rallies the nation round us, keeps up its spirit, & proves at home and abroad
that republicanism is not incompatible with decision." Should we
not take firm action, he warned, "the effect will be felt on the
principles of our govt. as well as on the character of those who
administer it." [21]

President Jefferson shared these sentiments. In February, 1806,
he explained the decision to contest British restrictions on the
American reexport trade from the West Indies to the Continent.
Submission to restrictions and seizure would feed foreign contempt for the American government and bring on aggression
everywhere. American economic pressure against Great Britain
would instill the proper respect. "The love of peace which we
sincerely feel & profess, has begun to produce an opinion in
Europe that our government is entirely in Quaker principles, &
will turn the left cheek when the right has been smitten. [T]his
opinion must be corrected when just occasion arises, or we shall
become the plunder of all nations."

Just three years before, the President had warned of "untoward events . . . sufficient to bring into doubt the competency of a republican government to meet a crisis of great danger, or to unhinge the confidence of the people in the public functionaries." Widespread seizure of American ships would have required that America fight, or would have shaken national confidence in both government and party. The President believed commercial restrictions would make it unnecessary to choose between these grim alternatives. He was more explicit in June, 1808, during the embargo. This measure was passed by Congress in December, 1807, and operated both to protect American vessels and sailors from seizure and to bring pressure on the belligerents for concessions. The Federalist party had bitterly opposed the measure. Jefferson's interpretation of Federalist motivation shows how he linked republicanism with the protection of American commerce. The "federalist monarchists," he wrote in 1808, "disapprove of the republican principles & features of our constitution and would I believe welcome any public calamity (war with England excepted) which might lessen the confidence of our country in those principles & forms." Seeking to discredit republicanism, they now pressed for repeal of the embargo, urged Great Britain to stand firm, and assured her that the United States must soon give way. "[But] we can never remove that, & let our vessels go out & be taken under those orders without making reprisal," he affirmed. Widespread unresisted seizure of American vessels would have been the very confidence-shattering calamity which Jefferson so anxiously desired to avoid.[22]

Other Republicans agreed that in order to disgrace the government and the party the Federalist opposition intended to force American submission to British maritime power. Ezekiel Bacon, a Massachusetts congressman, in 1808 declared: "I do most sincerely believe that it is the darling object of a Class of Politicians whose roots are planted in & about Boston, to see the present administration & Govt of this Country *humbled* before that of G. Britain." Elbridge Gerry in the same year denounced the Federalist leaders who, as he said, sought to unite the northeast "against the federal government, to represent it as despotic, to compel it to retrace it's steps, and thus to disgrace, to destroy the confidence of the people in, and to overthrow it." Joseph Varnum, the Speaker of the House of Representatives, in 1810 believed that the Federalist game was to win British aid and support for their subversive plans. Thus, to George Washington Campbell of Tennessee:

I have for a long time been convinced, that there was a party in our Country, fully determined to do every thing in their power, to Subvert the principles of our happy Government, and to establish a Monarchy on its ruins; and with a view of obtaining the aid of G. B. in the accomplishment of their nefarious object, they have Inlisted into her service, and will go all lengths to Justify and support every measure which she may take against the Nation: and I think with you, that Recent Transactions have rendered the fact so manifest, that the weakest Optics must be inveloped under a thick phelm which cannot deserne it. Much might be said on this head, but I forbare.[23]

But whatever the Federalist strategy as Jeffersonians conceived of it, it was abundantly clear that they could not abandon American commerce to foreign restriction and seizure. Too much was at stake—the happiness of all America and of mankind.

(2)

NO OTHER OPTION

The Republicans felt heavy responsibility in challenging British and French maritime practices. In their eyes the prestige of the Republic and of their own party depended on protection of American commerce against the restrictions and seizures of the European belligerents. They could have imagined no more momentous a task. But both President Jefferson and his chief adviser, Secretary of State James Madison, were confident that in commercial restrictions America possessed the means of instilling respect for her maritime rights. Great Britain and France had colonial possessions and national economies that depended on American foodstuffs and raw materials. The two powers relied on the American market for sale of their own exports—the textiles, pottery, glassware, and metalware of Britain; the fine clothes, fruits, wines, and brandies of France; the sugar, coffee, molasses, and spices of their colonial possessions. It seemed probable that they would concede much in order to maintain trade with the United States. Commercial restrictions, if "properly suited for the Executive hand" as Madison put it, could be negotiated to win European respect for American rights.[1]

Great Britain was initially the chief offender. Handicapped by manpower shortages, after 1803 the royal navy began impressment of sailors from merchant vessels. Many British seamen, in search of better conditions of work and pay, had deserted to American employment, and the royal navy sought to stop this drain on experienced manpower. Mistakes and abuses inevitably occurred and British boarding parties seized native and naturalized American seamen from American decks. Between 1803 and 1812 impressed American seamen numbered between 3,800 (those actually released by British authorities) and 6,257 (those claimed as impressed by the American government).[2] The British government also imposed restrictions on American carriers sailing between France, satellite Spain, and their West Indian possessions. The British government, invoking the formula of the Rule of the War of 1756, denied American merchants the right to participate in a direct wartime carrying trade which had not been open to them in time of peace. Americans evaded the prohibition by the subterfuge of paying duties at American ports and claiming they made two separate "broken" voyages open to them in peacetime.

In 1805 a British admiralty appeals court in the *Essex* case denied this practice as adequate proof of bona fide importation, a change of policy that British captains swiftly carried out in scores of seizures.[3] In 1806 there came more sweeping interdicts against American commerce. The ministry issued an Order in Council in May which declared the entire northern coast of Europe from Brest to the Elbe River under blockade, but provided for strict and uniform enforcement of this measure along a more limited coast (Fox's blockade). An Order in Council in January, 1807, proclaimed the blockade of all coastal trade between enemy ports on the European continent. Another Order in Council in November, 1807, declared all of Napoleon-controlled Europe under blockade as if by naval forces in a most strict and rigorous manner. All ships and goods, British excepted, that violated this Order were good and lawful prize. A second edict issued in the same month authorized neutral trade with the Continent, provided carriers first landed at a British port, entered their cargoes, and paid duty. The government narrowed the dimensions of its system in April, 1809, by opening Germany and the Baltic to neutral commerce, but imposed the blockade against Napoleonic France, French satellites (the Low Countries, northern Italy), and French colonies.[4]

Napoleon struck at American maritime commerce also, though not extensively until 1807. His navy shattered in 1805 at Trafalgar, he turned to economic warfare to force Britain to terms, a "remorseless war against English merchandise" as he put it. An edict issued at Berlin in November, 1806, initiated the famous Continental System. The Berlin Decree declared the British Isles in blockade and prohibited all trade including that of neutrals: all ships coming from the British Isles or carrying British goods were liable to seizure. The Milan Decree, promulgated in December, 1807, added a provision that ships submitting to British blockade regulations or permitting search by British vessels would be seized.[5]

The net effect of the British Orders in Council and French Berlin and Milan Decrees combined was to make all American trade with either belligerent open to seizure and confiscation. The two powers after 1807 harassed American commerce with equal ferocity. Secretary of State James Monroe estimated in July, 1812, that Britain had seized some 389 vessels since the Orders of November, 1807, while Napoleon had been responsible for 469 seizures—307 under the Decrees, 117 by satellites, and 45 since the announced repeal of his edicts.[6]

Protest and appeal characterized initial Republican response to British seizures and impressments. In 1803 and 1804 American officials at home and abroad sought to persuade the British government to modify its maritime policies. The Jefferson administration contended that the American flag protected all sailors from impressment—British and American alike—and that British captains had no right to search American vessels on the high seas for deserters. With respect to seizure of American vessels bound to or from French West Indian ports declared in blockade by the British government, the administration denied the legality of the Rule of the War of 1756 and claimed that no port could be considered as blockaded unless investing ships created an "evident danger of entering." The American government carefully confined itself to making a case by discussion and argument, hoping to obtain concessions but careful not to take any further action that might appear unfriendly or jeopardize relations. The British government made no move towards meeting American claims.[7]

In 1806, following the sudden rash of seizures occasioned by the *Essex* decision, Congress considered proposals to bar importation of British goods into the United States. After long debate and much division among members, the Republican majority passed in the spring a selective nonimportation act that prohibited import of such goods from Great Britain as could be obtained either in the United States or in other foreign countries. Suspended repeatedly by acts of Congress, the nonimportation act nevertheless represented the initial phase in the complex series of commercial restrictions that preceded the War of 1812.[8]

Still the British government refused to yield, giving no ground on the issue of impressment and offering little else on the other points at issue. The President felt obliged early in 1807 to reject the treaty negotiated during 1806 in London by the American commissioners, William Pinkney and James Monroe, a treaty which not only failed to give an explicit guarantee against impressment but pledged the United States to refrain from commercial restrictions against Great Britain for ten years. Nor did more stringent pressure produce concessions. One could expect little from curtailments on British naval vessels in American waters ordered after the brutal *Leopard* attack on the American frigate *Chesapeake* in June, 1807. But the sweeping Republican ban on all American exports and ship sailings certainly held hopes of a better result. The famous embargo, enacted in December, 1807, in response to news of stringent enforcement of the Berlin Decree against American shipping and of British intent to prohibit all trade with the Continent, sought to prevent an unwanted war, which widespread seizures would have required, and to bring economic pressure against the two belligerents. But neither Great Britain nor France showed the slightest sign of bowing to this economic weapon, nor of yielding to the repeated American claim that blockades to be legal under international law must be effectively upheld. Dispatches from the American ministers in London and Paris in the autumn of 1808 told of unsuccessful efforts to win repeal or modification of the Orders and Decrees in return for repeal of the embargo. Each power maintained the justice of its own system by right of retaliation against the illegal and prior measures of the enemy, and both belligerents claimed that it was the duty of the United States to secure prior justice from the other power.[9]

The embargo bore down severely on Americans everywhere. With all sailings and exports prohibited, the commercial life of the country reached a point of near paralysis during 1808. Ships rotted at wharves, sailors walked the streets in search of work, merchants idled, and all work associated with shipping and export ceased. Farmers and planters faced rapidly falling prices in a domestic market flooded with commodities. A smuggling trade of epic proportions got under way, and became a national disgrace.

The Federalist party, which had opposed the embargo in Congress from its inception, launched a bitter campaign of vilification and abuse against the measure and made alarming gains in the elections of 1808, doubling their congressional representation and tripling their meager presidential electoral vote of 1804. No one denied the Federalist charges that the embargo was painful, least of all Republicans who defended it as a necessary hardship and less costly than war. But Federalist claims that anticommercial sectional prejudices and pro-French biases inspired the measure were difficult to refute in areas where the Federalists had built strong organizations and commanded influence. To ease the pressure in the northeast, where the Federalists had won their greatest gains and now even openly threatened secession, the Republican majority in Congress, nearly paralyzed by its own internal conflict over policy, early in 1809 voted to terminate the embargo, turned down a proposal for contingent letters of marque, and rallied to a weaker measure of commercial restriction—the nonintercourse act.[10]

The nonintercourse law forbade all trade with both belligerents and their colonial possessions, closed American ports to their private and public vessels, and authorized the President to suspend the restrictions "in case either France or Great Britain shall so revoke or modify her edicts, as that they shall cease to violate the neutral commerce of the United States." At the same time it removed restrictions on all sailings and exports to non-belligerent countries—South America, China, Africa, and the Baltic countries. President James Madison, who succeeded Jefferson in the White House in March, 1809, notified the powers that his authority to restore trade would be exercised whenever either power ceased its illegal blockades; he also conveyed a warning of hostile American action against whichever belligerent did not follow suit. The Republicans, as these actions showed, intended to concentrate all efforts on the British and French edicts while relegating to secondary rank other unsettled issues —impressment, reparations for the *Chesapeake* affair, and the colonial carrying trade.[11]

Aside from considerations of national sovereignty and moral right which had become involved in all the issues, the Republican leadership anticipated a more serious threat to American overseas commerce from the Orders in Council and Berlin and Milan Decrees. The British and French edicts made all American vessels bound for the territories of either belligerent liable to seizure and condemnation. Without preventive action Republicans could foresee either sweeping seizure of ships and cargoes or monopolization of all American commerce under the pressure of British naval power. Either alternative was unacceptable. Impressment, in contrast, an issue that had dragged on intermittently since 1793 without provoking hostilities, seemed a less serious evil. The *Chesapeake* affair seemed on the road to settlement: the British ministry had already disavowed the *Leopard* attack and disclaimed all pretensions to search public ships for British sailors. Nor was the Rule of 1756 any longer at issue; it had been superseded and replaced by the system established by the Orders in Council. Hence the shift in the orientation of the Republican effort from impressment, the *Chesapeake*, and the colonial carrying trade, to the Orders in Council and Berlin and Milan Decrees —an emphasis that would last until war.[12]

Still Britain and France held fast. A temporary agreement made in April, 1809, between the British minister to the United States,

David Erskine, and the Madison administration, provided for settlement of the *Chesapeake* affair and traded repeal of the Orders in Council for an end to nonintercourse against Great Britain. But Erskine had violated instructions which set conditions never met by the American government, and the momentary hiatus in the contest with Great Britain was rudely terminated when Foreign Secretary George Canning disavowed his envoy's handiwork and rejected the agreement. So insultingly did Erskine's replacement, Francis James Jackson, conduct negotiations—accusing Madison of deliberately concluding an agreement with Erskine that he knew would be unacceptable to London—that Madison refused to receive him further and asked for his recall. Renewed efforts to induce a repeal of the French Decrees also failed.[13]

Under such circumstances, and in the knowledge that the nonintercourse law was due to expire by statutory requirement at the close of the session, Republicans coming to Congress in November, 1809, found themselves forced to devise new legislation. The measure eventually emerging in May, 1810, from a divided session was known as Macon's Bill Number Two. It removed restraints on trade entirely, but provided for restoration of restrictive measures against whichever belligerent failed to follow the other in repeal. In the event of either power revoking or modifying its edicts so as to cease violation of American neutral rights, the President was to announce the fact by proclamation. If the other power failed to follow suit within three months, sections in the nonintercourse act of 1809 that prohibited importation of goods and closed American waters to private vessels would take effect against that nation. By this action the government offered not to lift restrictions against whichever belligerent repealed its edicts but to impose them against whichever belligerent maintained its edicts after the other had repealed.[14]

It is quite evident that Madison regarded this legislation as ruinous and dishonorable submission. No longer did the government legally prohibit American vessels from trade with the belligerents, and either Great Britain or France might now seize

American vessels trading with the enemy. With Great Britain in virtual command of the sea, this meant that American vessels trading with France ran greater danger of seizure. The wise shipowner would send his vessels to British possessions only. Madison expected that Great Britain would shortly monopolize all American overseas trade.[15]

In September, 1810, word came from France that Napoleon intended to revoke the Berlin and Milan Decrees, an announcement formally made in the famous letter written by Napoleon's Foreign Minister, the Duc de Cadore, to the American minister in Paris, John Armstrong. The Cadore letter actually contained no positive statement of French repeal, but made the announcement in ambiguous language. Cadore affirmed that the Decrees would cease to have effect after November 1, "it being understood that" either Great Britain shall revoke her Orders, or the United States, "conformably" to the Macon law, "shall cause their rights to be respected by the English." The difficulty lay in the apparent conditions of this announcement. Did Cadore mean that the French Decrees would cease to have effect on condition that before that time either the Orders in Council shall have been revoked, or the United States shall have restored restrictions on British commerce and British shipping as authorized in the Macon law? [16]

The President took the position that this letter did announce an actual repeal of the Decrees as of November 1. On November 2 he announced to the world by proclamation that "the edicts of France have been so revoked as that they ceased on the first day of the present month to violate the neutral commerce of the United States." Under the terms of the Macon law, Britain now had three months to follow suit or suffer the consequences of renewed commercial restrictions. Unknown to the President was Cadore's confidential dispatch to his American minister confirming the conditional interpretation of his letter to Armstrong. The decision of Napoleon was "conditional," the Minister of Foreign Affairs told Louis Turreau, and its execution "will depend on the measures which the United States shall take if England persists in her orders of Council and in the principles of blockade which she has tried to establish." [17]

The President based his decision to announce repeal on both technical and political grounds. The Cadore letter, he reasoned, technically did not require a condition precedent on the part of the United States. The letter explicitly recognized that action taken by this country to cause respect for rights violated by the English would be taken "conformably" to authorization in the Macon law. Since the Macon law authorized no restrictions on commerce with one belligerent until three months after the President had proclaimed actual repeal of edicts on the part of the other, Cadore must have meant to announce an actual repeal on the presumption the United States would act three months later with restrictions against Great Britain. Thus Madison wrote to the American Minister in London, William Pinkney, in terms indicating belief in actual repeal: "You have been already informed that the Proclamation would issue giving effect to the late act of Congress, on the ground of the Duke de Cadore's letter to Genl Armstrong, which states an *actual* repeal of the French Decrees." To reinforce this interpretation, instructions sent to the American minister in France ordered him in dealing with the French government to presume repeal of the Decrees. The American government would assume (so read the instructions) that "the reservations under the expression 'it being understood' are not condition precedent affecting the operation of repeal." Armstrong was also quietly to drop the demand laid down in previous instructions that Napoleon must restore previously sequestered American ships and property as a condition to any action by the United States against Great Britain.[18]

It is difficult to imagine a man of Madison's shrewdness basing so momentous a decision solely on such flimsy grounds. Under normal circumstances he certainly would have waited for further confirmation of actual repeal of the Decrees, or at the very least clarification of the actual meaning of the Cadore letter. But the times were far from normal. Under the Macon law the nation had virtually given up the contest, meekly allowing Great

Britain to seize American vessels in trade with the Continent. The Cadore letter offered an opportunity to rescue the nation from this ruinous and degrading submission to British power. Under the pressure of renewed American resistance, Great Britain might possibly follow France in repeal of her system. At the very least, if these pressures failed to produce concessions from Great Britain, the United States would no longer be confronted with the alternatives of war with both belligerents or submission. All these reasons were implicit in the President's letter to Attorney-General Caesar Rodney requesting his presence at the capital to discuss legal aspects of the situation: "The new scene opened by the revocation of the Fr. Decrees, will I hope, terminate in a removal of the embarrassments which have been as afflicting as they have been unexampled. It promises us at least an extrication from the dilemma, of a mortifying peace, or a war with both the great belligerents." To Madison the Cadore letter offered advantages too great to risk by further investigation into the good faith of French repeal. It was better to act immediately, trusting to the prospect of American pressure against Great Britain alone to hold Napoleon firmly to the mark, than to run a risk of losing this opportunity to end the nation's submission. At best the policy announced by the President in his proclamation would set in motion events that might lead to a general settlement with Great Britain. At worst they would lead to war with her. In either event the Republicans would be protecting commerce and avoiding disgrace.[19]

On June 30, 1811, Augustus J. Foster arrived in Washington to begin negotiations on subjects at issue between Great Britain and the United States. The arrival of the new British minister, coinciding with the closing of the American ministry in London and the return of William Pinkney to the United States, shifted the scene of negotiation between the two governments to the American capital. Foster's reception was courteous and friendly. He found in the new American Secretary of State, James Monroe, "a tone & manner of the most mild & conciliatory nature."

He was honored at diplomatic dinners by the President and other Cabinet members. He noted on such occasions "a desire to impress upon me a favourable impression of the President's disposition towards His Royal Highness the Prince Regent." He could report "as great attention were shewn to me on my arrival as have I believe been paid to any foreign Minister who has been sent to this Country." [20]

These courtesies could not alter the unfavorable character of Foster's instructions from the successors of the Portland ministry, the Tory government of Spencer Perceval. Foster brought authority to settle British reparations for the *Chesapeake* outrage in 1807. On the subject of Fox's blockade of May, 1806, he could move a long way towards the American position by announcing that the blockade, if continued after any future repeal of the Orders in Council, would be an actual blockade maintained by an effective naval force. But on the matter of the Orders in Council his instructions bore demands that would admit of no accommodation short of complete American surrender. [21]

Pursuant to instructions during July Foster steadily and firmly denied that the Berlin and Milan Decrees had been in any way repealed. He argued that no evidence existed of such repeal and claimed that positive evidence existed to the contrary. Protesting the injustice of provisions in the nonintercourse act directed against British commerce when the French had not yet complied with the Macon law, he demanded their withdrawal and warned that unless withdrawn his government would retaliate with economic restrictions of its own. He seemed to advance still further when he set forth the terms Great Britain demanded of France as a right for repeal of the Orders in Council. Before the Orders could be repealed the Decrees must be revoked not only to the extent they declared the British Isles in a state of blockade, but to the extent they prohibited importation into the Continent of the productions and manufactures of Great Britain when owned by neutrals. This assertion denied an essential distinction made repeatedly by the Madison administration.

In November, 1810, Madison had carefully announced repeal
of the French edicts to the extent they violated American neutral
rights, but excepted by implication those parts of the Decrees
not in violation. Those parts of the Decrees which prohibited
American trade with Great Britain were clearly violations of
neutral rights. They had been repealed. Parts of the Decrees,
however, still prohibited trade between the Continent and Great
Britain, including ships and goods belonging to or made in
Great Britain. These were in effect, and legitimately so, as municipal regulations, just as the United States had the right to prohibit importation of goods from a foreign nation. Every nation
had the right to regulate commerce as it saw fit within its own
national jurisdiction, and this no other nation had a right to
deny.[22]

Madison and Monroe in their talks with Foster had steadily
and firmly maintained that France had repealed the Berlin and
Milan Decrees to the extent that they affected American neutral
rights. They denied the justice of demanding, as a right, repeal
of municipal regulations by the French government. With
Foster maintaining the exact contrary, it soon became apparent
to all concerned that the negotiations over the Orders in Council
were in a state of hopeless deadlock. Whereupon the President
and his Secretary of State suspended the talks and, according to
custom in the summer season, left the capital for their Virginia
country residences. Foster summed up in a dispatch to his superiors on August 5 the substance of his discussions with the two
Virginians. It had become clear to him, soon after beginning
discussions on the subject of British-American relations, "that
unless I could state that the Orders in Council were repealed,
our discussions, for the present at least, were likely to be fruitless." [23]

Looking back almost a year later, Monroe, who carried the
burden of the talks with Foster, wrote that he had done everything in his power consistent with American rights and interests
to reach an agreement with the British negotiator. This was true.
When Foster delayed settling reparations for the *Chesapeake*

affair until satisfactory explanations for the recent clash between the *President* and British sloop-of-war *Little Belt* had been made by the American government, Monroe might have made this a major issue. Instead, he showed "very little concern" about the matter. On Foster's explanation of the British stand on Fox's blockade he indicated that he and the President were "very well satisfied." He carefully avoided taking up the question of impressment. He conducted his part of the negotiation in a "tone & manner of the most mild & conciliatory nature." [24] But Monroe could not agree with Foster's claim that the Decrees as far as they affected American neutral rights had not been repealed, not only when there was no evidence that they had not been repealed, but when there was positive evidence that they had been repealed. The French government had been slow in releasing American ships seized under the Decrees before November 1, 1810, the date the Cadore letter set for repeal. This did not prove, Monroe maintained against Foster's contrary assertion, that the Decrees as they affected American neutral rights were still in effect. In fact, he argued, France's promise made in December, 1810, that the ships would be turned back on February 2, 1811, provided the United States complied with its part of the agreement and imposed restrictions on British trade, proved that the Decrees were no longer in effect. The French government had confiscated non-American goods from American ships come from British ports and seized in French ports after November 1, 1810. This, Monroe insisted, it had every right to do under the municipal provisions of the Decrees which did not affect neutral rights. The French government had imposed tariffs and other annoying regulations on American imports and exports. This, also, was within her rights of municipal regulation. [25]

More ominous was the apparent stiffening of demands on America made by Foster. To satisfy the British government, the United States had either to withdraw her own measures against British commerce, or force Napoleon to withdraw some of his. The former would be submission to British power and policy. The latter was clearly a device to force the United States to pry open Continental markets to British goods. It too was utterly unacceptable.[26]

Before leaving the capital for Montpelier the President issued a proclamation summoning members of the recently elected 12th Congress to Washington some weeks earlier than originally scheduled. The proclamation, printed in Joseph Gales's semi-official *National Intelligencer* in the final week of July, announced the new date as November 1. In the calm atmosphere of his country estate the President had ample opportunity to review recent events and determine a future course. For some weeks he apparently came to no final decision. Before leaving the capital at the end of July he had informed a former cabinet colleague of the failure to obtain repeal of the Orders in Council and of his plan to convene Congress in the fall, but gave no hint of future measures. A month later he was weighing the possibility that Foster might not have accurately represented the views of the Prince Regent. It was during the two weeks between August 23 and September 6—possibly during Secretary Monroe's visit in that interval—that he made up his mind to recommend war measures. A letter written by the Secretary of State after his departure shows that the two men agreed on some matter of high importance at this interview. Monroe cautioned the President against his usual visit to former President Jefferson at Monticello. Should the President visit his predecessor, just before the return to Washington, "it will be concluded, & probably so represented in the gazettes, that all the measures of the govt., at this important crisis, are adjusted at the interview. It will not be material that the idea is erroneous & false," said Monroe, accurately appraising Madison's lifelong difficulty in dispelling the fiction of subserviency to the sage of Monticello. "The impression will be the same as if the fact was true." [27]

Forty-five years later Joseph Gales of the *Intelligencer*, close in the confidence of the administration during the period preceding the war, recalled (with aid of a diary) the events of the summer and fall of 1811. In consequence of the failure of Foster's mission, he remembered, President Madison and others of his official family, particularly Secretary of State Monroe, decided ("within some two months prior to the commencement of the first session of the Twelfth Congress") that the nation had no choice but to fight. It was at that time both men "appear to have made up their minds that no option remained to this Government but open War with that of Great Britain, which had for several years been making covert war by her hostile edicts and her maritime supremacy upon the United States." [28]

Political enemies long maintained that Madison never made up his own mind on the matter of war until forced to it by political pressures. According to one myth he was brought to favor war only after militant members of his own party had threatened to oppose his renomination for a second presidential term. Another describes the President yielding to war only after military preparations and belligerent blusterings had made it impossible to back down without personal and political disgrace. Only in the last thirty years have these views been effectively contested, most convincingly by Irving Brant in his biography of Madison. Even so, the view dies hard, and it will aid understanding to review the case for Madison as the author of his own policy.[29]

There are the President's own personal letters written during the session. They leave no doubt that by the opening of the new Congress he had firmly made up his mind that the country had no alternative but to fight Great Britain or to submit to the Orders in Council. "The pretension of G. B. which requires us as a neutral nation to assert agst. one belligerent an obligation to open its markets to the products of the other, shews a pre-determination to make her orders in Council co-durable with the war," he told his minister to Russia, John Quincy Adams, in November, 1811. "The question to be decided, therefore, by Congress, according to present appearances, simply is, whether all the trade to which the orders are and shall be applied, is to be abandoned, or the hostile operation of them, be hostilely resisted." The "apparent disposition" of Congress is "certainly not in favor of the first alternative," he added with approval. In a reply to resolutions from the Tennessee legislature written late in December or early in January he reaffirmed his belief that war was necessary. "The necessity will be deplored by a people who have cherished peace in sincerety, because they are alive to the calamities which begin where peace ends. But they will meet those as not the greatest calamities when a surrender of their sacred rights & vital interests are the alternative." Finally, to Jefferson in April, 1812, on learning that even under the threat of war the British government would not repeal: "It appears that Percival &c, are to retain their places, and that they prefer war with us, to a repeal of the Orders in Council. We have nothing left therefore, but to make ready for it." [30]

There are also letters of confidential advisers. Secretary of State Monroe had perhaps the closest access to the President's thoughts. On December 6, 1811, we find him writing: "The govt. is resolved, if G. Britain does not revoke her orders in council, in a short time, to act offensively towards her. In fact not to remain inactive and at peace, while she wages war." On June 13, 1812, he wrote a long and revealing letter to the Virginia planter and agrarian philosopher, John Taylor of Caroline. The Madison administration had decided on war after the abortive Foster negotiation, Monroe explained.

Nothing would satisfy the present ministry of England, short of unconditional submission, which it was impossible to make. This fact being completely ascertained, the only remaining alternative, was to get ready for fighting, and to begin as soon as we were ready. This was the plan of the administration, when Congress met in November last; the President's message announced it; and every step taken by the administration since has lead [sic] to it.[31]

Nor did the President waver when Albert Gallatin, his Secretary of the Treasury and close adviser, advised against war shortly before Congress convened. It was probably safer to adhere to the present nonimportation law, Gallatin indicated in notes made on the preliminary draft of the President's opening message sent to Congress on November 5, 1811. Not that non-importation would bring Great Britain to terms; there was little chance of that. But war would involve the nation in incalculable risks. There would be great difficulty in financing the war and in raising troops, and the added burden of debt would weaken us and retard our economic growth at the end of the war. In addition, the military measures necessary for war—the taxes, inflationary spending, budgetary deficit, wartime economic restrictions, increase in the army—"must be unpopular and by producing a change of men may lead to a disgraceful peace, to absolute subserviency hereafter to G. B., and even to substantial alterations in our institutions." Better to remain as we are, "whilst we can calculate almost with certainty all the evils and inconveniences of the non-importation," than to yield national leadership to the Federalists, thus risking national independence and even republicanism.

That these were powerful arguments no Republican would deny. Yet Gallatin appreciated the perplexities involved, and as his notes indicate was not even fully convinced of the rightness of his own position. He knew well that a strong case could be made for the point of view that war was necessary. Since nonimportation would probably not shake Great Britain, admittedly national morale ("the spirit of the Nation"), or "an opinion that hostilities not repelled by corresponding measures would be still more pernicious than any possible effect of a war," may lead to a view that war is less dangerous than nonimportation. If this should prove to be the case, then ought not the President to consider further whether the tone of his proposed message to Congress was not overly belligerent? Was it wise to announce our determination to fight at a time when the nation was not prepared to repel a possible preemptive attack by Great Britain? The President saw merit in this final suggestion, and in the final draft removed and softened the most provocative phrases in his message. On the first point, however, that of war or nonimportation, it was Gallatin who changed his mind. Thus the Secretary of the Treasury wrote to Jefferson in March, 1812, that this was "an unavoidable war." He could only do his utmost to limit its evils, to make certain that "the United States may be burthened with the smallest possible quantity of debt, perpetual taxation, military establishment and other corrupting or anti Republican habits or institutions." Madison, on the other hand, remained firmly resolved.[32]

It thus appears that after the Foster negotiation the President reluctantly came to the decision that the nation had no acceptable policy left to choose but war. Ever since enactment of the embargo in 1807 Madison had hoped that repeal of edicts by one belligerent would induce the other to follow suit rather than see its rival become the sole beneficiary of American commerce and friendship. After the Cadore letter he had felt some hope that Great Britain might now be induced to follow the example of France.[33] But the Foster negotiation had dashed this feeling. In the course of the negotiation it had become abundantly clear that the Perceval ministry would not repeal the Orders despite withdrawal of the French Decrees insofar as they affected American neutral rights. The British government had shown clearly by its impossible demands that the Orders would last for the duration of the conflict with France no matter what the enemy did. Indeed, the British government had shown that the Orders were not, as claimed, in retaliation against Napoleon's Continental System, but aimed primarily at the United States, Britain's chief commercial and maritime rival. If her own merchants and shipmasters could not have access to Continental trade, then neither could their American competitors. Either the United States must pry open the Continent to British commerce, or, failing that, must become the economic vassal of Great Britain, trading only within her own imperial system and not at all with the Continent.

To effect these purposes Britain would seize and destroy all American shipping in trade with Continental Europe. In fact she was waging what amounted to "war" on American commerce, a war she had been waging four years under the cloak of retaliation against the French Decrees, but now exposed as a war of naked economic greed. Could the American government stand by passively while Great Britain accomplished her aims? Madison believed that it could not. But the problem was to find some way actively to resist British aggression. The embargo, nonintercourse, and nonimportation policies had failed to shake Britain from the Orders in Council. The prospect of commercial restrictions against France alone held out in the Macon law had failed to shake her. The prospect of war against France by the United States had failed. Thus Madison concluded that no other form of resistance remained but force. This is why Monroe wrote, as he did, that war was "the only remaining alternative" and "the only possible means of giving effect to the just claims of the Country on foreign powers"; why the President in his letter of November 15 to John Quincy Adams saw complete abandonment of trade as the sole alternative to war; and why Dolley Madison, the President's wife, told her sister that "Mr. Madison sees no end to the perplexities without [a war]." [34]

Firmly decided on war as the last remaining alternative, the President still did not close all doors to an accommodation with Great Britain. Until hostilities actually began he stood ready to welcome any arrangement with Great Britain which guaranteed security to American commerce in trade with the Continent. He had slight hope of a British concession, but continued to work for one even while the country prepared for hostilities. The government would plan strategy, raise troops, appoint army officers, stock-pile supplies, and strengthen defenses. If Great Britain still did not relent, then war would follow. [35]

Madison's opening message to Congress of November 5, in its revised and corrected final form, bore witness to these ideas. The message began with a discussion of the negotiations with Foster. Instead of replying to the repeal of the French edicts as they violated American neutral rights with similar action, Britain had denied the fact of French repeal and had advanced to new ground, demanding as "an indispensable condition of the repeal of the British orders that commerce should be restored to a footing that would admit the productions and manufactures of Great Britain, when owned by neutrals, into markets shut against them by her enemy." Fresh evidence of the repeal of the French Decrees against American neutral trade, conveyed to the British government, had resulted in no effective change in the British cabinet. Nevertheless, the President asserted: "To be ready to meet with cordiality satisfactory proofs of such a change, and to proceed in the meantime in adapting our measures to the views which have been disclosed through that minister will best consult our whole duty."

Barely touching on the fact that indemnity and redress for other wrongs (impressment and the *Chesapeake* affair) continued to be withheld, the President pointed out that under the authority of the Orders in Council British ships-of-war were harassing American shipping directly off our coast and even within American territorial waters. "I must now add," the President continued, "that the period is arrived which claims from the legislative guardians of the national rights a system of more ample provisions for maintaining them." Despite "the scrupulous justice, the protracted moderation, and the multiplied efforts" on the part of the United States to preserve peace with Great Britain, the British ministry "perseveres not only in withholding a remedy for other wrongs, so long and so loudly calling for it, but in the execution, brought home to the threshold of our territory, of measures which under existing circumstances have the character as well as the effect of war on our lawful commerce." In the light of this evidence of "hostile inflexibility in trampling on rights which no independent nation can relinquish," he concluded, "Congress will feel the duty of putting the United States into an armor and an attitude demanded by the crisis, and corresponding with the national spirit and expectations." [36]

Thus the President's recommendations for military preparations made to Congress on November 5 rested on British refusal to repeal the Orders in Council and her continued seizure of American vessels under this authority. Conspicuously absent in the message was any stress on impressment, an issue that has frequently been given equal weight as a cause of war in 1812.[37] Neither Madison nor his predecessor had pressed for settlement of this issue for four years since late 1807, when they had unsuccessfully tried to link the issue with their *Chesapeake* demands.

That impressment formed no major part of the presidential decision to recommend war preparations gains confirmation from the attention that Madison and Monroe gave to the Orders in Council as responsible for the coming conflict in their correspondence during the seven months preceding war. But in two major policy statements made at the very moment that the United States entered upon war the two men emphasized impressment as a practice that Great Britain must not continue.

On June 1, 1812, Madison sent a message to Congress in which he recommended a declaration of war against Great Britain. He began with an historical account of the unfriendly conduct of the British government towards the United States since 1803. Impressment, the hovering of British ships-of-war off American coasts, Fox's blockade of 1806, the Orders in Council, the Erskine repudiation, and most recently the John Henry secessionist plot and Indian attacks on the western frontier all received mention in a chronologically arranged account of British injustice and hostility towards the United States. Then the President narrowed the focus of his discussion to two issues—the Orders in Council and impressment, and the pernicious consequences of these two evils.

We behold our seafaring citizens still the daily victims of lawless violence, committed on the great common and highway of nations, even within sight of the country which owes them protection. We behold our vessels, freighted with the products of our soil and industry, or returning with the honest proceeds of them, wrested from their lawful destinations, confiscated by prize courts no longer the organs of public law but the instruments of arbitrary edicts, and their unfortunate crews dispersed and lost, or forced or inveigled in British ports into British fleets.[38]

After war had begun, moreover, the minimal conditions for restoration of peace set by the Madison administration emphasized both impressment and the Orders in Council. In instructions to the American chargé d'affaires in London, Jonathan Russell, drafted June 26, Secretary of State Monroe briefly discussed the recently enacted declaration of war. This measure had been produced by continued British aggressions on American rights and the presumption "that no favorable change of policy might be expected" from the British government. It was "impossible" for the United States to surrender their rights, and equally so "to rely longer on measures which had failed to accomplish their objects. War was the only remaining alternative; and that fact being clearly ascertained, you will find by the documents transmitted, that it was adopted with decision." Before the United States would agree to make peace the British government must repeal the Orders in Council, refrain from further paper blockades, make an end to impressment, and restore all American sailors already impressed.[39]

The President's war message and the instructions to Russell are not evidence which is inconsistent with the previous stress given the Orders in Council as the cause of war. Both the message and the instructions came at the very moment when new political and diplomatic considerations had risen to prominence in Madison's mind. Great Britain had refused all concession on the Orders in Council, and the United States was about to bring force to bear against her. What should the United States require as the price of a restoral of peace between the two nations? Would it be wise to agree to a peace which did not include a settlement on impressment, in addition to repeal of the Orders in Council? Unless Great Britain agreed to cease impressment of sailors, the country might have to go to war again in order to force her to do so. Would it not be less costly to settle this issue also in the present contest? A statement written by Secretary Monroe some months after war had begun shows that the Chief Executive and his advisers actually followed some such line of thought. News of the Liverpool ministry's conditional repeal of the Orders had reached America and the Secretary was defending the subsequent decision to continue the war over impressment. Monroe indicated that if Britain had repealed the Orders before the United States had declared war, hostilities would have been avoided. But now the situation was different. The impressment controversy must be settled before the United States would make peace. Monroe wrote:

In going to war all matters of controversy ought to be settled. Impressment is one of the first importance & ought not to be neglected. If we give it up now we sanction the practice. we wish our friendship with that country to be permanent; it is not wished to patch up a quarrel to begin anew in a year or two, but to have a lasting peace with it. To secure this, it will be necessary to settle firstly every difference.[40]

Coming at the moment of final congressional decision, the President's war message of June 1 seems to have been intended to perform two functions—one persuasive, the other diplomatic. Madison was not explaining how it happened that he was recommending war to Congress. That had become clear enough, at least to members of his party, in the preceding months. He seems rather to have been trying to rouse and to justify. Two weeks previous to the message, Congressman John A. Harper of the House Foreign Relations Committee had rightly predicted that the President's message would be "very argumentative." The President's long chronological account of British acts of hostility towards the United States put the worst possible construction on British policies and motives without mentioning settlements, the shifting course of negotiation, and possible alternative interpretations of British intentions. Against impressment, for example, the President said that the United States "have in vain exhausted remonstrances and expostulations," a statement that completely ignored the four-year hiatus in the effort to settle this issue. The Chief Executive made no mention of the final settlement of the *Chesapeake* affair in December, 1811, or of the fact that on Fox's blockade the two governments seemed closely in accord. Thus, to anyone who still thought Great Britain might yield, the long recital of "injuries and indignities which have been heaped upon our country" since 1803, would surely show that Britain was determinedly hostile, that nothing short of war could shake her. In following with a restatement of injuries caused by the Orders and impressment the President was answering the necessity of giving some indication as to which of the several grievances were most important and must be settled before he would agree to make peace. For, as Monroe's instructions to Russell made clear, the Orders and impressment would become the *sine qua nons* of peace once war began.[41]

Long after the war, in the twilight of life, Madison returned to the question of what had caused America to go to war in 1812. The aging statesman recalled in 1827 that during the very week when Congress finally voted war the British government had conditionally repealed the Orders in Council. Earlier British action, thought Madison, if it had been known in the United States before Congress took the plunge, would have saved the peace.

Had repeal of the orders been substituted for the declaration that they would not be repealed, or had they been repealed but a few weeks sooner, our declaration of war as proceeding from that cause would have been stayed, and negociations on the subject of [impressments], the other great cause, would have been pursued with fresh vigor & hopes, under the auspices of success in the case of the orders in council.

Impressment had been a major grievance in 1812, but the Orders in Council had held the key to war.[42]

Was there no other alternative than war? By 1812 there was indeed ample reason to believe there was no way out—short of giving up the contest. Matters of timing and strategy aside, the Madison administration had guided the nation into a situation where the final resort in controversies between nations—war—seemed the only method of resistance having any chance of success. Under the pressure of the nonimportation system, the British ministry had shown no sign of relenting; in fact, as it put forth new demands, it seemed even more adamant. Ultimately, on June 16, Foreign Secretary Castlereagh announced in Parliament the impending repeal of the Orders on a conditional basis —two days before Madison signed the war bill—an action as unexpected as it was six weeks too late to be known in America in time to keep the peace. For sixteen months, since February, 1811, the British government had stood firm against repeal in spite of nonimportation. So unyielding did it seem that not until May 9, 1812—one month before the declaration—did the American chargé d'affaires in London, Jonathan Russell, after repeated statements affirming the hopelessness of repeal, give the first intimation that the British cabinet might be weakening.[43] After failure of all other methods, from the embargo to earnest warnings of war to offers of unilateral restrictions and war against the opposing belligerent, what else remained?

Could anything have been done during the preceding years which might have made this ultimate choice unnecessary? Here the matter is more controversial. It has been argued that ratification of the Monroe-Pinkney treaty of 1806 might have prevented war, on the grounds that a diplomatic and commercial *rapprochement* would have tempered future British policy towards the United States. But what new advantages would such a treaty have brought Great Britain to induce her statesmen to treat the United States and its commerce more sympathetically? Monroe suggested the treaty would have encouraged British merchants to embark more extensively on trade with the United States, thus creating stronger pro-American pressures within Great Britain. But Great Britain and her dominions already exported to the United States goods worth nearly as much as all other countries combined, and her own exports in 1806 were roughly equivalent to what she sent us in the peaceful years of 1801 and 1802.[44] In any case, as subsequent events would testify, her Tory leaders did not consider American friendship and commerce as valuable as other objectives. Spencer Perceval and George Canning, the chief architects of the system of blockades, were more eager to ensure British commercial supremacy and retaliate against the Continental System than to maintain American commerce and friendship. On the outside chance that a treaty would produce a new British attitude, should Jefferson have given up protection of American sailors and surrendered for ten years the one weapon short of war that he believed would persuade Britain to yield, i.e., commercial restrictions?

In April, 1809, the Portland ministry replaced the Orders in Council of November, 1807, with new regulations that opened cracks in the British blockading system. The new Order in Council declared a general blockade against Napoleon, his immediate satellites, and all French colonies, but opened Germany and the Baltic countries to neutral commerce. It also sought to prevent discrimination in the sale of licenses to American vessels in trade with the Continent, and lowered or eliminated duties on American-borne goods required to pass through the British Isles to Europe. Did these points mark concessions towards the United States which President Madison might have accepted and turned into a general settlement with Great Britain? They probably did not. In 1802, 1803, and 1804 American trade with Germany and the Baltic countries represented about one-third of the value of trade with the countries still left under blockade by the Order. While the European conflict doubtless gave a stimulus to trade with these northern countries, the continued blockade of France, the Low Countries, and French-held Italy still constituted a major threat to American commerce. Madison, furthermore, could not have accepted this new regulation without undermining his entire position against future British blockades. Once he agreed to a partial blockade from Italy to Belgium (a coastline not even the British navy could claim to be able to seal effectively), the entire case against future "paper" blockades would have collapsed. Finally, Jefferson and Madison had repeatedly insisted they could permit no foreign government the right to regulate American commerce with a third power, which this Order, despite its more limited sweep, certainly did. If the Order of 1809 was a concession, it was with good reason never viewed as anything but unacceptable by the President.[45]

One may argue, as did Federalists, that commercial restrictions actually impeded settlement, that they raised obstacles to British concessions, and that negotiations carried on under their shadow were foredoomed to failure. Yet from 1803 to 1806, without the slightest threat of commercial restrictions, the Jefferson administration tried unsuccessfully to negotiate an end to impressment and British seizures. Could one really expect concessions from Great Britain without additional pressure? The real trouble lay in Republican failure to enforce commercial restrictions more strictly. A stringent nonimportation bill in 1806 might have produced a treaty more favorable to the American position at the end of the year, and would have afforded needed additional pressure on Great Britain at the time of the embargo. A more thorough enforcement of the embargo in 1808 might have resulted in real concessions. Even under the existing measure, with all its loopholes, by early 1809 Lord Auckland discerned "symptoms of a desire among the King's Ministers to give way." From the moment that Congress, alarmed by Federalist resurgence and threats of disunion, replaced the measure with a less stringent law, the possibility of Britain yielding to decreasing economic pressure from America grew more dim. When the British government finally did give way, it did so owing to a fortuitous depression, probably caused mostly by unrelated factors—the sudden collapse of the Latin American market and the tightening of the Continental System.[46]

One sure way of avoiding war in 1812 was to abandon the effort to protect American commerce against the Orders in Council. Opposition leaders, John Randolph of Roanoke and some Federalists, advocated this course. Jefferson and Madison believed this to be impossible, economically, morally, and, above all, politically. In economic terms, they believed it would mean loss of a substantial trade with the Continent, vital to American merchants and farmers and to maintenance of a favorable trade balance. In moral terms, they believed it would be wrong to abandon American citizens engaged in lawful occupations to the lawless rapacity of the European powers. In political terms, they believed it would have struck at American sovereignty and honor, and, most important of all, disgraced the Republican party and republicanism. Given prevailing conditions and climates of opinion—the need to build a strong economy, affirm national independence, maintain national morale, and support republicanism and the party of republicanism against its presumed enemies—could responsible Republican statesmen have made any other decision?

(3)

A RELUCTANT MAJORITY

Historians have long presumed the existence of a belligerent Republican faction, "the war hawks," genuinely bristling and warm for a war with Great Britain. Urged by economic grievances, expansionist designs, a hypersensitive sense of national honor, or simply the conviction that no other course remained open, these men, led by Henry Clay and John C. Calhoun, drove their more reluctant colleagues into a contest for which the country was ill-prepared. Federalist opponents of the war, men not privy to the views of Republicans, coined the term "war hawk." They relied on false appearances. No Republican ever really answered this description. There were differences among Republicans as to the time for beginning hostilities and initial strategy to be followed, but there is no firm evidence of reckless bellicosity either among Republican leaders or the great rank and file.[1]

Disunity and division characterized the congressional decision that in June, 1812, brought war with Great Britain. By a vote of 79–49 the House of Representatives authorized war on June 4. By a margin of 19–13 the Senate passed the measure on June 17. Ninety-eight members of Congress approved and 62 opposed the declaration of war. Casting an eye over the nation's nineteenth-century wars with Mexico and Spain, one notes that in 1846 and 1898 Congress twice again failed unanimously to agree on war. But neither of these later conflicts began with the national legislature so badly torn by conflicting sentiment, with majority and minority so close to balance.[2]

Sectional interpretations of pro- and antiwar motivation have dominated twentieth-century writing on the War of 1812. Modern historians with the notable exception of Bradford Perkins have viewed the division in sentiment as between a prowar south and west and an antiwar northeast. An economic interpretation of the causes of war holds that ruinously low cotton and grain prices in the south and west aroused war feeling against Great Britain and her blockade of Continental markets. An expansionist thesis locates the primary thrust of war sentiment in frontier aspirations for Canada and Florida. Historians explain northeastern opposition to the war on the basis of reluctance to give up profitable overseas commerce with Great Britain and fear of naval bombardment and military attack.[3] Although sectional interests played a part in the final war decision, this problem is more clearly understood as a party division than a sectional one. Contemporaries understood the line of division as primarily between Republicans and Federalists. A Republican congressman, Jonathan Roberts of Pennsylvania, noted that his party seemed "well disposed with a few exceptions" on the war question but that the Federalists remained "as mulish as ever" in opposition.[4] The war vote itself is more consistent with a party than a sectional interpretation. With some exceptions the congressional split followed party lines. All members for war were Republican while 40 Federalists and 22 Republicans who bolted from party ranks stood in opposition. A breakdown of the antiwar vote by geographical regions shows 31 Federalists from the northeast and 9 Federalists from the south—not a consistent sectional line-up. Of 22 Republican votes against war, it is true that 18 came from the northeast, only 2 from the south, and 2 from the west. But a geographical breakdown of the Republican vote for war shows 46 from the south, 12 from the west, and 40 from the northeast—again not a sectional pattern.[5]

President Madison and Secretary Monroe believed that the impasse over the Orders in Council could be broken only by a resort to force and that failure to bring force to bear against Great Britain constituted submission. Monroe in June, 1812, described this conclusion as follows: "Nothing would satisfy the present ministry of England, short of unconditional submission, which it was impossible to make. This fact being completely ascertained, the only remaining alternative, was to get ready for fighting, and to begin as soon as we were ready." A close study of the evidence has shown that Republicans in Congress shared this view.[6]

Indeed, the agreement between Madison, Monroe, and the Republican congressional majority is striking. Congressional Republicans joined the administration in the belief that matters had reached an impasse leaving no other solution but force. Nor was this consensus confined to men from any particular section of the country. Republicans from every major section—south, west, and north—held an identical opinion.

The letters of Jesse Franklin, a veteran Republican senator from North Carolina, illustrate how one member felt on the question. Franklin told a constituent in February, 1812, that diplomatic relations between Britain and America had reached an impasse leaving war as the only means of solving the difficulties.

We have nothing from GB that is in the Smallest degree Indicative of any Change in their measures towards the United States. our political Relations with her are perfectly at a Stand. nor do I at present see in what manner it is possible to extricate the nation from its Difficulties with her without coming to Blows.

Nearly two years later he explained his vote for war, stressing the failure of all peaceful efforts to bring Britain to repeal the Orders.

I voted for the war but not untill I believed that every effort had been made to preserve the peace of the nation that every point of the political compass had been trid. and every Honorable offer made to the present enemy, notwithstanding what may be said by those in the opposition.

Another group of important letters reveal the views of John Sevier, a congressman from Tennessee. Sevier, the epitome of a frontier type—Indian fighter, land speculator, and frontier-state organizer—gave an opinion to his son on Indian duty on the Tennessee border. The congressman believed that failure of all means short of war had left the country no choice but to fight or submit. In January, 1812, he wrote: "Our Government have tried negociation until it is exhausted, and there is no doubt in my mind the Executive have observed the most perfect uprightness, and impartial neutrality." Again, in April: "I don't conceive there can be a shadow of doubt remaining of War; we have had news from England as late as the 20th of March, and no appearance of any relaxation of their measures towards America; therefore one of two things, either *War* or *Submission*." [7]

Republicans from all sections of the country, in letters to relatives, local party leaders, and constituents, stated similar views. Members from the south, the northeast, and the west had come to believe that all means short of war had failed and that the country had no other alternative. The stand taken by Great Britain, revealed in the Foster negotiation, was the key to this conclusion. From a young congressman from Georgia, Bolling Hall, came the statement: "The documents accompanying the Presidents message which I presume you have recd and examined furnishes the most unequivocal proof, that we had no alternative but war or submission to England." From a young Pennsylvania member, Jonathan Roberts, came the opinion in November that "prospects for a termination of our disputes with Britain with[out] War are very small" and in June, that we would soon decide "whether war or submission should be the order of the day." The Kentucky senator, George M. Bibb, was in full agreement: "I do not expect any substantial benefit from negociation —and look to a war or a most base and disgraceful submission as the only alternatives." A Virginia congressman—explaining the factors that had brought the majority to war—told his constituents in July, 1812: "From the public documents communicated by the President to Congress at their meeting in November last, it was manifest that a crisis in our affairs with Great Britain had arrived when we were to select between the alternatives of national degradation or war." A northeastern Republican identified this view as the key to prowar sentiment. In a good position to judge accurately was the chairman of the House Committee

on Foreign Relations, Peter B. Porter of New York: "The great
body of the people judge & act correctly. They know that there
is no honourable course for this country to pursue but open &
determined resistance to British wrongs. They approve a war,
and will go every length to support the administration in it." [8]

Recent writing on the causes of war in 1812 supports this
position. Norman Risjord, Bradford Perkins, and Reginald Horsman, in publications that have appeared within the last three
years, agree in locating the basis for war in a feeling that the
peaceful policies of diplomacy and commercial restrictions, op-
erative since 1806, no longer offered hope of redress. Nevertheless, on the matter of when and how Republicans reached this
consensus, significant differences occur among these writers.
Risjord and Horsman see the process as one of gradual conversion, a process that began with the agitation of the "war hawks"
as early as 1809, then gathered strength and numbers as more
"conservative" Republicans gradually joined their ranks. Perkins, on the other hand, finds no "war hawks" until late 1811,
when by word and action a belligerent wing of the party began
forcing peace-minded "scarecrow men" and "moderates" into
hostilities. [9]

It is true that some Republicans had given up all hope in peaceful methods long before the Foster negotiation. George Washington Campbell, a senator of several years standing from Tennessee, was one. Campbell told a colleague in the winter of
1811–12: "There appears at present no honorable ground upon
which, war can be avoided—a change in the measures of G. Britain towards us could alone preserve peace—and there is no
stronger reason to calculate on such an event now, as than there
has been for several years past." After repeal of the embargo in
1809 William H. Crawford of Georgia also put no confidence
in anything less than war. At that time he had written: "When
the embargo is repealed, war, or submission is plain ground, but
all between, is mere whipping the devil round the stump." But
their numbers were limited to a handful. Wilson Cary Nicholas
of Virginia had resigned from Congress in 1809 rather than go

along with another try at peaceful measures. At that time he had written to former President Jefferson that few agreed with him.

As you say there now remains only war or submission. I suspect the administration is not for the former. With all its weight I do not know that congress cou'd be induced to make war In opposition to the wishes of the administration. the vote wou'd be small. with these sentiments you can judge how little probability there is that I cou'd have been of the least service. I am decidedly of the opinion that every expedient short of war is submission disguise it as they will and that such expedients will only tend to our embarrassment & disgrace.

Nicholas was a leading Republican in the House of Representatives. His resignation shows his near-isolation in 1809. By 1810 the number of Republicans for war had not appreciably increased. Joseph Desha, a Kentucky congressman, in February wished that "a little of the fire of 76, could be infused in congress," and believed that "imbecile measures will not do much longer." But he found few who at that moment agreed: "[S]omething must be adopted, to run us up together, we are too much divided, a small struggle would do it." President Madison, in January of the same year, observed the "diversity of opinions and prolixity of discussion in Congress. Few are desirous of war; and few are reconciled to submission; yet the frustration of intermediate courses seems to have left scarce an escape from that dilemma." [10]

Neither of the two most famous members of the 12th Congress —Henry Clay of Kentucky and John C. Calhoun of South Carolina—supported war until late 1811. Both men played important roles in the final march towards hostilities. Clay, as speaker, appointed the standing committees and almost certainly packed them with men who agreed with his views. During the session he worked closely with the administration and helped shape and guide much of its program through the House. A telling document in the Monroe papers shows Clay working out details with the Secretary of State for a brief embargo as a preliminary to war. Calhoun had an important share in the final drafting of the war manifesto and it was he who introduced the war resolution to be voted upon on June 1. Both men, as their letters and speeches clearly demonstrate, believed the country had before it only the two alternatives of war or submission. Clay in August, 1811, had believed war to be "inevitable" if Britain did not follow France in repealing her edicts. In November he wrote an acquaintance that we must have war with Britain. In December he voiced confidence that Americans would support the administration in its views and policies "now that war was the only alternative left to us by the injustice of one of the powers." Again, in February, 1812, he wrote of the coming war "into which we are about to be driven by the aggressions of England"; in May, of the war "brought upon us by the continued aggressions of a foreign government, and to avoid which every honorable effort has been made on the part of ours." [11] Calhoun too saw no other way out. Addressing the House of Representatives in December, 1811, he declared: "The extent, duration, and character of the injuries received; the failure of those peaceful means heretofore resorted to for the redress of our wrongs, is my proof that [war] is necessary." And again:

The question, even in the opinion and admission of our opponents, is reduced to this single point; which shall we do, abandon or defend our own commercial and maritime rights and the personal liberties of our citizens employed in exercising them? These rights are essentially attacked, and war is the only means of redress.

He wrote one month before war began that war had become necessary, but regretfully there was no other course: "War, I regret, has become unavoidable." The "same sense of the justice and necessity of the measures, which originally induced Congress to adopt them, will also coerce us to resort to that last redress of a nation's wrongs." [12]

There is no clear evidence that Clay and Calhoun had been for war before the fall of 1811. Contrary to frequent accounts, Clay had not pressed for war in 1810 when addressing Congress. True, he had at that time told the assembly that when commercial restrictions were abandoned he was for "resistance by the sword" and that the "conquest of Canada" was "in your power." But he also made it clear in the same speech that the time for forcible resistance had not yet come. He had then proposed either a more stringent nonimportation law or congressional authorization for arming merchant ships to take effect after another negotiating attempt. In the early months of 1811 he intimated that Britain might still repeal her Orders in Council. In August, 1811, he told a party associate that repeal was possible, but that if Britain did not follow France's example in repealing her edicts, war would be "inevitable." During the war session he said again and again, in public and private statements, that war had now become necessary owing to British intransigence.[13] Nor did Calhoun advocate war before the fall of 1811. Nowhere in the recently published first volume of his papers is there any indication that before that time he believed war necessary. His biographer, Charles M. Wiltse, hypothesizes that Calhoun campaigned for Congress in 1810 on a war program.[14] Yet during the war session Calhoun showed considerable concern as to how his constituents were taking the prospect of a coming British war. His letters suggest he did not know just what kind of response the war would evoke in South Carolina. Would he have been unsure of public reaction had he campaigned and been elected on a war platform? There are other indications that he shared the position of Clay and the great majority of other Republicans. "Experience," he told a friend, had proved commercial restriction and negotiation to be "improper for us." Their effects had been "distrust at home and contempt abroad." Again, he told a correspondent in May, 1812, that war "has become unavoidable," military preparations having been no more successful in bringing England to yield than all other efforts.[15]

Furthermore, members made it very plain that Republican support for war rested on the view that now no other course had become possible. Military preparation was a matter "on which we have no choice but to act," said Jonathan Roberts of Pennsylvania. The President had called for military legislation "under circumstances that present no alternative but a vigorous preparation for resistance, or, as has been frequently observed during this debate, 'unconditional submission.' " Nathaniel Macon of North Carolina declared that "to attempt another negotiation would be useless; every effort has been made in that way that could be made. Indeed, no one has yet said that he wished another. Is there a man in the House that wishes another attempt at negotiation, or one that wishes to go to war if it could possibly be avoided?" Perhaps Felix Grundy of Tennessee gave the best testimony on the matter:

At the opening of the present session of Congress, the President informed us that every effort to settle our differences with Great Britain by friendly negotiation had been employed without effect. Under such circumstances, as every other expedient had failed, we determined that the only justifiable course left was to put the nation in arms, and by force redress the violated rights and honor of an injured and insulted people.

As Bradford Perkins has accurately perceived: "Most congressmen came to Washington in the fall of 1811 unpledged, probably undecided." [16]

Precisely when and how did the Republican majority reach the view that no alternative remained but war? A close study of congressional correspondence for the period November, 1811, to June, 1812, showed that widespread agreement developed among Republican members during the first month of the session. In July, 1811, after the position of the British government had been fully developed through negotiations with Foster, President Madison had issued a proclamation summoning Congress some weeks earlier than originally planned. During late summer, at Montpelier in Virginia, he had reached his decision for war. His recommendations, together with the documents exchanged between Monroe and Foster in their July negotiations, greeted Congress at its November convening. But the President did not state clearly his personal reasons for recommending force. His message recommended military preparations, but did not analyze in detail the reasons for making this recommendation. Great Britain, Madison noted laconically, had refused to repeal her Orders and had taken a new and more advanced position that indicated greater intransigence than ever. This action led him to believe that Congress would feel the necessity of putting the nation "into an armour and attitude demanded by the crisis."

The facts communicated by the President threw congressional Republicans into a quandary. They agreed a "crisis" was at hand. Nonimportation had failed to shake Great Britain. Now that the Napoleonic Decrees as they affected American neutral commerce no longer seemed in force, Britain's defense of her own system as retaliation was untenable. Yet in addition to denying the fact of French repeal, Foster had indicated that Britain had no intention of repealing her Orders even if she were to accept, as fact, repeal of the French Decrees. France must repeal her Decrees to the extent they prohibited importation into the Continent of productions and manufactures made in Britain when owned or carried by neutrals. So impossible did this demand appear that its very existence proved Britain would not yield. Meanwhile, on the high seas, British cruisers seized American vessels not complying with the Orders in Council—according to one report in circulation, 100 were lost within six months. Republicans agreed it was necessary to do something to protect American commerce. As George Poindexter, delegate from the Mississippi Territory, observed, shortly after the President's message had been received by Congress: "We cannot tell what will be done, until the Committees report. No one has suggested a specific measure; but all agree *that something must be done*." In a similar state of mind Felix Grundy told the Governor of Tennessee that "something must be done, or we shall loose [sic] our respectability abroad and even cease to respect ourselves." [17]

To observers, the month following the President's message seemed a period of much confusion. Actually, it was a time of slow groping towards common ground, a time when members revolved, canvassed, and discussed various opinions and possibilities. Congressman Thomas Cooke of New York noted on November 6 that "many Voices" were for war but that "more"

knew not what they wanted. Nearly two weeks later opinion
was so incoherent that Nathaniel Macon could confess to perplexity in writing the news of Congress to Joseph Nicholson,
the Maryland Republican:

I see you are for war, and must observe to you, that it seems much
easier to form opinions, at home than here at this place. we are nearly
all too wise or too mysterious to form hasty conclusions; it is however probable, that there is not more than five or six opinions amongst
us, varying from open war to repealing the present restrictive system.

Among those quickly reaching a decision that war was necessary
was Henry Clay. As early as the previous August he had been
over the possibilities and foreseen "inevitable" war if Britain
continued to hold fast; he must have made up his mind the moment he learned the contents of Foster's hand. Perhaps Republican members he picked for the Foreign Relations Committee
—Porter, Calhoun, Grundy, Desha, John A. Harper of New
Hampshire, and Ebenezer Seaver of Massachusetts—had arrived
at a similar conclusion; would he have chosen a majority that
did not agree with him or the President? [18]

In this situation, as Congressman William Lowndes of South
Carolina observed, "the want of some controuling or at least
concentrating influence" was "very obvious." On such a basis
members could predict that impending committee reports would
afford the necessary rallying point. Calhoun noted that members
were "generally very anxious as to the course that will be persued" and predicted that the report of his committee "will in
a great measure determine the course that will be persued." The
committees in both House and Senate invited the Executive to
discuss its views in detail. Charles Tait of Georgia, a member of
the Senate committee, told how Secretary of State Monroe appeared before his group and explained "with utmost frankness
the views of the Admin," giving assurances that "the utmost
harmony prevails in the Cabinet and that they mean bona fide
to enter into the Contest" unless Britain relaxed. Likewise the
Secretary appeared before the House committee, where he made

known as one committee member put it, the *"motives,* the *views* and the *wishes* of the Executive." [19]

On November 29 Chairman Porter of the House committee presented the report of the Republican majority. The report reviewed past efforts to induce repeal of the Orders in Council —embargo, nonintercourse, and nonimportation laws, repeated negotiations and appeals to justice—all unsuccessful. It restated what everybody knew, that Britain had not only refused to admit the fact of French repeal of edicts affecting American neutral rights but had demanded that France repeal provisions affecting British trade with the Continent as a precondition of her own repeal. It stated what everybody knew too, that Britain was seizing and condemning American vessels. Also it cited, as the second of "the great causes of complaint against Great Britain," the impressment of American seamen into the British navy, a practice it described as "carried on with unabated rigor and severity." The time has come, the report proclaimed, when we "must now tamely and quietly submit, or we must resist by those means which God has placed within our reach"—armed force. Despite the emphasis given impressment Porter made it clear in an explanatory speech that this issue had not been the basis of the decision to recommend war. The refusal of Great Britain to repeal the Orders in Council, a refusal made abundantly clear in the negotiations carried on with Foster in July, had caused this action. "The committee, Mr. P. said, after examining the various documents accompanying the President's Message, were satisfied, as he presumed every member of the House was, that all hopes of accommodating our differences with Great Britain by negotiation must be abandoned." Presumably the committee emphasized impressment in order to help justify the recommendation for war and also to lay the groundwork for war aims the Republican leadership intended to pursue after the fighting had begun: repeal of the Orders in Council, no further paper blockades, no more impressment, and return of all impressed American sailors.[20]

During November members had looked towards the impend-

ing report of the Foreign Relations Committee as a crucial deter-
minant of future events. All signs point to the report as fulfilling
its predicted function. Even before formal presentation, members, aware of the contents, had begun rallying to its stand. On
November 21 Congressman Peleg Tallman revealed what com-
mitteemen had been saying, "that it will be best for this country
to go to war with England & take Canady nova scotia &ce."
Attributing the origin of these ideas to the Executive, Tallman
discerned growing willingness among members to support them:
"whether we have war or not will I belive all lay with England
for you may rest assured that Messs. Madison & Co. are Determined not to relax an Inch & I belive a large majority of Congress will Go with them all lengths—if England has no objection to war." [21] With presentation of the report on November
29 opinion began moving swiftly towards a consensus. It is clear
that the document made an impact on Republicans and brought
into sharper focus incipient ideas and tentative positions.[22] A
sudden confidence of Republicans that there would be war reveals the rapid development of agreement. In mid-November
Roberts of Pennsylvania had complained that the "house wants
men to take the lead" and had confessed: "In politics I know not
whether to say we shall have bold & great measures or not." The
day following the report, November 30, he could write with
assurance: "I think these principles will go into effect—& they
must speedily lead to peace or War." A week later on December
8 he told his brother: "Congress will declare War against Britain if she does not do us justice before we rise. I shall vote for
it." Following the report other members were confident that
Congress would declare war. On December 2 Harper of New
Hampshire affirmed: "I feel no hesitation in saying, that the
present Session will not be closed, without an *arrangement*, or
an actual *war* with Great Britain." Clay on December 21 wrote
to an acquaintance who had recently been at the capital: "The
War preparations are advancing with the support of an immense
majority; and I think the spirit you witnessed in their favor when
you were here is not at all diminished." Many other Republicans

believed with George Poindexter of Mississippi that "We shall assuredly have war." [23]

There were Republicans—very few at most—who did not back war until well along in the session. By then Congress had gone so far that retreat from war seemed impossible without absolute disgrace. John Smilie of Pennsylvania admitted that at the beginning of the session he had been for commercial restrictions, not war. He had been against the 25,000-man army, "but as the House have determined otherwise he would now go to war—if we now recede we shall be a reproach among all nations." It is doubtful that there were many others. Calhoun, who certainly should have known, believed that a majority had felt the "justice and necessity" of war measures from the very beginning of the session. It is doubtful that there were many "bluffers" among those Republicans who originally supported measures of military preparation, hoping Britain would retreat under the threat of hostilities but having no idea of war if she did not. Members frankly and openly expressed hopes that military preparations still might possibly produce repeal. William Findley of Pennsylvania and Hugh Nelson of Virginia both avowed that military measures might prevent war, but both men were clearly willing to vote for war if threats proved unsuccessful. But this was true of virtually all Republicans who clung to a dim hope that preparations might possibly produce British repeal and would have rejoiced in such an event. Calhoun expressed the party sentiment when he wrote in May, 1812: "War, I regret, has become unavoidable. I did hope, England would have returned to a sense of justice, when she saw this country determined to avenge her wrongs." [24]

No Republican member genuinely hoped for war or joined the consensus that war was now necessary with any other feeling than deep reluctance and regret. Thus Nathaniel Macon asked the rhetorical question of his congressional colleagues whether there was "a man in the House" who "wishes to go to war if it could possibly be avoided?" John A. Harper avowed: "I pray to God, that he may open the eyes of the British Government to the interests of their renowned nation, and save us, them, and the world, from the evils of the impending conflict." Jonathan Roberts accurately perceived this mood when he wrote in January: "There seems to be no disposition to relax our war measures but I beleive every body would be exceeding glad to remain at peace. the federalists seem sanguine the orders in council will be revoked. I confess I hardly allow myself to hope it." [25] These men did not minimize or close their eyes to the disadvantages and evils of war. Historians have portrayed the leaders as bellicose, fervent, and heedless as to the evils of war. A reading of their correspondence suggests that this does not do them justice. A few Republicans foresaw danger in a standing army, a swollen national debt, corruption of public virtue, and a possible alliance with Napoleon. All foresaw hardships and dangers in war— casualties, expenses, taxes, and commercial and business losses. The nation's military and naval establishments were weak. Thirty years had gone by since the nation had fought a war, and few men were experienced in supply, recruitment, strategy, and tactics under actual war conditions. There was great concern as to whether public opinion would wholeheartedly and unitedly support war against Great Britain at this time with all the hardships and sacrifices it entailed, and which Federalists were bound to exploit.[26]

Calhoun, for instance, was particularly anxious on this score, and expressed fervent hope that Americans would show courage and patriotism in support of the war. "God grant that the people may have sperit to maintain our interest and honor in this momentous period." When word arrived that his own constituents were well disposed, he seemed relieved: "I rejoice to hear my constituents are ready to support the cause of the country with so much Zeal; and that they so clearly perceive the necessity of Taxes. With such a state of the publick sentiment we must succeed; we will cause our rights to be respected." But at the moment of the declaration he seemed again to have doubts: "It will be useless to ma[ke] comments on this great [event?] made necessary by British injustice; I hope the courage and patriot-is[m] of our people, will make it as fortunate as just." Calhoun showed his anxiety in other ways. He kept a close watch on military preparations, called at the war department to learn the progress of recruiting, showed relief when informed of advances in stock-piling military supplies, and betrayed regret and discouragement at the slow pace of preparation and lack of vigor and leadership in the Executive.[27]

Henry Clay was aware of many difficulties and dangers ahead. Following news of the battle of Tippecanoe between Governor William Henry Harrison's army and the Shawnee Indians at the Prophet's town early in November, 1811, instead of calling for immediate chastisement of hostile tribes, he expressed hopes that "as the Indians were repulsed, they will not be disposed to prosecute the War. It will certainly add to our embarrassments if we have to carry on a war with them, as well as their good friends, the English." One enemy at a time was certainly enough, even for the sanguine-tempered leader from Kentucky! Indeed, Clay took no easy view of the matter. Against advocates of 10,000 or 15,000 additional troops he urged authorization of 25,000 men, holding that only a force of this strength, with the 10,000-man army already authorized, would be sufficient to defend our coasts and invade Canada. He kept a close eye on lagging military preparations. Despite congressional enactment of the 25,000-man army, in March he suggested to Monroe that the President recommend provision for a new 10,000-man short-term volunteer force. This would "furnish a force in itself highly useful," and additionally, circumvent constitutional objections against employment of state militia on foreign territory, thus leaving "a certain quarter of the Country disposed to fly off without even a pretext for dereliction." At the same time he recommended a 30-day embargo to warn the country of imminent hostilities and "above all powerfully accelerate preparations for the War." One suspects that he worried about public support for this war: "This country only required resolution and a proper exertion of its immense resources to command respect, and to vindicate every essential right." But the problem was, did the people have these necessary qualities? Clay thought they probably did, but he was not altogether certain: "God grant us a happy result to this new & untried experiment to which the only free government upon earth is about to be subjected! That such will be the issue of the contest I entertain no doubt if the people possess the fortitude and firmness which I believe they do." He referred to the expiration date of the embargo as the period when the American sloop *Hornet* would return "with good or bad news" of British reaction to the new American stand. He certainly did not take war lightly.[28]

Calhoun and Clay were perhaps the two most influential members during the war session—the former as acting Chairman of the House Foreign Relations Committee in the final months of peace, the latter as Speaker of the House. Other Republican members showed much concern as to wartime dangers and difficulties. Charles Tait of Georgia believed that war "is deeply to be regretted," and that we "ought not, if we could, conceal from our view the inconveniences, the suffering, not to say calamities which must necessarily be attendant on a War with G. B." William W. Bibb of Georgia wrote: "So much do I deprecate a war at the present time, and under the existing circumstances of Europe, that I have had great difficulty in bringing my mind to the 'sticking place'; but I consider it unavoidable (unless the steps of our adversary be retraced) without a sacrafice greater in its extent, than will be the calamities of war." William Lowndes of South Carolina was obviously concerned when he told his wife in early November that "the situation indeed of the country is so embarrassing as to divert the attention from individual difficulties." Israel Pickens of North Carolina told a constituent that "I could not have come [to Congress] in a more serious & critical moment." Jesse Franklin affirmed "that there is not a man in the nation woud be more rejoiced than myself to see some event that Shoud render our Military preparations unnecessary but we must make the best of a bad Bargain." Stevenson Archer of Maryland wrote: "War is a calamitous event, & is at all times if possible to be avoided."

Samuel L. Mitchill of New York affirmed that the time had come when "we must combine our strength, try our resources, and atchieve all we can. We must, on this just & necessary occasion, encounter a war, with all its privations, contributions and hardships." Charles Turner of Massachusetts, in describing efforts of the Republican majority to prepare the country for war, exclaimed: "On them rests the tremendous responsibility; I feel its pressure; as we need, so I trust we shall have the prayers of all, who wish well to their Country." Felix Grundy of Tennessee, so often held up as the epitome of irresponsible bellicosity, wrote that the present Congress would "do more *harm* or *good*" than any session for some time, that he would "endeavor to pursue a consistent course, and one which shall in my opinion promote the prosperity of the Country," and that "A Seat in Congress, at present, is too responsible a Station to be even tolerably pleasant." George Washington Campbell of the same state confessed that the prospect of avoiding war was "very gloomy," and later implied that no Republican took the war lightly when expressing the hope that there would be none whose "*fears*, & *apprehensions*" would overcome "their *resolution* & *judgment;* and make them shrink from the contest"—for the sake of "the honor of our Country—& of human nature." [29]

It was quite true that a good deal was said in debate to suggest that some Republicans were spoiling for a fight with Great Britain. Men did wax belligerent, they did ignore or minimize the evils of war, and they did predict quick and easy victory. They talked heatedly and emotionally of accumulated British aggressions on national rights and honor—Orders in Council, impressment, British-incited Indian attacks, the *Chesapeake* outrage, and much else. In vivid colors they painted the horrors of American sailors enslaved on British men-of-war and of Indian scalping raids against frontier women and children, the indignity of American vessels seized on our own coasts, the insulting repudiation of the Erskine agreement, and the growing hardship of the southern and western farmer. They seemed eager for war, for a chance to get revenge for half a decade of unredressed injuries and insults. Yet one should consider the situation they were then facing. The country needed to be aroused. The recruitment of men for the new army, the subscription to the $11,000,000 loan, and the conversion of business operations to a war footing all required that the war seem credible and worthy of sacrifice to private citizens. But how were these objects to be met, except by oratory that received a wide circulation through the newspapers? The President's statements were infrequent and couched in restrained, almost cryptic tones. No new blatant insult, like the *Chesapeake* affair or the Erskine repudiation, had occurred in 1811 to stir national feeling. Britain had once again refused to repeal her Orders, but in terms requiring a better understanding of the complex web of diplomacy than the ordinary citizen possessed. A British envoy had laid out his government's position in an exchange of notes with an American secretary of state which are not easy even for the historian to understand. When many men, Federalists, were telling their friends and constituents that the war was a fraud, the task of rousing the country became even more difficult. When even Republicans suspected the sincerity of colleagues, the task must have seemed monumental. Henry Clay well understood the difficulty. His principal argument for a brief embargo in March—as "a measure of some vigor upon the heels of Henry's disclosure"—was to "give tone to public sentiment," to repress "indiscreet speculation," to enable the prudent "to put under shelter before the storm," and, above all, "powerfully" to "accelerate preparations for the War." [30]

One should consider other motives also. While Congress had as yet no official stenographer and kept no record of its debates, such speeches as were given publication in newspapers probably reached more readers than do speeches made in Congress today. Initially printed in the *National Intelligencer*, the administration organ generally considered the most reliable reporter by Republicans, these speeches would be printed and reprinted by other newspapers in town and country the nation over. Not that many Americans subscribed at this time to such journals, but every tavern and coffee house took one paper at least, and customers could there follow the speeches of their representatives at the capitol. The opportunities in the situation should be obvious. While motivation is extremely difficult to prove, there is the case of Jonathan Roberts, a freshman congressman from Pennsylvania. Roberts was reluctant to embrace war—"every body would be exceeding glad to remain at peace," he told his brother. Yet it was not inconsistent with this opinion for him to wish to seem "active" on his first introduction in the national legislature, or to worry lest a speech of his would be so placed (in the *Intelligencer*'s account) as to appear "to little advantage." Observers like Levi Bartlett, the son of a famous New Hampshire statesman and the brother of a congressman, probably were right when they surmised that members often spoke with an eye to the gallery.[31]

Possibly, too, members were seeking to justify their conduct before constituents. Would voters approve their decision for war simply on the basis of Britain's refusal to repeal the Orders in Council? Should they not be reminded of the long catalogue of unredressed aggressions by this hostile power? Public letters, hot with indignation at countless British atrocities, pointed to this end. John Clopton of Virginia drafted a letter of this kind, cataloguing British aggressions and demanding war in bellicose language. The Virginia congressman sent this letter to an acquaintance, and had him read it "to as many as he can" at the coming meeting of the county court. The letter "may be of advantage" he told his son. Yet Clopton certainly (his personal papers make clear) was reluctant to go to war, and believed it necessary only as a last resort. Felix Grundy wrote warm letters for public perusal and for newspaper publication; his confidential letters were far less flamboyant.[32]

Finally, heavy concentration of belligerent speeches during the December debates suggests the possible operation of another motive. A faint hope remained that Great Britain only needed convincing that the Republican majority genuinely meant war and she would repeal her Orders. Was it not well therefore to show her we meant business? For more than a month, members outdid themselves in recital of British wrongs and in threats of war. This led George Poindexter of the Mississippi Territory to write angrily: "I am so much disgusted with the repetition of our wrongs, and the *windy* storm, which, is sped from Capitol Hill to, Canada, Novescotia, and even, to Halifax, that I am sick to loathing, of, the most eloquent attempt, to present them, in a new, dress to the imagination." By January, when the time for more such warnings to have effect had pretty well passed, speeches became more moderate. Federalists, taking note of the shift in tone, erroneously believed that Republicans meant to back out of war. As one Federalist noted at the end of January, the "war fever" seemed to have "all evaporated," an observation that confirmed his opinion that the war had all along been a bluff. Even Felix Grundy, for example, whose emotional call to arms in December became perhaps the most oft-quoted speech of the session, late in the winter delivered a sober, careful, and moderate analysis of the basis of war.[33]

In summary, the speeches of individual congressmen afford a false impression of eagerness for war. Fiery, belligerent, and oblivious of the consequences as they may seem at first glance, they give a less accurate picture of prevailing reluctance than do private letters. With some such possibilities in mind William Plumer of New Hampshire at the beginning of the session asked a senator to write him privately concerning the news of Congress. Plumer had once been in Congress himself, and would have appreciated the need for a skeptical view of congressional oratory. "By the National Intelligencer, which I regularly receive, I obtain a pretty full account of the debate votes & proceedings of Congress; but it is from private letters only that we can obtain information of the motives views & designs of the Administration & of Congress."[34]

On the existence of a conflict between "war hawks" and "peacemen" within the party, the evidence is also far from conclusive. There was no consistent division within the party over war measures—the army, navy, taxes, or recess—that might reveal such a struggle; the same men may be found on both sides of these issues at different times. There were Republicans who were very suspicious of "bluffers" in their own party—Grundy was one. But suspicion does not prove fact. Grundy was suspicious of Madison and Monroe who were not bluffing, even though at times they might seem to have been.[35]

The great majority of Republicans—south, north, and west—rallied to the idea of war when party leaders had assured everyone that all honorable, pacific measures had been tried and that no choice remained between war and submission. This meant confidence that Jefferson, Madison, and their advisers had earnestly and honestly sought accommodation with both belligerents. It meant acceptance of Henry Clay's avowal: "Not a man in the nation could really doubt the sincerity with which those in power have sought, by all honorable pacific means, to protect the interests of the country." Or of John Sevier's claim: "Our Government have tried negociation until it is exhausted, and there is no doubt in my mind the Executive have observed the most perfect uprightness, and impartial neutrality." In 1812 only men who trusted Jefferson and Madison in their leadership of party and country held such sentiments. These were administration Republicans, men who had agreed with the Virginians on the main outlines of their domestic and foreign policies and who trusted their personal competence and devotion to the Republic. This did not include Federalists, antiadministration Republicans like John Randolph of Roanoke, or Clintonians. But that is another story.[36]

To say all this is not to disclaim the importance of leadership in the Republican march towards the final June declaration of war. Clay and Calhoun deservedly won reputations for their role in shaping and guiding the Republican war program through the Congress. Their energy and determination impressed members of both parties at the time, and their contribution to the business of legislating the means of war was vital.[37] Without their presence Congress might have become paralyzed in squabbles over the details of war legislation. Nor is it contended that Republicans were generally agreed on the manner and timing of hostilities. A sizable group in the party wanted an undeclared limited maritime war instead of the full-scale hostilities that a declaration of war would bring. Some of the same men, and others, wanted to postpone hostilities until the nation was more adequately prepared. But these were differences over strategy, not over the fundamental question of war or peace. It is contended, however, that the main body of the Republican party did not separate into two factions that differed during most of the session over the question of war or peace; that the great majority of Republicans reached a consensus that no acceptable peaceful alternative remained between the end of July, 1811 (the Foster negotiations), and the end of November, 1811 (the report of the House Foreign Relations Committee); and that the great majority came to this decision with no little regret and reluctance, however eager some might appear in their speeches. Given these conclusions, perhaps the time has come for us to relegate a misleading term—"the war hawks of 1812"—to the realm of partisan misunderstanding and historical mythology.

There remains a crucial problem. Republicans rejected submission and chose war. They regarded this choice as a choice between evils, and they took the lesser—war. They were reluctant to go to war. They would have been happy to avoid it. What might they have anticipated from submission that outweighed the risks and evils of war? Why did Republicans prefer war as a less dangerous course than submission?

(4)

THE REPUBLIC IN PERIL

Congressman Jonathan Roberts of Pennsylvania had expressed belief that "every body would be exceeding glad to remain at peace." Congressman Nathaniel Macon of North Carolina had implied the same when he asked rhetorically whether any man would wish to fight if war could be avoided. The statement of Congressman John Harper of New Hampshire: "I pray to God, that he may open the eyes of the British Government to the interests of their renowned nation, and save us, them, and the world, from the evils of the impending conflict," struck a keynote for the party as a whole. The repeated expressions "we are driven to war," "we must fight," "we have no choice," reflect these feelings. Up to the very moment war began the party would have welcomed, with great relief, news of British repeal of the Orders in Council.[1]

Understandably, Republicans had not found it easy to decide for war. William W. Bibb of Georgia spoke for many colleagues when he confessed to "great difficulty in bringing my mind to the 'sticking place.'" He deprecated a war "at the present time, and under the existing circumstances of Europe," as an aid to Napoleonic ambition to conquer the world. He may have considered, as did colleagues, a number of other evils. The nation would suffer from losses in men and materials; the country was young and could ill afford loss of population and wealth. Casualties would occur, however brilliant the strategy or skillful the conduct of battle. A stoppage in all trade, a fall in revenue, a decline in agricultural prices, and destruction of shipping and war materials would probably occur. All these adversities, undesirable in themselves, might well culminate in alienation of public opinion and a Federalist victory. "Is there not some ground to fear a reverse of public opinion?" asked Charles Tait of Georgia, "I think there is." In Republican minds a "change of men," as Secretary of the Treasury Gallatin put it, might "lead to a disgraceful peace, to absolute subserviency hereafter to G. B., and even to substantial alterations in our institutions." [2]

War might possibly have other pernicious effects. A swollen national debt, the probable outcome of prolonged hostilities, in addition to the check it would give to national growth, would threaten republican government. Creation of a large standing army cast another gloomy prospect. War would corrupt "our habits, manners, and republican simplicity," thought Hugh Nelson of Virginia. There was a chance of being driven into the arms of Napoleon during the course of the contest.[3]

There was also concern over the outcome of the war. The nation's military and naval establishments were weak. Harbor defenses and fortifications stood in disrepair. Few men had experience in meeting problems of supply, recruitment, strategy, and tactics. There was concern as to whether Americans would volunteer in sufficient numbers to allow effective military operations, and whether they would pay taxes or subscribe to the loan. What if Great Britain bombarded coastal cities or invaded at some weakly defended point? What if the expedition against Canada should fail? Would not this lead to the "change of men" that all Republicans so greatly feared? [4]

Obviously, there were major dangers. Logically, submission must have involved still greater evils if Republicans considered war preferable. In the phrase of Bibb of Georgia, he considered war "unavoidable, (unless the steps of our adversary be retraced) without a sacrafice greater in its extent, than will be the calamities of war." A "sacrafice" greater than the "calamities of war" would prove great indeed. Other Republicans showed less restraint. Joseph Desha of Kentucky declared that "it would be folly in the extreme to depend upon negociation any longer." Israel Pickens of North Carolina averred that "evils incalculable must visit our country, if we continue to slumber." David R.

Williams of South Carolina asserted that "indifference is criminal" and that submission would be "a ruinous and disgraceful course." Jesse Franklin of North Carolina wrote after the declaration that peace any longer would have been "Criminal." The President himself reportedly said that "anything was better than remaining in such a state" of ruinous peace.[5]

Not until June, 1812, eight months after the session began, did Congress take up the question of actually voting a declaration of war. Meanwhile, Republican leaders showed anxiety lest the nation fail to resist the Orders in Council by force. Their feelings indicated the extreme peril in submission. Felix Grundy of Tennessee, concerned over the decision, wrote that he was "hoping for the best & fearing the worst that can befall our Country." William Blackledge of North Carolina exclaimed on the matter of congressional energy: "God forbid they should prove to be the 2d edition of the 10th [Congress]." During the fortnight of debate on the war resolution, Roberts wrote emotionally that "the suspense we are in is worse than hell!!!!" Even the sanguine-tempered Clay of Kentucky betrayed strong feeling in his avowal that "*all* is at hazzard." [6]

Republican leaders outside of Congress also felt anxiety. Elbridge Gerry, Governor of Massachusetts, thus wrote on learning in June of House approval of the war resolution: "God grant to the Senate the same Wisdom & fortitude. Our anxiety is great, in a state of such awful suspense; but we have great confidence in a majority of its members." Henry Dearborn, a Massachusetts Republican leader and commander of the northern army, confirmed that the "Republicans of New England, with few, if any, exceptions, as far as I have the means of knowing, are extreemly anxious for the ultimate discision of Congress on the question of war." Thomas Rodgers, a Pennsylvania Republican editor and party leader, deemed the American people now "ripe for the contest, and to delay would be jeopardizing all." John Binns, another Pennsylvania Republican editor, confided that "I wait in confidence but not without my fears & forebodings, to which I give no tongue." Richard Rush, newly appointed Comptroller of the Treasury and close observer of congressional affairs, had perhaps the most expressive words. On May 16: "I think *all* is at stake on our holding on." On May 24: "We are gone" if we hesitate. On June 9: "What a time of anxious, most anxious, suspense it is? what fears, what doubts, what bodings, what hopes, for our common our beloved country, now fill the bosoms, and throb the bosoms of all?" [7]

It is natural to wonder at such expressions. What kind of prospect haunted Republicans as they considered the consequences of submission? What dark perils lay in store for the nation from a continuation of peace?

The prospect of continuing economic adversity had influence on members. Some southern Republicans thought the British blockade had caused price decline in cotton and tobacco which in normal times had been able to reach buyers in France, the Low Countries, and Italy. John C. Calhoun of South Carolina saw in the low price of cotton "the hand of foreign injustice." David R. Williams of the same state directed a "curse" at the one who had "meddled" with the cotton and tobacco export; the most recent crop was rotting at home in the hands of the grower, "waiting the repeal of the Orders in Council." Langdon Cheves of South Carolina asserted that the blockade of Continental markets explained the depression in cotton and tobacco. But it would be a mistake to put great weight on sectional interests. These men also stressed the economic implications for the entire nation. Calhoun wrote of the contest as involving important national rights and national interests, and in speeches called attention to losses not only in agriculture but in commerce too. Williams averred that the British system was "levelled at your most valuable interests," and "in a pecuniary point of view" carried "poverty and wretchedness everywhere." Cheves called for war for the protection of commerce, "the second great interest of the nation" and vital to the prosperity of agriculture.[8]

The economic consequences of submission worried Republicans from other areas of the country. Men foresaw continuing depression in agriculture and commerce. They predicted a large loss in tariff revenue as the result of continuing economic stagnation. William King of North Carolina asserted that we must fight for the right to export our produce—"the deprivation of which strikes at the very foundation of our prosperity." Roberts of Pennsylvania declared that to give up "our fair export trade" was to affect adversely "the great resources of national strength." Henry Clay of Kentucky declared that "if pecuniary considerations alone are to govern, there is sufficient motive for war." [9]

Despite this evidence, however, one should not overemphasize the economic motive. The private correspondence of individual members does not stress economic considerations. Leaders such as Calhoun gave equal emphasis to both "national honor and interest" in letters explaining the need to protect American maritime rights. David R. Williams of South Carolina remarked that the British system "in a pecuniary view" was harmful, but added that "in every other [point of view] it ought to be spurned with detestation." Some Republicans even denied the importance of assuring American trade with the Continent. Jesse Franklin of North Carolina complained that overseas commerce should have been left from the very beginning to fend for itself without government protection.

I have always been of opinion that the united states true interest was as it respected our Commerce—after Laying on proper Discriminating duties upon Tunage &c to have left its Regulation pretty much to the Custom House and insurence office. Particularly in such a state of things as has existed in Europe for years passd. But such has been the thirst of our Citizens for foreign Commerce and such their unbridled avarice in pusuit of Commerce and extravegant profit that they have run into great extream, and perhaps rather exsesably Carried the government a Long already too far.[10]

Men also weighed in the balance against submission the question of America's sovereignty. Many Republicans believed that surrender to the Orders in Council would be to yield a portion of national independence. The right to regulate one's own commerce on the high seas was the exclusive prerogative of every truly independent nation. "Practically considered," said Williams of South Carolina, the operation of the Orders in Council "is the exercise of supreme legislation over us, involving not only all the attributes of legitimate sovereignty but despotism direct." When it is considered, said Pickens of North Carolina, that the right of carrying our products to foreign markets belongs to the independence won by the patriots of the Revolution, "the duty on us becomes indispensable, to protect it unemcumbered for posterity, who have a fair claim to the valuable inheritance." Grundy of Tennessee wrote that "Our Fathers fought for and bequeathed liberty & Independence to *us* their children," and that a firm and manly effort "will enable us to transmit to *our children* the rich inheritance unimpaired." [11]

Furthermore, to yield a portion of sovereignty would only encourage further infringements. "Further forbearance," argued Tait of Georgia, "would but invite further aggression and . . . no nation ever did preserve its independance and its Rights which did not repel with spirit the first incroachments on them." Clay made this point in debate. Yield to the Orders "and to-morrow intercourse between New Orleans and New York—between the planters on James River and Richmond, will be interdicted." The "career of encroachment is never arrested by submission. It will advance while there remains a single privilege on which it can operate." Pickens of North Carolina declared:

History affords no instance of a nation securing, or successfully resisting encroachments on its sovereignty, when this resistance has been weak and timid. On the contrary, does not all experience show, that in proportion as a nation is found regardless of injuries, even of minor consequence, in that proportion have exactions been made upon it.

The same thought led John Sevier of Tennessee to write that the time had again come "to contend for our Independency." [12]

A concern for national honor also led Republicans towards war. Many anticipated that failure to resist would degrade and demoralize Americans. They could reason from their own sense of honor. Senator Thomas Worthington of Ohio considered "the Point of Honour" as the crux of the controversy and told Augustus J. Foster, the British minister, that "he would rather live on a Crust in the Interior than live degraded." William Eustis, the Secretary of War, gave eloquent testimony of the humiliation he would feel if the country failed to fight. Answering George Logan, the famous Quaker pacifist who had written opposing war, Eustis avowed that this could only mean "submission with disgrace." On what honorable basis could a new negotiation be initiated? "Describe what you imagine might be said. Look at it after it is written—and see if a check of disgrace does not follow every word. Lay aside every sense of honor & national pride in your men. imagine them perfect courtiers who will speak with out a blush—but remember they are to speak the language of an honest decent long abused nation." Therefore, Republicans could easily project how fellow citizens would react to submission. "[S]omething must be done" avowed Grundy of Tennessee in November, 1811, or we shall "cease to respect ourselves." General Henry Dearborn described the shame Americans would feel, writing during the June debates: "[I]f the Senate should ultimately negative a vote of the House for war, we may hang our harps on the willow, and hide our heads in the dust, for we shall have no character left, worth contending for." [13]

Even so, when Clay warned that "*all* is at hazzard," when Grundy feared "the worst that can befall our Country," when President Madison exclaimed that "anything was better than remaining in such a state," concerns larger than assured commerce, national sovereignty, and national honor were at stake. Republicans thought of themselves as defenders of republicanism against enemies both at home and abroad. Certainly the economic consequences of submission concerned many. Certainly the threat to national independence caused worry; certainly, too, did the matter of personal and public self-respect. But Republicans in 1812 feared above all else that submission would threaten their control of the nation's political life and draw odium down upon republican government. No other possibility could have so overweighed the predicted dangers and evils of war, or evoked such dire forecasts at the thought of submission.

Republicans anticipated peril to the Republic from party disgrace and the loss of political power to the Federalists—from "a change of men." Having taken upon themselves the task of defending the nation's commerce, independence, and honor against foreign aggression, Republicans could foresee that their own party would bear the brunt of public scorn if they now gave up the struggle. Thus John Binns, the Philadelphia editor, wrote on the eve of war: "The honor of the Nation and that of the party are bound up together and both will be sacrificed if war be not declared." Now that all measures short of war had failed, the administration and its Republican supporters in Congress must embrace war, or court disaster at the polls. James G. Jackson of Virginia, a former congressman writing from retirement, warned President Madison, his brother-in-law, of this danger: "I am rejoiced that the crisis has produced a corresponding attitude because I fully believe the national spirit & the national honor demand it and if the Government were now to succumb—what with the pressure from abroad & at home—it would be crushed to annihilation." William Crawford, a Pennsylvania congressman, feared the downfall of the administration. Writing the President he urged more vigorous direction in leading Republicans to war—"the only safe & honorable alternative which offers to preserve [the nation's] independence." For "even among those who profess to have *only* the same objects in view, so much diversity of sentiment prevails; that some means to unite their views & their efforts, appears essential to the immediate preservation of the government." From John Sevier, the famous Indian fighter and Tennessee congressman, came in May, 1812, another forthright statement of the danger: "The Government have exhausted every measure to support peace, and an honest and impartial neutrality, but all in vain, and in my opinion nothing but a war can possibly save the *Government*, and the *Nation*." One may imagine Sevier's thoughts on the subject of submission: surrender of "our Independency," a change of men, Federalist betrayal of the Republic.[14]

Federalist taunts during the session fed these fears of political

disaster. Barring a last-minute British concession, actions and
words had firmly committed the Republican majority to war.
Federalists in Congress and throughout the country responded
with scoffs and derision: the ruling party had neither the intention, the courage, nor the ability to make war, and would never
do so. Under such an attack Republicans felt the precariousness
of their position still more keenly. Governor Gerry expressed
a common view in describing opinion in Massachusetts: "The
anxiety here is great for the final decision. The opposition in-
creases with delay, & predicts that it will terminate in vapour.
This would produce on the one part a compleat triumph, & on
the other an overthrow." In April a movement got under way
in Congress for a brief adjournment previous to the final decision. Some Republicans feared this might divert the march towards war. John A. Harper, the New Hampshire congressman,
wrote in a private letter: "In my opinion, if we have a recess, we
shall have no war, but complete disgrace"; and again on the same
subject of a recess: "[Y]ou may well consider that the friends
of the government feel anxious."

Roberts, the Pennsylvania congressman, predicted disaster
from an adjournment which seemed to him "as settling the question of peace and war in favor of peace." When it became likely
that the measure would pass, the Pennsylvanian moved to disallow compensation to members during their absence from the capital. "Every consideration of a personal & public nature engaged
me to oppose it—When it seemd that no hope was left but thro
the weakness or the error of our friends we were to be thrown
prostrate before our enemies—I movd to disallow any compensation during the recess." Not only did he think adjournment
would leave the President alone at a dangerous time—"worse
than all it would have been taken as evidence of the indecision
of Congress & of an anti warlike spirit in the public councils."
It is understandable that Roberts should have greeted the final
decision for war with satisfaction. His party had given the lie
to Federalist propaganda. The declaration of war was "a great
point gain'd. . . . The Feds & their Foster are both at last de-

ceiv'd. They persuaded themselves that war could not nor dare not be resorted to & with all the warning they at Last are by surprise." [15]

If Republicans foresaw party dishonor in submission, would not disgrace also fasten itself to the form of government that permitted such weakness? Ever since the Revolution American leaders had been conscious of the unproven capacity of their republic to function effectively in the jungle of international life. The question was still unanswered whether a government made up entirely of elected members possessed enough unity of purpose and firmness of will to give full protection to vital national interests—by force if necessary. Years of temporizing and postponement in the face of European maritime aggression—negotiation after negotiation, restriction after commercial restriction—had deepened doubts as to the competence of the present American form of government. Perhaps, after all, republicanism was (as Washington once put it) "ideal & fallacious." Thus, Henry Clay, deploring the fear of British power in the "councils of the nation" and its influence on the retreat from the embargo in 1809, referred to "that dishonorable repeal which has so much tarnished the character of our Government." It was of the utmost importance to dispel all doubt as to the capacity of republican government and to avoid giving any further proof of weakness.[16]

Republicans warned that submission would disgrace not only their party but also the government. Some tentatively made their predictions. Gideon Granger of Connecticut, the postmaster general, in December, 1811, confessed: "I cannot perceive the grounds on which we can remain at peace without a change of measures which will dishonor the Administration and possibly the goverment." Others voiced more certain opinions. Joseph Gales, Republican editor of the nation's leading newspaper, the semiofficial *National Intelligencer*, avowed that the standing of republican government had become involved in the issue of war versus submission. "Not only the rights of the nation, but the character of the government, are involved in the issue," he wrote. "The deliberations of Congress 'at this momentous era,' will, perhaps, do more to stamp the character of genuine republican governments, than has been effected in this respect since the creation of the world." Congressman James Pleasants of Virginia believed firmness imperative for the reputation of the government. Pleasants wrote in 1812 that he failed to see "how it can be any thing else" than war. Remarks made during debate explain his rejection of submission. He pointed to a growing feeling at home and abroad that the American government was unable to stand firm on its own resolves and urged the importance of dispelling this impression. "A very general impression has been produced on foreign Governments, and indeed on this people also, that our councils are so vibratory, so oscillating, that we are incapable of carrying into effect our own resolves." It was "of the utmost importance to us that that impression should be done away, almost at any hazard." It was "the interest of no party, but of the whole people, that our own character should be fixed; that we should no longer be the sport of foreigners, nor an object of distrust to our own citizens." Congressman Hugh Nelson of Virginia stated the great importance of refuting impressions of weakness. Great Britain and France believed (he told constituents in July, 1812, explaining his vote for war) that our republican government was "inefficient and incompetent to exert the power and energy of the nation, and to assume the attitude and posture of war."

[To] repel these unfounded imputations, to demonstrate to the world and especially to the belligerents, that the people of these states were united, one and indivisible in all cases of concern with foreign nations, to shew that our republican government was competent to assert its rights, to maintain the interests of the people, and to repel all foreign aggression, were objects with me of primary importance. My conduct as your representative has been regulated entirely by these great and important considerations.[17]

Talk of war and military legislation led to more such expressions. To retreat from these pledges to fight would be sure proof of weakness. John McKim, Jr., a Maryland merchant and party leader, lamented "so much unsteadyness in the Councils of the Nation," and exclaimed: "If the Stand that is now Taken is departed from, Without bringing England to Justice, we may as well give up our Republican Government & have a Despot to rule over us." Calhoun of South Carolina warned of the harmful effects of submission on the prestige of the government: "I think the friends of the country of whatever politicks, must see, that it is impossible for us to receede without the greatest injury to the character of the government." Congressman Burwell Bassett of Virginia warned that there was "nothing so much to be guarded against in this government as vacillation," and that there was "more now at stake than the mere question of war or peace"; if we failed to fight now "the people never would believe that Congress or the Government possessed energy enough to support their rights." [18]

Such expressions reveal how Republicans linked the prestige of republicanism to the issue of war versus submission. Submission would demonstrate that republican government lacked energy, staying power, the ability to organize and bring to bear the will and strength of the nation. In the event of submission, would republicanism survive? It seemed possible that it would not. Proven inability to ensure such vital concerns as the economic interests of citizens, national sovereignty, and national honor might destroy the faith of all America in the republican form of government.

A government must afford protection to the personal economic interests of its citizens if it wishes to keep their loyalty, urged John Roberts, a Pennsylvania Republican, in April, 1812. Otherwise, citizens will not give the government their confidence and support.

[T]he Circle I am acquainted with have pretty much made up their minds to meet a War—Town & Country say our condition cant be worse than it has been and it is to the Representatives of the Nation we now look—and I think with [Edward] Gibbon [the historian]

"that that Government which is found too weak for the protection
of its Citizens, will be found to[o] weak and unworthy [of] their
protection."

Calhoun repeatedly expressed such a view. The Carolinian believed it to be a prime duty of a government to give protection
to its citizens. Unless it did so, he implied, it could not long exist.
Speaking to the House during the war debates, Calhoun declared
that the government must "protect every citizen in the lawful
pursuit of his business"; that the citizen "will then feel that he
is backed by the Government; that its arm is his arms; and will
rejoice in its increased strength and prosperity." Calhoun told
Augustus J. Foster, the British minister, at a Washington state
dinner, "that the Merchants would put up with any wrong and
only thought of Gain, but a Government should give Protection." Calhoun's personal correspondence shows that he believed American opinion to be dissatisfied with the protection
afforded by the government. The South Carolina congressmen
felt that a long period of negotiations and commercial restrictions had caused disillusion at home and contempt abroad. All
efforts had failed to maintain respect for "national honor and
interest." Negotiation and restrictions "might suit an inconsider-
able nation, or one that had not such important rights at stake.
Experience has proved it improper for us. Its effects have been
distrust at home and contempt abroad." He therefore hoped
that Congress would stick to its "salutary resolve" of military
preparations.[19]

Following the declaration of war Calhoun returned to this
point. Great Britain had repealed her Orders in Council on a
conditional basis, but now the issue was impressment—the protection of American seamen against compulsory service in the
British navy. In a scathing attack on continued Federalist obstructionism, Calhoun warned that such opposition could paralyze the war effort. When governments failed to protect citizens, they failed in their most essential function and forfeited
public confidence. Indeed, those responsible for obstructing the

operations of republican governments had commonly been among the first to exploit ensuing public discontent to their destruction—an obvious allusion to suspected Federalist purposes.

The evil [of partisan opposition] is deeply rooted in the constitution of all free governments, and is the principal cause of their weakness and destruction. It has but one remedy, the virtue and intelligence of the people—it behooves them as they value the blessings of their freedom, not to permit themselves to be drawn into the vortex of party rage. For if by such opposition the firmest government should prove incompetent to maintain the rights of the nation against foreign aggression, they will find realized the truth of the assertion that government is protection, and that it cannot exist where it fails of this great and primary object. The authors of the weakness are commonly the first to take the advantage of it, and turn it to the destruction of liberty.[20]

A government must also assure national independence. If British infringement of American sovereignty went unchallenged, would not this weaken the attachment of the people to a government found unable to protect so vital an interest? Richard Leech, a Pennsylvania leader, made this point to a party colleague: "I confess I feel the most painful anticipations. How is it possible that a Govt. can have the respect & Confidence either of its own Citizens or of Foreign Nations which is afraid to do any thing more than *talk* about its Independence & its rights?" John Campbell, a Virginia leader and state representative, wrote his brother late in 1812 that he had been for war in order to demonstrate "the stability of the government" and prove its capacity "to support our independence," concluding: "Time will soon test the durability of republican governments and shew the truth or falicy of the maxim that man is incapable of self-government." Among members of Congress Nathaniel Macon of North Carolina declared that the nation must now fight to protect its sovereignty or place its destiny in the care of some authority other than the present government. "If we cannot fight by paper restrictions, we must meet force by force. It we cannot do this, it is time we put ourselves under the protection of some other Power." [21]

Finally, there were Republicans who foresaw that Americans would not undergo dishonorable and degrading submission without reacting against the cause of their shame. Submission would depress national honor to so low a level that citizens would seek another kind of government to restore their sense of self-respect. National pride—"the national spirit" as contemporaries called it—had to be supported if Americans were to remain loyal to republicanism. James Jackson of Virginia, the former congressman, expressed this point of view. At the time of the *Chesapeake* affair he had written to Madison, who was then Secretary of State:

[A] tame submission to such outrages will disgrace the Government & its Friends: it will be the signal for every species of insults, until the national spirit, broken, sunk, & degraded: will return with loathing & abhorrence from the Republican system we now so fondly cherish & take refuge against such wrongs in a military despotism, where another Buonaparte, or a Burr will give Law to the Republic.

What was true in 1807 was no less so in 1812. Among members of Congress, Roberts of Pennsylvania stated this view in debate. Submission, he declared, "must not only affect us, in the great resources of national strength; but it must break the spirit of our citizens, and make them infidels in the principle of self-government." [22]

Thus Republicans saw in submission great danger to republicanism. A government found unable to protect such important concerns as the personal economic interest of citizens, national sovereignty, and national honor might well forfeit public support. But these dark warnings of waning confidence remain tantalizingly obscure as to ultimate processes. Precisely how the Republic would fall is rarely discussed in available source material. Perhaps men were not entirely clear in their own minds how the catastrophe would occur. A few hints point to concrete possibilities. Jackson of Virginia clearly predicted that a man on horseback would come to rescue Americans from the depths of humiliation, "another Buonaparte, or a Burr." David Campbell, a Virginia Republican, also anticipated the rise of a military dictator. Demoralized by submission, wrote Campbell, Americans will "crouch to the oppressor like the slaves of Europe, and then, a violent, unprincipled & misguided rabble become fit instruments for some designing and desperate leader to commit acts, the cruelty of which the world has not yet seen an equal." Edward Fox, a Pennsylvania Republican, foresaw demoralization, increasing factional squabbles, the disgust and despair of "well disposed men," and ultimately such disorder that "any change will be readily agreed to that will promise quiet and tranquility." Wilson Cary Nicholas of Virginia, writing in 1813 when the American war effort had stalled, warned that domestic enemies of republicanism might persuade the American people to adopt a different government.

[O]ur feebleness and imbecility now will invite agressive attempts to conquer us hereafter. Perhaps the greatest & most pressing danger to us is that it may lead to a change in our government which will lose the confidence and attachment of the people. It may not be difficult to induc[e] them to believe that a government that can neither defend the persons nor the property of the Citizens nor preserve the national character and honor is not worthy of their support. Altho as in this case the failure may justly be ascribed to the wickedness of some and the folly of others.

Other Republicans feared a Federalist return to power. In the event of submission, so these men believed, the Federalist party, whose leaders presumably championed monarchy and aristocracy, would gain popular favor. William Plumer of New Hampshire, a former Federalist turned Republican, predicted Federalist gains among disillusioned citizens. Congress must remain in session one month longer, he wrote to Congressman Harper at the end of April. "By that time the Admin will have information on which they can rely from England, whether that haughty nation will do us justice, without an appeal to arms. If she refuses, one of two things will follow, Congress will declare war, or the government of our Country will be *degraded*—degraded so that *hosts of tories will* emphatically *be* found *in private life*." Indeed, thought Plumer, a war declaration "must necessarily

produce a great change in public opinion & the state of parties—
British partizans must then either close their lips in silence or
abscond." Again, in May, he deplored the spectacle of so many
members obtaining leave of absence, feared a quorum might not
be raised on the war question, and exclaimed: "But we must not
despair of the Republic—a steady firm undeviating prudent spirit
will save us from our fears." The danger seemed real enough.
Even if Federalists gained control only in the northeast, they
could secede from the Union and rejoin the British empire.[23]

Finally, there are the views of President James Madison and
his chief adviser on foreign policy matters, Secretary of State
James Monroe. The President was opposed to submission because of its ruinous economic effects. He felt that surrender to
British blockade of the Continent would hurt all classes of people
in America. The British market would continue to be over-
charged with American exports, causing low prices for farmers and planters. Disproportionate imports from Great Britain
"would drain from us the precious metals, endanger our monied
Institutions; arrest our internal improvements, and would strangle
in the cradle, the manufactures which promise so vigorous a
growth." The "Ship owners & Shipbuilders and mariners" must
be equal sufferers in the cramping effect of British blockades
on commerce. The President saw other evils in submission: national dishonor and the betrayal of independence. "It would be,"
he wrote, "a voluntary surrender of the persons and property
of our Citizens sailing under the neutral guaranty of an Independent flag." Furthermore, it "would recolonize our commerce
by subjecting it to a foreign Authority; with the sole difference
that the regulations of it formerly were made by Acts of Parliament and now, by orders in Council."

At the Constitutional Convention in 1787 Madison had labored
to save republicanism. His efforts to organize opposition to the
Federalists in the 1790s had been to save this precious form of
government. In 1812 he was again concerned. Richard Rush,
a Pennsylvania Republican, famous in later years as a diplomat
and cabinet member, was the newly appointed Comptroller of

the Treasury. Rush believed that further submission to British Orders in Council would destroy republicanism as a system of government for all time and that Americans must therefore resort to war. "Being the only republick, the destinies of that sort of government are in our keeping. Should we stand by and see it longer debased by submission, or sordid avarice, its cause is gone forever." Moreover, being "the first republick," that is, "genuine popular democratical government" at war since antiquity, Rush believed there to be "proportional considerations to animate us to great deeds, and hold out to us prospects of glory." In a drawing-room conversation with the President, Rush had propounded these two ideas. Madison, reported Rush to a correspondent in April, 1812, "fell in with them, particularly the last, which he thought should animate." Here the President, in agreement with the concern behind Rush's first proposition, stressed the second, possibly to suggest means of arousing national enthusiasm. But the future of republicanism was not far from his thoughts, as other evidence reveals. It was Madison's concern that dictated a passage in the Annual Message of November, 1812, where he reviewed the course of British aggression.

To have shrunk under such circumstances from manly resistance would have been a degradation blasting our best and proudest hopes; it would have struck us from the high rank where the virtuous struggles of our fathers had placed us, and have betrayed the magnificent legacy which we hold in trust for future generations.

There was also the Second Inaugural Address in which the President stated that war had not been declared by the United States until all hope of accommodation had been exhausted, "nor until this last appeal could not longer be delayed without breaking down the spirit of the nation, destroying all confidence in itself and in its political institutions, and either perpetuating a state of disgraceful suffering or regaining by more costly sacrifices and more severe struggles our lost rank and respect among independent powers."

There was also, we may infer, fear of Federalist resurgence

in the President's mind. His wife, Dolley Madison, seems to say so in a letter to her sister, Mrs. Anna Cutts, wife of Congressman Richard Cutts of Saco, Maine. Congressman Cutts had been on leave during much of the session, and Mrs. Madison was urging her sister to persuade Richard to return to Washington. The President's brother-in-law was needed to help the party in the coming vote on war. "You may rely upon it, if Mr. Cutts does not come it will be a disadvantage to him as well as to his party—some of them have reproached him already, but he will be here, we hope, just in time—not a moment too soon, it is supposed, to give his vote for War." [24]

Madison's Virginia compatriot and chief adviser was James Monroe. The prestige and security of republicanism depended on successful defense of maritime rights, wrote Monroe during the war debates. The Federalists demanded repeal of all commercial restrictions and surrender of our commerce to British regulation. "But where," asked Monroe, would this act of submission "have left the U States? & what effect would it have had on the character—, & destiny of our republican system of govt? My idea was that such a step would have put it in great danger if it had not subverted it eventually." Likewise, to rely further on measures which had failed to accomplish their object, "while war is carried on, on the other side, is equally unworthy the character & inconsistent with the true interests of the U States." In an interview with the British minister in the month before war Monroe expressed a belief that America must now fight, or he would despair of the present republican form of government. As Foster recorded:

Mr. Monroe confidentially spoke of the impossibility there was for this Government now to recede without a change of any kind on the part of England. He even said that he should feel like a man disgraced and ashamed to shew his face, if after the steps which were taken they were now to submit; that they had no ground on which to stand but upon continuing their present course; that should they submit now it would be impossible ever again to speak about neutrality or neutral rights; that they might as well be without a Government at once and that he for his part would rather quit the

United States at once and go somewhere else where there was a Government that could make itself respected.[25]

The enthusiasm of the Republican response to news of the war declaration is a measure of men's anxiety over possible submission. One might have expected hostilities against the world's most formidable naval power to have aroused somber thoughts of coming difficulties and dangers. Initial responses were, on the contrary, exultant. An unconfirmed report of the congressional declaration of war prompted Thomas Rodgers, the Pennsylvania editor, to exclaim: "The news last night cheered me; for I was, I confess, very much afraid of the Senate. If the news is true we hear, the Republic is safe, and all must now rally round the standard of our country." Celebrations, parades, illuminations, resolutions, and salutes testify to the emotions released by the congressional action. Governor Gerry of Massachusetts expressed the feelings of many. He wrote to President Madison soon after receiving news of the declaration: "War is declared, God be praised, our country is safe." A stranger, observing these events, could easily have concluded that war was just over, not just beginning.[26]

It remained for Henry Clay to sound a more realistic judgment. Clay in 1810 had referred to repeal of the embargo as "that dishonorable repeal which has so much tarnished the character of our Government." Clay in 1810 had written a party colleague in the Madison administration of his "great solicitude for our Country & for our cause." Now Clay in 1812 believed that "*all*" was "at hazzard." Submission was a "potion of British poison actually presented to our lips." But war could be fatal also. The simple fact of a declaration by no means assured the fate of republican government. A long, difficult, and perilous road lay ahead. Once the government had shown itself capable of declaring war, it must show itself capable of waging war. The fate of the world's only republic, Clay implied, might depend on the fact: "God grant us a happy result to this new & untried experiment to which the only free government upon earth is about to be subjected! That such will be the issue of the contest

I entertain no doubt if the people possess the fortitude and firmness which I believe they do."

It is therefore understandable that men should have viewed the War of 1812, its beginning and outcome, as demonstrating that the American Republic could function effectively in international life. Reviewing the recent contest in a speech delivered in 1816, Henry Clay could thus avow:

Have we gained nothing by the war? Let any man look at the degraded condition of this country before the war; the scorn of the universe, the contempt of ourselves; and tell me if we have gained nothing by the war? What is our present situation? Respectability and character abroad—security and confidence at home. If we have not obtained in the opinion of some the full measure of retribution, our character and Constitution are placed on a solid basis, never to be shaken.[27]

The second war with Great Britain had proved, if it accomplished nothing else, that the Republic was not utopian.

(5)

THE TRIALS OF PREPARATION

To the great majority of Republicans war seemed necessary in 1812 because the alternative to war, submission, presented unacceptable consequences. There were grave risks and evils in war, Republicans well knew; there were greater risks and evils in continuing peace. Broadly speaking, most Republicans felt that American policy and diplomacy had reached a point where force was necessary. But among them there arose during the session sharp clashes as to how force should be brought to bear on the adversary with greatest effectiveness and with minimal danger to the nation.

Ever since the 1790s James Madison had regarded commercial restriction as an instrument of diplomacy, a method of inducing recognition of American neutral rights by the European belligerents. This was the idea expressed in his phrase "a commercial weapon . . . properly shaped for the Executive hand." [1] After the failure of negotiations with Foster in July, 1811, the complete inefficacy of this weapon in the present situation became apparent. In turning to the alternative of force he did not abandon vital concepts in the previous policy. He had conceived of commercial restrictions as an aid to diplomacy—so now did he think of war. While preparations for war advanced he would use, in a last-minute effort to induce concessions from Great Britain, the threat of war. If this failed, armed force would win concessions.

The President announced the first phase of this policy on November 5, 1811, in his opening message to Congress. He recommended that Congress enact such legislation as would prepare the country for war and promised "to meet with cordiality" a repeal of the British Orders in Council as they affected American neutral rights. Secretary Monroe soon after appeared before the House and Senate Committees on Foreign Relations and made known Executive views on strategy. The nation should prepare to fight both on land and sea. It should make ready regulars and volunteers for military operations against Canada. It should prepare naval vessels and privateers for use against enemy shipping. The Secretary specifically recommended an increase in the army by 10,000 men, and an authorization to the Executive to call out 50,000 volunteers and to issue letters of marque and reprisal. Hostilities should not begin, however, until after the sloop-of-war *Hornet* had sailed to Great Britain and returned. This would serve a dual purpose of affording enough time for military preparation and for news of this preparation to have an impact on the British government. If the British government under the prospect of war *then* did not repeal the Orders as they affected the United States, the occupation of Canada and disruption of her commerce would create the necessary stimulants.[2]

The President came to believe that threats might stiffen rather than soften the attitude of the British councils. Accepting criticism of his November 5 message made by the Secretary of the Treasury shortly before delivery, Madison removed from the working draft all expressions that seemed provocative and promised hostilities before the end of the current session. Threats might have the unwanted effect of antagonizing the British government. They might make it politically impossible for the ministry to retrace its steps, however much it might wish to avoid war. The President also agreed that an announced future deadline for the commencement of hostilities might lead an adamant British government to strike immediately before the nation had adequately prepared. After reading the President's draft message Gallatin recommended that if the President intended to use the threat of war to induce the British to repeal,

the recommendation must be so framed as not to convey any threat too offensive to their pride to be digested, and yet to carry a conviction that war must be the final tho' not immediate effect of their not receding. (I say not immediate, because if they considered it as such & concluded not to recede they would strike at once). It may be impossible to frame a recommendation precisely to that effect. but that proposed in the message may be improved.

Gallatin's recommendations formed the basis of Executive policy until well into the spring. Thus Isaac Coles (former private secretary to Jefferson during his presidency and guest of the Madisons at the White House in early December, 1811) could remark, on the basis of conversations with members of the Executive and Congress, that "little expectation is entertained here that Great Britain will ever consent to retrace her steps and it seems to be the policy of the Govmt to avoid for the present any useless threats or menaces which might preclude her from doing so." [3]

In recommending less provocative language, Gallatin implied that this might make it difficult to convey credibility to the British government. The Secretary shrewdly perceived that a line between the language of provocation and the language of weakness was a thin one. In 1812 the line was particularly hard to draw. Madison and Monroe were not successful.

In personal discussion with congressional committee members on Capitol Hill, Executive officials indicated that if Britain did not recede by the return of the *Hornet* war should be declared. At the same time, seeking to avoid a seeming ultimatum, both Madison and Monroe refrained from publicly setting forth this policy. The President's opening message recommended that the country be put "into an armor and an attitude demanded by the crisis" but made no explicit statement regarding actual consequences if Britain should not repeal her Orders. Following Secretary Gallatin's suggestion, Madison removed or softened such phrases in the message as "direct & undisguised hostility," "authorizing reprisals," and an allusion to the lapse of the present session, the presumed deadline for beginning war. The President, in a published reply to a Tennessee address, in January referred to war as a necessary alternative in case Britain should not yield, but made no statement as to the actual time war should commence.[4]

Editorials in the semiofficial *National Intelligencer* also lacked clarity. Joseph Gales, editor of this famous paper, was certainly working closely with the administration in the early spring of 1812, and probably did so throughout the session. Not until January, two months after the President's message, did the *Intelligencer* clearly explain that Madison had meant actual war when he recommended military preparations in November. An editorial on the President's opening message, printed on November 7, correctly explained Republican sentiments when it held that "[not] only the rights of the nation, but the character of the government, are involved in the issue"; and that the present session of Congress would "do more to stamp the character of genuine republican governments, than has been effected in this respect since the creation of the world." It said nothing explicitly as to how or when Congress was to accomplish such a task. Subsequent issues printed warlike letters and speeches, but without editorial comment. Not until January did the paper make it absolutely clear that Madison had "decidedly" meant war in November. Not until early spring did the *Intelligencer* explicitly state that war would be declared before the close of the current session of Congress. Editorials denied Federalist charges that the war was just a bluff. Not until April 7 did the *Intelligencer* print an unsigned editorial written by Secretary of State Monroe setting a date for hostilities by the expiration date of the 90-day embargo. On April 14 the paper finally announced that the return of the *Hornet* was "the period when the measures of our government would take a decisive character, or rather their final cast." [5]

The President and Secretary of State showed similar lack of clarity in their communications to the only official liaison between the American and British governments—the British minister, A. J. Foster. In November, 1811, before the *Hornet* set sail, Foster had several private interviews with the two men which he recorded in dispatches. The President on one occasion talked in general terms of the "embarrassing" position in which the country found itself and said that "anything was better than remaining in such a state." Madison at another interview "hinted darkly at motives for the conduct of Great Britain which he would not however suppose out of respect for His Majesty's Government, not wishing to impute to them any but such as could be honorably argued." Secretary of State Monroe spoke of the two governments as on the eve of "variance," and intimated that if unpleasant consequences ensued they would not be imputable to the United States. But in their final interview before the *Hornet's* sailing Monroe, shown the record of their previous conversation, strongly denied intending any threats or menaces and asked the Englishman to remove any that might be found there. Foster in subsequent interviews met with equivocation. Responding to the minister's protests against threatening speeches of Republican congressmen, the Secretary told him "that it was to be expected the members, exasperated as many of them must be, would speak their minds in rather warm language, but deprecated my looking upon their use of angry terms as a threat on the part of the Government." [6]

In March, 1812, Madison made public certain documents purporting to show that an English spy, John Henry, had been sent to the United States by high-ranking British officials to foment disunion. The Henry affair caused a national sensation. When Foster called on the President to discuss the matter, Madison told him vaguely that the affair "might produce a good effect by bringing matters in a more peremptory manner before His Majesty's Government." When Foster called on the Secretary of State to inquire further as to the effect these disclosures would have on relations between the two governments, Monroe told him "he really could as yet say nothing to me on the subject, from which I am plainly to infer that the public pulse is to be felt upon this business before the Government act." [7]

Such delicacy, however, did not inhibit congressional Republicans. A glance at contemporary newspapers or the *Annals of Congress* will show that some Republicans belligerently threatened immediate war with Great Britain if she did not yield. Many urged war in highly menacing and violent language. Republicans and Federalists alike took note of these violent appeals. Foster lodged a formal complaint with Secretary Monroe over the threatening character of the language used in Congress. But as we have seen most Republicans did not want war and would have welcomed British repeal. Whether seeking to rouse the country, win personal reputations, justify positions, or convince Britain of congressional determination, Republicans, though in public far more bellicose and threatening, were at one with the Executive in their private views.

Among other Republican members there was disapproval of such behavior. George Poindexter of Mississippi was annoyed at the volume of oratory pouring forth from Congress day after day. Congress should be passing legislation in preparation for war, not wasting time harping on British wrongs. "We shall assuredly have war," he wrote in December. But he was "much disgusted with the repetition of our wrongs" and "sick to loathing, of, the most eloquent attempt, to present them, in a new, dress to the imagination." Hugh Nelson of Virginia was also critical. Time spent in violent war speeches meant less spent for effective preparation of necessary legislation. Intemperate threats against Great Britain "will place her in a situation not to recede: but driving her to the Wall, she will have no alternative but to fight." Addressing the House he had warned against taking too high a tone.

The object of my speech was, to arrive at the same End—the redress of our Grievances, by peaceable means if practicable, if not then by war; which the committee proposed. I was opposed to vapouring and bullying; but wished by a steady and deliberate step to march up firmly to the object. I recommended calmness firmness and deliberation, instead of passion, warmth heat and Intemperance. I thought we ought to look the subject fully in the face, with all its calamities, and all its consequences, and not leap blindfold into a Pit, and heed then to Heaven to draw us out of it.[8]

Such contrast in style and tone among Republicans led many observers to make false estimations of the true situation within the party. Foster, tragically, was one. From outward appearances Foster concluded that Republican councils were deeply split over war. One faction, the "war party," composed of the most violent and outspoken members (Felix Grundy among them) was hot for war. Their motives? Foster endorsed John Randolph's charge that some were for war "because in that case their Hemp would sell well"; some "because they would obtain contracts for supplying the troops: many wish it, I am inclined to believe, for mere amusement, their puerile imaginations supposing it would be but an agreeable march to take possession of Canada." Another faction, "moderates," were fearful of the consequences of a war with Britain and opposed it, but went along with the war program in the hope of bluffing Britain into repeal of her Orders in Council. A third group, headed by the administration, did not know what it wanted, but shaped its course according to the political barometer, its main purpose being, as Foster put it, "a desire always to accommodate their tone to the varying humour of the majority in Congress upon whom depends so much of their popularity." On the basis of this analysis, Foster made varying predictions as to the likelihood of war. When it seemed that the Federalists, with the avowed purpose of overturning the administration, would join war men in voting a declaration, Foster warned the ministry that war might be declared immediately. When the war temper of Congress seemed to abate, he predicted the administration would not be pushed into war and that Great Britain might do as she like with the United States. When neither faction seemed to predominate, he simply confessed himself unable to forecast the outcome.[9]

The Federalists, also, believed their political opponents to be torn by disagreement over the war question. Federalists arrived in Washington in the autumn of 1811 believing, as Josiah Quincy of Massachusetts had once put it, that the Madison administration could not be "kicked into war." Outward appearances during the course of the session did not effectively deny this assumption. Calls from the Executive for military preparation did not necessarily mean that a determination to fight actually existed. Vague public pronouncements by the President and by the

National Intelligencer suggested a careful effort to avoid commitment to war.[10] Bellicose statements by some Republicans, on the other hand, led Federalists to discern a faction genuinely for war. In some cases it was not until after enactment of the embargo in April, 1812, in other cases not until after the President had actually made his formal recommendation to Congress for war, that Federalists came to believe that a majority in the party could be brought to vote for war.[11]

There was additional cause to think war would not take place. In the original estimate of regular troops needed to supplement the authorized establishment of 10,000 men, the administration recommended an increase of 10,000, to be enlisted for one year. Many Republicans supported this recommendation, but the Senate defeated the recommendation and voted an increase of 25,000 men, to be enlisted for five years. Here was further evidence of peace sentiment within the party. A large increase in the regular army would go a great way towards committing the country to war. An army of that size could not be enlisted for five years and then not be used without major political repercussions. The administration plan called for two-fifths that number for one year's service—a far less binding commitment, presumably reflecting an intention to avoid war. If enactment of the 25,000-man additional army proved the strength of the war party in Congress, other signs indicated that the peace men still held positions of great strength. More than two months elapsed before Congress actually authorized the raising of these troops. Over four months elapsed before the Senate approved nominations of officers for the new army. Not until the last week in March, after officers had been confirmed and received notification, did actual recruiting for the new army slowly get under way; and not until about the same time did military supplies begin to arrive at procurement points. The fact that nearly five months after Congress convened new troops and supplies still did not exist strongly indicated that the Republican peace party continued to be dominant.[12]

Federalist members told Foster on several occasions during the

first months of the session that the Republican administration
and many Republicans in Congress opposed war. (Such information could only strengthen Foster's own impression.) On February 1 two Federalist leaders, men whom Foster did not identify,
called on the envoy and gave him their estimation of the political
situation. According to Foster's account, they began by "expressing their Conviction of how embarrassed I must be, to form
a correct opinion of the State of Things here, and to manage so,
as neither to appear to laugh at the ridiculous Situation of this
Government, nor yet to shew so little Sagacity, as to be seriously alarmed." Next, they proposed a most remarkable plan.
Foster should recommend to his superiors that the Orders in
Council be steadfastly maintained. In this way the administration would be pushed "to the Edge of the Precipice" of war—
to the benefit of the Federalists. Either the administration would
refuse to fight, and so disgrace itself in the eyes of the country,
or it would go to war and quickly prove its incompetence to
carry it on. As if to make certain that this plan would be brought
to the attention of the proper authorities in Great Britain, another Federalist wrote to Francis J. Jackson, the minister whose
insulting conduct in 1809 had occasioned an administration re-
quest for his recall. The author of this letter urging Britain to
hold fast to the Orders was Alexander Hanson, editor of the
Federalist newspaper, the Baltimore *Federal Republican* (his
office was attacked by a Republican mob soon after the declaration and Hanson barely escaped with his life) and a frequent
visitor on Capitol Hill. Hanson wrote:

The only way to dislodge the prevailing party from the post of
power, is by saddling them with a war which they have neither the
means [nor] the ability to conduct, or by allowing them to place
themselves in a situation . . . which would expose their weakness
and pusillanimity, and render them contemptible . . . in the eyes of
all mankind. The first situation, I believe . . . they could not be
kicked into, while we enjoy the delightful spectacle of seeing them
decoyed or turned into the other, like a flock of geese into a pen. We
have them snug enough, and if they make their escape the British
government will have to answer for the crime of rescuing them.[13]

Congressional Federalists and their political lieutenants did not confine their views to secret communications with British officials. They also made them known to fellow citizens. They assured correspondents that the administration had been bluffing in its call for military preparations. The call was a gasconade, an effort to frighten Britain into repeal of the Orders, a move to strengthen the commercial restrictive system with troops. There was no intention of fighting if Great Britain held firm. The prediction of a Delaware Federalist was typical: "War is all in my eye, orders off or on. But what will Mad[ison] do, if E[ngland] don't relieve him?" On the basis of such reports, received from presumably reliable congressional sources, state leaders passed the word in their localities. Federalist newspapers quickly picked up the formula that the war talk was ridiculous, mere vaporing. The Hartford *Courant*, a leading New England paper, affirmed that "our administration only wishes for the continuation, the extension, and the more rigid enforcement of the restrictive system, rather than for war: and this too is probably the secret wish of the majority of the *orthodox* democrats." True, there were Republican "war hawks" all "red-hot" for war, but the President would probably be able to control them. The Baltimore *Federal Republican* sounded a party keynote in lines ending:

> As to powder and bullets and swords
> For *use* they were never intended,
> They're a parcel of high sounding words
> But never to *action* extended.

Editor Hanson of the *Republican* labeled the war a mere "scarecrow," a call for troops to enforce the restrictive system, a "Terrapin War"; his contemptuous phrases found their way into other Federalist newspapers. While a few Federalist journals apparently took the war seriously—the *Alexandria Gazette* warning the party of the boy who cried "Wolf"—the more usual newspaper reaction was disbelief and ridicule. A major segment of public opinion refused to believe in the intended war.[14]

Fairly considered, there was much sense in this outlook. After such events as the *Chesapeake* affair and the repudiation of the Erskine agreement there had been no war. Why should there be one now when no insult had occurred? The embargo of 1807 and the nonintercourse law of 1809 had not ended in war but in more commercial restrictions. Why should not the same thing happen again? Neither the President's own pronouncements nor editorial columns of the *National Intelligencer* had unequivocally committed the government to war in the near future. And there seemed to be no particular urgency about raising troops or supplies—at least judging from outward appearances. Both logic and events seemed strongly to confirm the Federalist prediction.

Understandably, then, Americans throughout the land—Federalists, independents, even Republicans—came to believe that war was not to be. In heavily Republican areas, there was probably less skepticism, but wherever Federalists were active there was strong disbelief in the likelihood of war. A Philadelphia Republican observed in December, 1811, that in that city: "Vessels are lading daily for English ports and merchants will not beleive we shall be involved in war untill it commences." Editor Binns of Philadelphia in April, 1812, anxiously sought reassurances from Congressman Roberts that Congress was serious: "What is the opinion now as to war? There are thousands who will not believe Congress are in earnest. This has a baleful influence upon our Country." Plumer of New Hampshire reported as late as May that "many people, even Republicans, do not yet beleive the govt is in reality preparing for *actual War*." Worried Republicans warned repeatedly against believing the war was a fraud. Among Republicans in close personal touch with members of the government there was confidence, but thousands of other men drew their information from less reliable sources and would not believe in a coming conflict.[15]

Among the incredulous were men who could well expect serious financial losses from war. These were merchants and manufacturers deeply involved in overseas enterprise. New York and Pennsylvania export merchants continued to buy wheat, flour, rye, and ashes throughout the winter and early spring in anticipation of a market in Spain and Portugal where the Duke of Wellington's troops were fighting a French army. To meet the merchant demand for flour, millers continued to buy wheat for processing. When Congress in early April passed a 90-day embargo as a preliminary to war many merchants and millers still held large supplies of these foodstuffs. The Republican editor, Thomas Rodgers, described a typical situation to Congressman Roberts. Both men had warned flour millers in the Delaware Valley against believing Federalist propaganda. Their warnings had been in vain. "I told some of them that they were purchasing too much wheat, but they had more confidence in Levi Hollingsworth, and other federal factors than in what you or I said. They will now suffer for their folly and credulity." [16]

Furthermore, shipowners had continued through the winter and early spring to send vessels loaded with foodstuffs to the Iberian Peninsula and Great Britain. Conditions for this sort of enterprise had seemed favorable: markets had been good, demand for carriage had been keen, and insurance rates had remained unchanged. Even with a notice of the April embargo, scores of vessels had hastily set sail before enforcement began. Many of these vessels when June came would still be at sea on return voyages. If war began at that time, there was danger that British warships cruising off the American coast would seize them.

Finally, there was the predicament of thousands of incredulous export merchants in commercial towns along the Atlantic seaboard—Portsmouth, Boston, New York, Philadelphia, Baltimore, Alexandria, Richmond, Charleston, and Savannah. Exporters of foodstuffs to Britain and the Iberian Peninsula, they had preferred to reinvest their receipts in British manufactured goods which the nonimportation act barred from entry into the United States, rather than bring their capital home through other less profitable means. Stephen Girard, the famous Philadelphia merchant, had begun securing his property early in 1811, purchasing American bonds and bank stock on the European market and storing his British goods in relative safety on Amelia Island in Spanish Florida. The Republican merchant

John McKim, Jr., of Baltimore, believed receipts could have been converted into specie and brought home—though at a less favorable rate of return than for value received in manufactured goods. But many merchants had paid no heed to Republican warnings and had operated on the assumption that peace would continue and that trade between the two countries would eventually return to a normal basis. Consequently, they now owned goods in British warehouses totaling millions of dollars—estimates of value ran from $25 to $100 million. Bankers were also involved, having furnished initial capital to many merchants. With the onset of war, there was great danger the British government would freeze, even confiscate, these assets.[17]

Moreover, the country was wretchedly unprepared militarily when Congress declared war. Many things caused this situation. Two months elapsed in authorizing the new army and two more in nominating and confirming officers; officers had to recruit but could not begin without commissions. The government lacked experienced administrators and planners. (Secretary Eustis sent a hurried call in January for the newly appointed commander of the armed forces, General Henry Dearborn: "Your knowledge and experience are rightly appreciated and will have a proper influence in determining what can be effected and within what time.") The sheer physical difficulties of communication among officials and contractors delayed preparation. (Richard Rush, comptroller of the treasury, gave a hint of the problem in Washington: "My *local perplexities* are also *immense*, owing to the distance at which people are scattered.") Acute shortages of clothing and equipment held up recruiting. (A Baltimore officer: "The want of Clothing Arms &c &c: together with music and a recruiting Sergeant has prevented me from commenceing the recruiting service since my arrival here— Every effort has been made to obtain music—but without success." An officer in Louisiana: "I am in a most lamentable condition for recruiting here—no blankets no coats no drum and to cap the climax no funds. I shall try and travel over what appears like impossibilities. I know I shall find the road ruff.") The new army required all new equipment. (By mid-March Tench Coxe, the purveyor general, had been able to procure one-half million yards of linen. He then had to arrange for this material to be cut and stitched into uniforms: "*I am proceeding and shall proceed with all my strength. one part of the business retards another.*") [18]

Surely widespread public incredulity explains to a very considerable extent the lagging state of military preparation. At the beginning of the session there were 5,500 men in uniform, 10,000 being authorized in the old army. Eight months later the count had inched forward to nearly 7,000. Officers in charge of recruitment complained that fifes and drums to stir national feeling had been unavailable—sure signs of public apathy. Men do not flock to the colors unless they expect war. Skepticism and incredulity ate deep into the morale of the armed services. An officer on board the frigate *Congress* off Hampton Roads actually submitted his resignation, offering as one reason the belief that "preparations for war are carried on so slowly and with so much indifference that I am convinced that the administration does not intend to declare it." Men charged with recruiting, building fortifications, and gathering supplies, often felt little urgency. General Dearborn told Secretary Eustis of his efforts to hurry governors, officers, manufacturers, and contractors to press their preparations. Governor Tompkins of New York was bending every effort: "I wish all our Govrs. would do as well. Williams will take too much time in preparations. I am urging him on, but he cannot be made sufficiently sensible of the necessity of having everything done in the course of five or six weeks." [19]

Between April and June, after newly appointed officers had received their commissions, it had been possible to raise for the new army by the most optimistic guess some 4,000 to 5,000 recruits. (No firm data was actually available on the new army. Worthington of Ohio believed the unofficial estimate of 4,000 to 5,000 too high; he estimated the new army at 3,000.) Together with the old army, which now stood at 7,000, this meant perhaps 12,000 regulars under arms when Congress declared war. More than half of these were raw and untrained. Units of the

old army had taken up stations throughout the country in posts
and garrisons. An army under the command of General Dearborn was near Albany preparing to invade Canada. At the
moment it was still in the first stages of organization—untrained,
ill-equipped, and in want of men and supplies. The only army
ready for operations was a small force of some 1,200 volunteers
and 500 regulars under General William Hull, slowly making
its way through the Ohio wilderness to Detroit preparatory to
an attack on the British post at Amherstburg.

Defensively, the country was almost helpless. On the exposed
Michigan and Ohio frontiers settlers expected to be swept from
their homes by a British-organized Indian uprising. The town
of Calais, Maine, was defenseless. The northern Connecticut
Valley was wide open to attack from Canada, and settlers in
Coos County, New Hampshire, feared raids by exiled Revolutionary War Loyalists and St. Francis Indians near the border.
Settlers living on the frontiers of New York State near the
Niagara and St. Lawrence lines were defenseless and feared
British-inspired Indian attacks before they could obtain protection. Forts and garrisons protecting towns and cities on the coast
were pitifully undermanned. A report from the Inspector General's office based on May 1 returns revealed this story: 143 men
garrisoned New Orleans; 175 protected Charleston; 193, New-
port; 131, Boston; 119, Detroit, with 430 more expected; 88,
Michilimackinac; 85, Fort Wayne; 53, Fort Dearborn. The figures on New York were the most encouraging; there 901 men
stood duty. Responsible men, however, believed New York to
be so feebly defended that a single British frigate could with
impunity lay the town under bombardment. The commander
of forces in the vicinity, Brigadier General Bloomfield, a Federalist, was believed to have deliberately delayed preparations in
order to wreck the administration. A Republican army officer
wrote in alarm to Secretary Gallatin that Bloomfield had told
him "that if the Government would precipitate into war without preparation, they must abide by the consequences, that the
recruits here are raw & undisciplined, that no officer could risk

his life & honour with them." The officer had confirmed the city's vulnerability. In such a situation he could well "tremble for the fate of the City." [20]

The public incredulity became apparent to Republican leaders in the capital. Lowndes of South Carolina was anxious over the situation, particularly the effect war would have on merchants: "We hear from all Quarters that the people do not expect war. And I look forward with great uneasiness to the shock which an unexpected declaration of it will give to the mercantile class." Speaker Clay and Secretary Monroe together agreed to a short embargo prior to the declaration as a warning measure. Clay thought an embargo of this kind would "give tone to public sentiment," warn citizens "to put under shelter before the storm," and "above all powerfully accelerate preparations for the War." Following a formal recommendation by the President for a 60-day embargo, Congress early in April enacted a law of 90-days duration. Shortly thereafter the *National Intelligencer* ran a series of articles (actually written by Secretary Monroe) explaining fully and explicitly the administration position and exhorting the country to make ready for hostilities. On April 9 the first of these appeared and declared that war must follow the embargo. On April 11 appeared a second, an historical account of the policies and negotiations leading to the present impasse, and on April 14 still another, an announcement of the expected arrival of the *Hornet* as the period of decision. More editorials of this nature followed at regular intervals. [21]

One could have predicted the result of these measures. Merchants and millers in New York and Pennsylvania felt dismayed as they faced the embargo with large quantities of perishable goods for export on hand. Men quickly drafted and circulated petitions for relief—practically anyone could sign. The Federalist millers of Northampton County, Pennsylvania, searched widely for signatures. Rodgers, the Republican editor, had "no doubt but they can prevail on many farmers to put their names to their memorials, but those very men, in my opinion will not act with them at the next election." The grain merchants and millers of New York City memorialized Congress for relief. Some 700 grain and flour merchants of Albany, "citizens of all political distinctions," begged for relief. After the embargo, they affirmed, grain values had fallen by nearly one-half in that city. Thousands of riverboatmen and sailors were jobless—the Hudson River grain vessels they worked all idle.

Mechanics and Labourers whose business was immediately connected with, and dependent upon the Mercantile interest are deprived of their usual mode of procuring subsistence. But your Memorialists, forbearing detail, need only say, generally, that it is difficult to conceive the scene of distress and ruin which this Law is producing in the State of New York, generally, and upon no section does it operate more severely than upon your Memorialists in the City of Albany, the greatest inland Depot of Produce in the United States.[22]

The news of the impending war staggered merchants with manufactured goods in British warehouses. They appealed for postponement of hostilities and suspension of the nonimportation act. Four hundred and fifty-five Boston merchants petitioned on April 24: "The importance and necessity of this measure, to the interest of a large class of citizens, as well as to the resources of the country, are too evident to require any illustration." Seventy merchants of Portsmouth, New Hampshire made a similar appeal: "As for ourselves, we beg leave, respectfully, to represent, That, in the event of a rupture with Great Britain, before we can withdraw thence our effects, our mercantile capital will be almost utterly annihilated, and the greatest individual distress must be the inevitable consequence." Some 80 signees petitioned from New York City: "Your Memorialists look with great anxiety to the probable fate of this property from Public Confiscation or private bankruptcy in the event of a War between the two countries, and it would be greatly advantageous both to the owners and to the nation to regain and secure it at home before this event may deprive them of it forever." Forty-five merchants of Alexandria, Virginia, and 146 merchants of Philadelphia, Pennsylvania, appealed. There were scores of others.[23]

There was clamor from other interests for postponement of

a declaration of war. Philadelphia and Portsmouth merchants with ships at sea on voyages to Great Britain and the Peninsula and to China, India, and the Orient urged members to delay hostilities until their vessels safely reached home port. Fear ran high in areas expecting possible immediate attacks from a declaration of war. Ohioans believed they faced hostile Indian attacks against farms and settlements in the north-central and northwestern parts of the state. New Yorkers imagined great danger from raids of Canadians and Indians across the borders at either end of Lake Ontario and from a naval bombardment of their greatest city. From these and other vulnerable areas came appeals for postponement of hostilities until preparations were more advanced, until militia companies could be equipped and moved into position, regular units brought into defensive station, fortifications strengthened, and cannon emplaced.[24]

To add further to Republican difficulties during the final weeks of peace, there now came unsettling news concerning France. In November, 1810, Madison, on the basis of the ambiguous Cadore letter, had announced French repeal of the Berlin and Milan Decrees to the extent they affected the neutral rights of the United States. By virtue of this announcement a nonimportation law had gone into operation against Britain. Eight months later the Madison administration had publicly announced Great Britain to be the single target of military action. Yet France continued to molest American commerce.

In July, 1811, Joel Barlow, the Republican poet and publicist, had gone to France on an official mission of negotiation. His instructions reiterated the presidential position that the Berlin and Milan Decrees had been repealed insofar as they affected American neutral rights. No American vessel trading with the British Isles had been seized or condemned on the high seas by France; no American vessel had been condemned for visit and search by British vessels or for seizure and imposition by British authorities. But the instructions also indicated that France was still not acting as she should act towards the United States: she had imposed exorbitant duties on American goods imported into France and required that two-thirds of return cargoes be in silks

and one-third in wines, she was causing expense and incon-
venience to American ships by continued harbor delays and
official investigations, and she had not yet agreed to pay indem-
nities for ships seized and confiscated previous to repeal of the
Decrees. Barlow's efforts to obtain commercial concessions and
reparations in accordance with his instructions met with delays
and vague generalities from the French government. He got
nowhere.[25]

In January, 1812, there came word of French seizure and burning of American merchantmen in the Baltic Sea and en route to
Great Britain. In mid-March news arrived of the burning of
American merchantmen by French frigates whose commanders
had reportedly said they had received orders to destroy all
vessels bound to or from British-held Lisbon. All these events
conspired together to undermine the administration position
vis-à-vis the two belligerents. Why should Britain be singled out
as the special target of American counteraction when France
also was molesting American neutral commerce? Had France
actually repealed her Berlin and Milan Decrees as they affected
the United States? And if she had, was she not replacing them
with equally destructive policies against American commerce?
These were obvious and logical questions which demanded answers. They were a cause of great anxiety.[26]

Finally, there developed in the final weeks before war a mount-
ing Federalist-led campaign of opposition to the whole concept
of war against Great Britain—now or at any time. Up until
early April Federalists had taken a posture of ridiculing Republican intentions but not actively opposing the war. So lightly
did they treat the whole war program that some even voted for
individual items as necessary for peacetime purposes. The warnings of early April changed all that. Aroused to activity by the
near-certainty of war, Federalists in states from Vermont to
Virginia began to flood Congress with petitions against war.
One batch of nine Federalist petitions bearing the signatures
of some 600 Maryland tobacco farmers reached Congress two
days before the final Senate vote on war. A similar document

bearing 1,150 names arrived from New Bedford, Massachusetts on June 8. A Federalist-controlled town meeting in Boston's Faneuil Hall accepted and forwarded a report and resolutions against war. This sudden activity was in noticeable contrast to months of relative inaction. Roberts of Pennsylvania found comfort in the idea that Federalist disillusion had come so late—too late to cause the trouble an earlier opposition would have made. "There is great activity in Virginia in circulating memorials against the war with England— Luckily the unbelief of the opposition in the seriousness of the majority in going to war has prevented them from using that activity to oppose it at an early stage that might have been found exceedingly embarrassing." [27]

These Federalists sounded all possible arguments against the declaration of war. The war was absolutely unnecessary and easily avoidable, they maintained. Not all possible alternatives had as yet been tried. The war was impolitic and inexpedient. The country was wretchedly unprepared for war. Our maritime and land frontiers were defenseless, easy targets of attack. Merchants and shipowners would sustain disastrous losses. Britain would certainly sequester the millions belonging to our citizens in that country and would sweep our vessels from the sea. France was burning and confiscating our vessels on the high seas, and there was no good proof of repeal of her Decrees. How could we single out Great Britain in the face of France's outrageous conduct? Would we become the allies and satellites of Napoleon? Under such circumstances how could a war against Great Britain be in any way justified? The political implications of these memorials were clear. The Boston town meeting made them explicit. "The power of the country is yet in the hands of the people. Union, energy, and resolution will cause the public opinion to be respected. Our constitution affords the means of saving our country, by changing the men and measures which have brought upon us our present embarrassments." [28] In the face of all the evidence, could Republicans safely ignore such arguments?

(6)

BY LAND OR BY SEA?

All Republicans well knew the grave consequences of war. As June and the deadline for hostilities approached, these evils seemed to multiply. A June declaration of war might result in loss of millions in mercantile property that could otherwise be saved. A June declaration might result in devastation of the unprotected northern frontier and eastern seaports. War against Great Britain alone, when France was still mistreating American commerce, would greatly weaken the case against Great Britain and give color to charges of French influence within the administration. Any one of these consequences could alienate thousands of citizens, many of great political and financial influence. The war effort would suffer. The Federalists would gain ground. They might even win control of all New England and New York and organize a secessionist movement as they had come near to doing during the embargo crisis. Men who felt these anxieties most keenly came from constituencies likely to suffer from the evils of an immediate declaration of war against Great Britain—constituencies in Ohio, New Hampshire, Massachusetts, New York, New Jersey, Pennsylvania, and Maryland.[1]

To avoid these dangers Republicans conceived of alternate plans. One would have put off a declaration of war until military preparations had further advanced and would have suspended the embargo and nonimportation laws to relieve pressure on the mercantile community. The other would have authorized immediate or contingent limited maritime war against one or both belligerents in the form of reprisals against enemy shipping by American ships-of-war, armed merchantmen, and privateers.

While the first plan would obviously pacify merchants and

give time for further military preparation, the second had an
appeal that was less clear. Advocates of maritime war believed
that hostilities limited to the sea would intensify pressure against
Great Britain but with less chance of provoking full-scale retaliation against American mercantile property and cities than
an open declaration of war. Such a war would confine American
land forces within American territory, thus affording more
troops for defense of frontiers and seaports; invasion of Canada
would come later if hostilities continued. In the event of British
concessions, the President might terminate hostilities by executive order, and thereby avoid delicate, costly, and time-consum-
ing negotiation over a peace treaty. If the enemy refused to
make concessions, or chose to enlarge the area of conflict on
his own initiative, the country would close ranks in full support
of an all-out military effort. Finally, inclusion of France in hostilities, immediately or contingently, would give the lie to
charges of French influence in the administration, and, furthermore, create incentives for concessions from one belligerent
through the prospect offered of unilateral American action
against the other.[2]

With good reason, the two plans, with minor variations in
detail, made sense to worried Republicans from areas concerned.
Local Republican leaders in letters to colleagues in Washington
urged their adoption. From Philadelphia, Manuel Eyre, though
approving the embargo, suggested to Congressman Roberts a
delay in hostilities until autumn, and a suspension of the nonimportation act. Would it not be best "to procrastinate the time
of making war until we are better prepared to strike the first
blow with effect—late in the fall and winter British Ships of
war cannot encounter the tempestuous weather on our coasts
without almost inevitable destruction—by that time the enlistments of our new army will have greatly progressed & our sea
ports better fortified?" From New York, the merchant John
Jacob Astor, just beginning his climb to wealth and fame, told
Secretary Gallatin that many people he knew favored suspension
of all commercial restrictions and arming merchant vessels: "we

are full of Speculation and conjecture as to the measures to be next adopted by government. Some say war with england others with france & england while Some belive that all restrictions on commerce will be taking off & that our merchant vessels will be permitted to arm. this I belive would meet the more genral approbation." [3]

A strong Republican minority in Congress rallied to these plans. Congressman Thomas Sammons of New York belonged to "a minority who are gaining that would not wish to engage in a war unless wee were attackted on our own teritories or brought on by our enemies, before wee are prepared with an army and would for the present remove all restrictive measures for export and emports." The plan to begin hostilities with letters of marque also won support. Nathaniel Macon of North Carolina tentatively predicted late in April that hostilities would begin with letters of marque—"necessity will prevent any invasion of Canada untill the regular troops can be raised and assembled." His forecast, admittedly guesswork, reflected the appeal of limited maritime war. Some members espoused both plans. Josiah Bartlett, Jr., of New Hampshire favored an outright postponement, but preferred letters of marque to a declaration of war; Samuel L. Mitchill of New York City, on the other hand, preferred the maritime measure to postponement. [4]

Both plans, however, met firm opposition from administration congressional leadership. In the House, Calhoun, acting chairman of the Foreign Relations Committee in Porter's absence, on June 3 brought forward a bill authorizing a declaration of war against Great Britain. The bill declared a state of war to exist between the United States and Great Britain and her dependencies, and authorized the President to make use of the entire land and naval forces of the nation to carry the war into effect. On June 4, after delaying tactics by the Federalists and John Randolph of Roanoke had failed, the bill passed the House. No Republican, save the party renegade Randolph, would move either postponement or limited war. A minority of Republicans, as Secretary of War Eustis reported, would have voted for letters of marque had anyone formally proposed this plan. But no one in the House wished to take the responsibility at this critical point of initiating the measure over the opposition of administration leadership. Randolph's obstructionist motion postponing the entire question of war until the following October lost by an overwhelming majority; Federalists and only some half a dozen Republicans from New Hampshire, New York, New Jersey, and Pennsylvania supported it.[5]

The Senate, where the administration leadership faced open rebellion, was less cooperative. Throughout the session, Senate Republicans had been at odds with each other over policy. On the one hand, Senators William H. Crawford of Georgia, George Washington Campbell of Tennessee, and George M. Bibb of Kentucky had led some dozen or so other senators in loyal support of administration recommendations and requests. On the other, five antiadministration senators had refused to follow this leadership and had sought adoption of their own individual plans. It is difficult to say just why William Branch Giles of Virginia, Samuel Smith of Maryland, Michael Leib and Andrew Gregg of Pennsylvania, and John Pope of Kentucky were in revolt and just what they were trying to accomplish. Resentment at administration support given to opponents in party feuds partly accounts for the revolt. Giles was angry at the appointment in 1811 of James Monroe, whom he had long suspected of pro-British sympathies, to head the State Department. Smith, Leib, and possibly Gregg were incensed at the favor shown Albert Gallatin with whom they had been feuding over patronage and control of state party machinery. Pope and Clay were rivals in Kentucky party politics, and the new influence enjoyed by Clay in the administration may account for Pope's hostility.

Honest differences over foreign policy were also responsible for the break. Smith, Giles, and Leib, putting little stock in commercial coercion after repeal of the embargo, had favored instead a policy of building up the nation's military and naval forces and negotiating from strength. They regarded Gallatin's apparent passion for economy as the cause of continuing administration support for commercial restrictions and failure to increase adequately the strength of the armed forces. Pope, Smith, and Giles disapproved of the weight put on the Cadore letter, and in the face of continuing French maritime depredations believed the United States to be in a false position vis-à-vis the two belligerents. From such differences, these senators had come to doubt the competence and integrity of the Madison administration. They believed the President to be personally weak and incapable of exercising firmness and sound judgment. They believed him under the control of self-serving cabinet colleagues. They believed him to be unfit to lead his party and his country safely through the jungle of international politics. During the course of the session they had doubted his willingness to face up to the trials of war. They ridiculed openly his military estimates and won the necessary votes for an increase in the new army from 10,000 to 25,000 men. They challenged his financial plans as ill-conceived and inadequate. Believing the nation must now resort to force, they apparently sought to maneuver Madison into such a position that he could not retreat from war without personal disgrace. Yet when it became evident that hostilities would commence in a June declaration of war against Great Britain, they seized the initiative and openly sought to force a revision of strategy more in line with existing military, diplomatic, and political conditions.[6]

The President sent a formal recommendation of war to Congress on June 1. The House took only one day to pass a war bill introduced by Calhoun. In contrast, the Senate spent thirteen days in bitter dispute on the measure.

The war bill reached the Senate on June 4 and immediately went to a special committee of seven senators. Four days later, on June 8, the committee reported the bill together with "sundry communications, confidentially made to them, from the Treasury and War Departments on the subject." The reports from these agencies showed a nation poorly prepared both for defense of cities, coasts, and frontiers, and for an immediate invasion of Canada. To bring the point home to colleagues, the Federalist

James Lloyd of Massachusetts won approval of a motion to distribute copies of the reports among interested senators.

These were preliminary skirmishes. On June 10 the serious struggle began. On that day Gregg of Pennsylvania offered a motion limiting hostilities against Great Britain to the sea. The motion instructed the committee of seven to replace the war declaration with a carefully limited conveyance of authority to the President to issue letters of marque and reprisal and to send the navy into action against British shipping. This motion carried on the following day by four votes, seventeen to thirteen. In the majority were six administration Republicans from states vulnerable to the military, economic, and political risks of an immediate declaration of war, two supporters of the antiadministration Clintonian faction, Giles of Virginia, Leib and Gregg of Pennsylvania, and six Federalists.

The committee of seven pursuant to Gregg's motion on June 12 reported a bill embodying the plan of limited maritime war against Great Britain. Proceedings took a new turn when Pope of Kentucky interjected a motion to include France in the maritime war. The motion won support from Giles and Smith of Maryland, but the opposition of Gregg and Leib of Pennsylvania defeated the proposal by a margin of two votes. The Senate then returned to the original bill as reported by the committee. On the question to strike out the declaration of war for the purpose of amending the bill with limited maritime war amendments, the Senate deadlocked, in a tie, sixteen votes on either side. To break the tie, Leib won approval of a roll-call vote on the measure, hoping that publicity would force a shift to the safer ground of limited war. But the lines held firm, again the Gregg plan failed to win a majority, and again the Calhoun war resolution stayed intact.

Just one day previously the Gregg plan had commanded a four-vote majority. The addition of two negative votes cast by senators who had been absent the previous day, Richard Brent of Virginia and Jonathan Robinson of Vermont, and the switch into opposition of Giles, who wished to include France in hostilities, explain this shift in balance. By the thinnest of margins an equally divided Senate defeated the plan to limit hostilities against Great Britain to the sea.

From this moment on the movement against the declaration of war began to crumble. Continuing the fight, on June 15 Obadiah German of New York, a Clintonian senator, moved to postpone all consideration of the Calhoun bill until the following November. With the support of only two administration Republicans from vulnerable constituencies, two Clintonians, and six Federalists, the motion failed to pass. Leib then moved to amend the House bill so as to authorize maritime hostilities against Great Britain immediately and against France at a specified future date if she failed to produce unequivocal evidence of the repeal of her Decrees. The proposal lost by three votes. On June 17 Giles, whose opposition to the Gregg bill had been partly responsible for its defeat, offered an amendment authorizing immediate maritime hostilities against both Great Britain and France. This proposal lost by four votes. With all possible combinations now exhausted, the question on the declaration of war carried at last, nineteen to thirteen. Voting in the majority were administration men, Giles, Gregg, Leib, and Smith of Maryland. In opposition were the Federalists, two Clintonians, four administration Republicans from vulnerable areas (Howell of Rhode Island, Lambert of New Jersey, Reed of Maryland, and Worthington of Ohio), and the antiadministration senator, Pope of Kentucky.[7]

This episode, in which the House declaration of war very nearly lost in the Senate, aroused intense feeling among Republicans. On the final day of Senate wrangling, Roberts of Pennsylvania wrote emotionally to his brother that the two Pennsylvania senators, Gregg and Leib, were so deep in "iniquity" as to deserve the tar and feathers of a "suit of '76." "Leib ought to [be] kicked & scuffed by every honest [man] & if he says three words to me I'll take pains to kick him." Perhaps "some of Fosters bills of exchange has dropp'd in the Senate. I know not when we will return. the suspense we are in is worse than hell–!!!!" The wonder is the affair should have been so little understood at the time. Three days after the tension was over and the country was at war, Roberts explained the conduct of his Pennsylvania colleagues on the basis of petty vindictiveness and personal ambition. "Gregg & Leib at last voted for war but [not] till they had disclosed their feelings to be fully against anything Madison might be for. Leib is I apprehend a devoted Clintonian. Gregg is fixing his cap for Snyder's chair thro' federal aid as he got his Senatorship. . . . The poor devils like fallen [illegible] have lost all wishes but to do mischief." Other administration supporters—Secretary of State Monroe, for example—also attributed the fight against the war declaration to unworthy motives, and some historians have followed a similar line.[8] Much evidence, however, indicates that in their fight against an immediate declaration these senators acted in the national interest as they conceived it to be. From March, 1812, until well into 1813 their actions consistently reflected serious concern over threatening foreign and domestic developments. Colleagues who knew their views understood them to be in the national interest. The senators frequently disagreed seriously among themselves on detail, unlikely conduct in men interested only in obstructionist tactics. Finally, the senators thought of themselves as actually working for the welfare of party and country. For these reasons it would appear they felt genuine concern over the prospect of a full-scale declaration of war under an incompetent administration when the nation was insufficiently prepared. They hoped to save the situation in the various ways they proposed.[9]

Why then did congressional leaders oppose a plan that would have been so welcome to colleagues from north and east? It seems doubtful that strong opposition came from anyone in the Cabinet. In the spring before war, as a result of French difficulties, Madison took up the question of whether to take forcible action against France as well as Great Britain. In the President's view there was positive evidence rebutting the thesis that France had not repealed her Decrees, but her conduct seemed deliberately intended to give Great Britain a pretext for continuing the Orders, and she had not yet satisfied American demands on spoliations and commercial relations. Was it expedient to include France in the forthcoming hostilities? War against both belligerents might hasten a peace with either by holding out the hope of unilateral war with the other, and it would give the lie to Federalist charges of French partiality. But the President concluded that triangular war was likely to create more difficulties than advantages. There was a good chance that neither belligerent would make the required concessions immediately and that the United States would have to contend with the two most powerful nations in the world instead of one. This would present a host of new difficulties which the Federalists would turn against the administration. Hence both Madison and Monroe opposed the idea of a triangular war.[10]

Changes in the planning of the war against Great Britain alone had more appeal. Secretary Monroe took the lead in pressing for postponement of land operations in favor of operations confined to the sea. On June 1, the very day the President sent his war message to Congress, Monroe intimated his conversion to the strategy of limited maritime war. "I am convinc'd that it is very important to attempt at present, the maritime war only," he wrote in a hasty note to Secretary of the Treasury Gallatin. He feared difficulty in getting approval from the Foreign Relations Committee in the House, and also from other leaders. Would Secretary Gallatin see Senator William H. Crawford of Georgia before coming to the President's this morning, "to confer with & explain to him the policy of the plan preferr'd?" How far Monroe actually got with the limited maritime war plan it is difficult to say. There is some indication that the President and other Cabinet members were favorably disposed towards the plan, if they did not actively press or formally agree to it. Congressman William Lowndes of South Carolina, a close associate and messmate of Clay and Calhoun, in 1819 recalled that members of the Executive had urged replacement of a war declaration with letters of marque. As far as he could recollect, none of the Cabinet, excepting perhaps Secretary of the Navy Paul Hamilton of South Carolina, had been averse. Moreover, Monroe's note to Gallatin suggests that the secretary of the treasury was sympathetic: would Monroe have asked his colleague to speak to Crawford had he not thought he was friendly? Whether President Madison was for or against the idea it is not possible definitely to say. It does seem unlikely that his Secretaries would have urged the plan on congressional leaders had they not thought he was at least receptive to it.[11] Whether agreed to or not by the Cabinet, it is clear that congressional administration leaders would have none of the plan. Lowndes very explicitly recalled in 1819 that Senator Crawford and other congressional leaders, on talking the matter over carefully, had refused it any support; Lowndes himself had been in the discussions and had opposed the change. Clearly it was Crawford of Georgia, Bibb of Kentucky, and Campbell of Tennessee who led the fight in the Senate against the movement to confine operations to the sea.[12]

The men who led the Senate fight against the change in strategy came from states where problems of preparation and political control were not nearly so difficult and worrisome as in the states of the north and east. Crawford of Georgia, Campbell of Tennessee, and Bibb of Kentucky had far less to fear from an immediate declaration of war on the lives and property of their constituents than did colleagues from other areas. Unlike Ohio and New York, a wide belt of intervening territory and the Ohio River protected Kentucky and Tennessee from an immediate attack from Canada. Georgia had a commercial center in Savannah, but the importance of this coastal town was small enough to justify an expectation that she would not be a primary target. None of these areas had many merchants who would suffer from an immediate declaration. Most important of all, the Federalist party in these states was practically nonexistent. None of the conditions were present which urged men from the northern and eastern states to favor limited maritime war.[13]

Thus, in the calculations of men from the south and west,

the dangers from an immediate war declaration did not weigh so heavily as for northern and eastern colleagues. Overbalancing this danger was another consideration. Abruptly to alter the character of the war in the way proposed would be a dishonorable retreat from an advanced position. After authorizing a land army and military appropriations, was Congress now going to confirm the presumed lack of firmness in republican government? [14]

Another point counted heavily in the calculations of Crawford, Campbell, and Bibb. The savage battle between the forces of Governor William Henry Harrison and the Shawnee Indians at the Prophet's town in November, 1811, had touched off great excitement in the west and had turned public attention to the Indian confederacy forming under the Indian leaders Tecumseh and the Prophet. The Prophet had faced Harrison with some 700 braves and had inflicted heavy casualties before abandoning the battle. Harrison had subsequently boasted that as a result of the encounter the Shawnee allies had begun to desert and "that our frontiers have never enjoyed more profound tranquillity than at this time." Small-scale Indian atrocities, however, continued—scalping raids, kidnappings, cattle killings—and the frontier remained in an uproar. The heart of the trouble seemed in Canada. Reports told of large numbers of Indians visiting the British fort at Amherstburg eighteen miles below Detroit where the notorious Indian agent Matthew Elliott plied them with arms and munitions. Canadian Indians equipped with British muskets reportedly circulated among restless Creeks and Chickasaws in western Georgia and northern Alabama. As the murders continued, panic swept Ohio and Indiana, and settlers streamed back across the Ohio River or fortified themselves in hastily constructed blockhouses. A Kentucky settler watching the exodus exclaimed: "The contemplation is truly painful, nay, shocking to humanity; but I greatly fear, so long as G. Britain by her possessions on our continent and her bribes and largesses, retains the means of controling the conduct of the whole of the Lake Indians, nothing less than extirpation will permanently tranquilize our frontiers." It was natural that a projected invasion of Canada should have met with warm approval in south and west. With the rendezvous at Amherstburg destroyed, large areas of Canadian territory occupied, and communications between the Indians and their presumed British allies severed, the Indians would quickly cease their attacks. Crawford, Campbell, and other members from southern and western constituencies clearly shared these sentiments. Both Crawford and Campbell in opposing the maritime plan urged the policy of acting offensively against the British in Canada in order to deal with the Indian menace. If the government restricted hostilities to the sea, they argued, the frontier would still suffer from Indian attacks instigated by the British. Was it not better to put an end to these attacks altogether by striking at the heart of the trouble? [15]

It has been difficult for historians to take seriously the proposals for limited maritime war that nearly won Senate approval on the eve of hostilities. Some have viewed the affair as a maneuver to embarrass the administration; others, as the last-ditch attempt of peace advocates to save the country from the worst horrors of a dreaded conflict. It is more correct to accept and evaluate the various plans for what their advocates professed them to be—superior strategies for the opening of hostilities. These men wanted to lessen the chances of an immediate British assault on the property and persons of constituents, with all the political evils such an event would bring. Their proposals, if adopted, would doubtless have won wide approval from worried voters in the localities concerned. Yet it is hard to see why Great Britain, anticipating attacks on her own seaborne commerce in a maritime war, would have refrained from assaulting American commerce and carrying the war to the American mainland. It was also unrealistic to suppose that any of the maritime war combinations would have reconciled the Federalists to the war. Even if Britain had broadened the war on her own initiative, Federalists would have blamed Republican opponents for starting the fray. Nor would immediate or contingent inclusion of France in the hostilities have won the desired support of Federalists. Henry Clay correctly advised a correspondent who wanted inclusion of France in the war that it was "in vain, by such a step, to attempt the conciliation of the Feds." [16] America's best chance of victory lay in an effective campaign against Canada in which she could bring to bear her overwhelming manpower. If it was desirable to make further preparation before invading Canada, this was better left to the responsibility of the Executive and his military advisers, not to self-appointed senatorial experts whose legislative contrivances would have limited the government's strategic flexibility and undermined its effort to raise and train an army.

Southern and western members wished to begin war with land operations; a number of northern and eastern members believed that war should begin on the sea. Does this mean, as some historians believe, that expansionist desire for Canada and Florida played an important role in bringing on war in 1812? [17]

In the early weeks of the session Republicans evinced much interest in Canada. The administration recommended an invasion of Canada as the most effective method of bringing Great Britain to terms. Canada was to be a bargaining counter, traded back to Britain for repeal of the Orders in Council and a satisfactory agreement on impressment. Rather than see the provinces of Upper and Lower Canada permanently in American hands, Britain would cease her maritime aggressions.[18]

For some Republicans, however, Canada held other interest. War with Great Britain would probably bring on many evils— burdensome taxes, an increased debt, casualties, commercial dislocation, and the like. But if the United States acquired the Canadian provinces as permanent possessions there would be many offsetting advantages. Annexation would sever British contact with the northwestern Indians, permit unrestricted American navigation of the St. Lawrence River, afford new facilities to the New England fishing industry, secure the nation from British intrigue and espionage, bring new revenue from trade, remove a competitor in the fur trade, provide new farm land,

and add political power to the northern section of the Union. To Republicans these were benefits of great intrinsic value, but they were also desirable for political reasons. They would make the war and the Republican party more popular in areas deriving greatest advantage from annexation. The idea thus aroused greatest enthusiasm among western Republicans who wanted to eliminate fur trade competition in the upper Mississippi Valley region and put a permanent end to British influence over the northwest Indians and among northeastern Republicans ever alive to the political struggle with the Federalists.[19]

Republican congressmen discussed these concepts freely and openly during the first weeks of debate. Felix Grundy of Tennessee was among the first to argue the advantages in adding the Canadas to the Union:

The war, if carried on successfully, will have its advantages. We shall drive the British from our Continent—they will no longer have an opportunity of intriguing with our Indian neighbors, and setting on the ruthless savage to tomahawk our women and children. That nation will lose her Canadian trade, and, by having no resting place in this country, her means of annoying us will be diminished.

He then went on to show how Canada would help preserve the Union. It would maintain "the equilibrium of the Government. When Louisiana shall be fully peopled, the Northern States will lose their power; they will be at the discretion of others; they can be depressed at pleasure, and then this Union might be endangered." John A. Harper of New Hampshire also pointed to advantages in annexation of Canada:

The northern provinces of Britain are to us great and valuable objects. Once secured to this Republic, and the St. Lawrence and the Lakes become the Baltic, and more than the Baltic to America; north of them a population of four millions may easily be supported; and this great outlet of the northern world, should be at our command, for our convenience and future security.

For a time, indeed, annexation seemed so strong a possibility that the postmaster general, Gideon Granger of Connecticut, felt moved to write when discussing the evils war would bring: "As a counterballance for these evils, we shall doubtless acquire the Canadas and other northern british possessions, which are of great importance to Ohio, Michigan, Indiana, Illinois—Pensylvania and all the States to the east." [20]

Months later, in mid-May, 1812, Harper of New Hampshire addressed an extraordinary letter to his long-time correspondent, the governor-elect, William Plumer. The great question on war or peace would be taken in June, he announced. The President would probably send a heated message to Congress denouncing British aggressions and asking for war. The Committee on Foreign Relations would bring forward a war manifesto and a declaration of war. It would probably also recommend letters of marque and reprisal, and an address to the Canadians promising them protection in their lives, property, and religion and pledging incorporation of Canada into the Union. The latter measure, the incorporation pledge, was his own personal proposal, sponsored by no one else, and one that was costing him much effort. But he did not want to fight several years for the Canadas only to give them back in a negotiation. Unless Congress would pledge itself that "once conquered, they shall be retained, I will never give my vote to send an Army there." Concluding, he remarked knowingly: "It would be arrogance in me to attempt to offer a person of your intelligence, any arguments in favor of such a measure, as it regards a policy to be pursued towards our own citizens, or towards the Canadians." [21]

Was the annexation of Canada the New Hampshire congressman's price for a vote in favor of war? Considered in the context of the intraparty controversy over a land or sea war, Harper's letter indicates he was weighing different strategic concepts, not considering whether to vote for or against war. He carefully told Plumer that without an annexation pledge he had "no idea of having a war for several years to conquer the British Provinces"—that he would "never give my vote to send an Army there." But he did not say if Congress refused the pledge he would vote against letters of marque and reprisal, a plan he also noted as about to be brought forward by the Committee. A war to take Canada would cost much blood and treasure. A war limited to the sea might well be less expensive and, in light of existing preparations, from military and political points of view, less dangerous. In war involving an invasion of Canada Americans would want assurance that their sacrifices would be amply repaid—through annexation and all the benefits annexation would bring.

Moreover, no one was consistently more adamant than Harper in insisting that force be brought to bear against Great Britain. He publicly committed himself to war: "There *must*, there *will* be a change of measures," he avowed in a speech carried in newspapers all over the country. Even before there was any question of pledging the annexation of Canada, he had threatened to bring forward a war resolution on his own responsibility if Congress shied from the contest. He bitterly assailed a proposed recess on the ground it would mean "no war, but complete disgrace." To have refused his vote for war in some form, whether by land or by sea, would have been utterly inconsistent with all previous statements.[22]

But at the same time he was deeply concerned as to how public opinion in the northeast would react to war. He had read gloomy letters from Governor Plumer warning that the Federalists stood a good chance of winning the state elections in Massachusetts and New Hampshire. Consequently he joined colleagues in recommending postponement by the Republican-controlled legislature of forthcoming congressional elections in New Hampshire for as long as possible. He was quick to believe a report that a "systematic plot" was forming in New York State to secede from the Union as soon as war began. During the final week of peace he was subjected to great pressure from several colleagues. The Clintonian senator from New Hampshire, Nicholas Gilman, told him that war was not yet necessary. The congressman from the Portsmouth district, Josiah Bartlett, Jr., told him that his constituents wanted a delay in the war until ships could reach home and property in Great Britain be secured. Considering these pressures, he told Plumer, "I think I have pursued a tolerable *strait* course. At least I possess an approving conscience." [23]

Harper's scheme for mitigating the evil effects of war in the northeast never got off the ground. He was utterly unsuccessful in bringing Congress to promise retention of even an acre of Canadian soil. The most the House would accept was his resolution authorizing a presidential proclamation pledging security to the Canadians in their lives, property, and religion in the event of invasion. This resolution said nothing about annexation, and was clearly a military measure designed to obtain Canadian cooperation during the invasion and occupation. Feeling safe from the usual pillage and persecution of invading armies, Harper believed, the inhabitants of the northern provinces would be more likely to assist rather than resist the Americans. Sent to the Senate two days after final congressional action on the war bill, it failed to pass.[24]

Congress never came close to voting the measure that Harper labored to obtain. In point of fact there had been strong opposition to annexation of Canada from the very beginning. There had been opposition from Republicans like Postmaster General Granger who clung to the Montesquieuian doctrine that republics must be of small area in order to survive. "But will not the addition of these Territories accellerate a dissolution of the Union?" he wondered anxiously. "Or can it spread securely over the continent? I fear, I doubt." Southern Republicans, unfriendly to the idea of an increase in northern political power and seeing nothing in the annexation of Canada that would benefit their own constituents, opposed the plan. Hugh Nelson of Virginia was cool to the idea. "The New Yorkers and Vermonters are very well inclined to have upper Canada united with them, by way of increasing their Influence in the Union," he observed wryly during the December debates. Against it also were men who believed the war could be fought more successfully on sea than land. A Canadian campaign would not bring Great Britain to respect our commercial rights, wrote Jesse Franklin of North Carolina. No doubt conquest would "do her emence Injury" by cutting off her naval supply and fur trade and ruining her influence with the Indians. But even "if all this Shoud be Crownd with the most Complete Success it Does not settle the dispute about which we are now like to get to war, that is our *Commercial Rights*." Presumably, the United States could bring Great Britain to terms only on the sea, where armed merchant vessels, privateers, and ships-of-war would resist her depredations and attack her commerce. And as for "Territory," exclaimed the Carolinian, "God knows we [have] enough already. More than we can cultivate or sell." [25]

Some Republicans believed an annexation pledge would even seriously obstruct the effort to bring Great Britain to respect our rights on the sea. The administration intended, after war began, to demand as the minimum price for peace both repeal of the Orders in Council and an end to impressment. It looked on Canada as a bargaining piece to be traded off, just as previously it had offered to trade commercial restrictions for repeal of the Orders. But once a pledge had rendered Canada nonnegotiable, its diplomatic value was at an end. Doubtless there were members of Congress close to the administration who shared this view; certainly there were prominent state leaders who did so. Thomas Ritchie of Virginia, the well-known editor of the famous Richmond *Enquirer*, believed an annexation pledge detrimental to the diplomacy of the war. On July 21, 1812, he published an editorial which balanced the military advantages in an annexation pledge against the diplomatic disadvantages. If we pledge our faith to incorporate Canada into the Union, wrote the editor, the Canadians "will many of them, be ready to join us. Our point will be gained by *half* the *force*, and in less than half the time." But some "difficulties occur to this plan, in the attainment of the great objects of the war." On the other hand, if we invade the Canadas without a pledge, "the opposition will be infinitely greater—every man will be a soldier, every house a fortress." Therefore, proposed Ritchie, in order to maintain freedom to bargain Canada for our maritime objectives without at the same time losing the aid of sympathetic

Canadians, we should pledge a guarantee of full protection against British reprisals to those citizens lending us assistance. We should pledge "that for whatever aid the Canadians may give us, they shall not eventually suffer; and a peace shall not be made which does not secure them a complete *amnesty* for this conduct; that there shall be no *confiscations*, retributions, &c &c."

The administration and like-minded Republican members of Congress would support Harper's resolution pledging protection to the Canadians in their lives, property, and religion. Brought to the Senate by its sponsors (Harper of New Hampshire and James Fisk of Vermont) it there received the full backing of administration leaders—Crawford, Campbell, and Bibb. But against it stood Federalists and Clintonians who had voted against the war, the five antiadministration opponents of immediate land war, a scattering of senators from vulnerable areas of the northeast, and Franklin of North Carolina, perhaps still convinced that Britain could be defeated only on the sea. Their votes defeated the measure.[26]

Despite the collapse of all his Canadian plans, John A. Harper stood with the majority in voting a declaration of war. He might well claim recognition for a "tolerable *strait* course." Obviously other more important considerations than Canada had decided him for war.[27]

Did desire for Florida lead members of Congress to vote for war? Both the Jefferson and Madison administrations made repeated and unsuccessful efforts to obtain the provinces of East and West Florida from Spain. In 1805 President Jefferson sent James Monroe on an unproductive mission to Madrid to negotiate a cession of the Floridas. President Madison encouraged disaffection and revolt in the Spanish provinces and by 1811 part of West Florida west of the Perdido River had declared its independence and passed into possession of the United States. The same year General George Mathews, sent to East Florida to foment disaffection against the Spanish regime, invaded the province in a fruitless attempt to overthrow the existing authority.

The General bungled matters by issuing a proclamation of libera-
tion and invading the province from American soil with American land and naval forces. Embarrassed by the obvious aggression
in this action, the President in the spring of 1812 disavowed
Mathews and ordered a general withdrawal from the area.[28]

The southern borderland, annoyed at the refuge that Florida
afforded to deserting Negro slaves and at Spanish inability or
unwillingness to stop Indian raids from the province, looked
with high favor on these attempts. Among members of the 12th
Congress, Georgia's William H. Crawford, William W. Bibb,
and Charles Tait supported Mathews and were deeply disappointed at Madison's repudiation of his actions.[29] The prospect
of hostilities with Great Britain gave an added incentive for an
American military occupation of Florida. There was the danger
that Great Britain would use her role as protector of the Spanish monarch, Ferdinand VII, to occupy Florida with her own
troops. British forces in that province could sow discontent
among southern slaves, attack the coastal commerce of the southern and western states, and incite the southern Indians against
the frontiers. Permanent British possession, a possible outcome
of occupation, would conceivably make it altogether impossible
to acquire Florida. Even if Florida remained in Spanish hands
there seemed justification for American occupation in the fact
that British vessels were using ports in the province and that
Spanish authorities had presumably armed and incited Indians
against American settlers. Consequently, the Georgia delegation
and other southern and western members of Congress wanted a
military occupation of the province just as soon as war began.[30]
President Madison agreed to this strategy and drafted a message
(apparently not actually sent to Congress) that recommended
a congressional grant of authority for the immediate occupation
of Florida. The President requested that this authorization bear
a stipulation that such an action would be "subject to future
amicable negociations for adjusting all differences between Spain
& the U.S."[31]

Still, no one could have been sure that Congress would agree to military occupation of Florida, even if subject to negotiation. Given the sentiments of many, a vote for war on the assumed basis of the occupation and annexation of Florida would have been a risky proposition. Florida belonged to Spain. Would those who wished to confine hostilities against Great Britain to the sea, on grounds that the country was unprepared for immediate offensive operations, agree to seizure of territory belonging to a friendly nation? Did we want war with Spain too?

Immediately following the declaration of war, legislation authorizing the occupation of Florida passed the House and went to the Senate. This bill authorized the President to take possession of all Florida territory not yet held by the United States, to institute temporary government within the area, and to take necessary measures for the preservation of the security of the inhabitants. Further, the bill specifically announced that the area designated for military occupation was to be subject to future negotiation between the United States and Spain. In the Senate, Crawford on July 2 attempted to revive the measure for aiding land operations against Canada. As an amendment to the pending Florida bill he moved to authorize the President to establish temporary government within the Canadas in the event of conquest, and to direct him to take necessary measures for protection of the Canadians in their property, liberty, and religion. At the same time, announcing to the world that the primary purpose of the Canadian expedition was to serve negotiation not to annex Canada, Crawford's amendment provided that the principles upon which such temporary government shall be established should form no obstacle to the restoration of peace between the two nations, the United States and Great Britain. Brought to a vote on July 3, the combined Florida-Canada bill received support from advocates of land operations. Antiadministration advocates of sea war, Clintonians, Federalists, and four administration Republicans from vulnerable areas combined to defeat the amended bill, thus ending this effort to authorize occupation of Florida and facilitate a successful Canadian invasion.[32]

The attractions of Canada permanently in American hands

did not disappear in the months that followed the war declaration. Both Secretary of State Monroe and Speaker Clay would have liked Canada had it been possible to obtain it. Clay went so far as to say that "if Canada is conquered it ought never to be surrendered if it can possibly be retained." But whether retention was even remotely possible depended on the success of American arms. Clay recognized the elementary rule that one's bargaining position depended on one's military position at the time of negotiation, and that it was therefore impossible to say in advance whether a transfer of Canadian territory would be part of the final settlement. "The *state* of things is undergoing continual changes, and we must judge of the conditions of peace, when peace comes, not by the present state, but by that state of things which shall exist when it is negociated." But no one believed the war should be continued solely for Canada alone once Great Britain had shown willingness to settle the maritime issues.[33]

During the war debates, and subsequent to the declaration of war, Federalists and John Randolph of Roanoke charged that the War of 1812 was an expansionist war. Assigning principal responsibility for the war to the "war hawks," they denounced the war as one intended for the conquest and annexation of Canada and Florida. These charges Republican leaders vigorously denied. Calhoun of South Carolina, on at least four known and separate occasions, refuted the notion that this was an imperialist war. Roberts of Pennsylvania publicly repudiated the charge that Florida was the intended object of the war. In private correspondence Republican leaders were equally explicit and equally firm. Secretary Monroe, who surely should have known, wrote Taylor of Caroline that in case of war "it might be necessary to invade Canada, not as an object of the war but as a means to bring it to a satisfactory conclusion." Speaker Clay, also an authority on congressional motivation, wrote privately to a friend: "When the War was commenced Canada was not the end but the means; the object of the War being the redress of injuries, and Canada being the instrument by which that redress was to be obtained." [34] There is no reason to doubt these statements, and every reason to believe them. Republicans were willing to give their votes for war even without assurance that either Canada or Florida would ever be annexed. In the face of many obstacles it is doubtful that anyone voted for war primarily on the basis of a future annexation of these areas. Other concerns of far greater importance were responsible for the war.

(7)

ANTIWAR REPUBLICANS

Despite the sharp conflict over strategy in the ranks of the party, the great majority of Republican members of Congress ultimately supported the declaration of war. For them, the perils of remaining at peace under existing circumstances clearly outweighed those of war, whatever the strategy adopted. But in the final polling a significant minority of twenty-two Republicans cast votes against the war declaration. How are we to explain this division within the party?

It is clear that to at least some Republicans the objection to the declaration was primarily to its timing. These members came from constituencies where there were grave dangers in a war for which the country was inadequately prepared. All would have voted for the war had they deemed the nation adequately prepared, but all opposed the timing of a June declaration as perilously premature. The risks in a full-scale war seemed to overbalance the risks of postponement.

The argument against a June declaration was a powerful one for members of the New York delegation in the spring of 1812. Slow enlistments and lagging defensive preparations left exposed and vulnerable to attack New York's long northern frontier and the vital seaport of New York City. Large groups of export merchants, with investments in the domestic grain market and in British manufactured goods, were clamoring for relief prior to the opening of hostilities. Lending these conditions particular force was the danger of Federalist resurgence presaged by spring elections in which the Federalists had gained control of the lower house of the state legislature. The threat was sufficiently acute to bring even Peter B. Porter, chairman of the House Foreign Relations Committee, to desert his colleagues. Early in April Porter astounded members by coming out against the 60-day embargo recommended by the President. The country was not prepared for war and he could not agree to a measure looking to war before we were ready. Indeed, he "did not believe it was possible to commence it with safety within four months from this time." Moreover, an embargo, enacted just at this moment, would be "of immense injury to the State of New York, on account of their flour which has gone to market."

Called to New York by Governor Daniel Tompkins to serve as quartermaster, Porter kept up the pressure to postpone hostilities. To Secretary of War Eustis, he urged postponement on frankly political grounds. Not that war had become any the less necessary and unavoidable: "The great body of the people judge & act correctly. They know that there is no honourable course for this country to pursue but open & determined resistance to British wrongs. They approve a war, and will go every length to support the administration in it." But the safety of the Republican party demanded prudence—"to ensure the continuance of this support we ought to *deserve* it." To make war at this time would be "an act of *madness* fatal to the administration" when "we are completely exposed to attacks in every quarter." So exposed was the city of New York that two British frigates with one regiment of men "might, in two hours, take possession of every fortification erected for the defense of our Metropolis & turn the guns upon the town." Governor Tompkins, he added, agreed. The two New York Republicans had just discussed the matter, the Governor frankly affirming opposition to war at this time. The country was unprepared, and the British navy would have fine sailing weather for operations against our cities if we declared war before autumn. "He would [as Porter reported] consider a declaration of war as an unfortunate measure in the present unprepared state of the country; and independently of the state of preparation, he thinks the *season of the year* peculiarly unpropitious to the commencement of hostilities with G. Britain." [1]

Porter was struggling with war preparations in New York

State when Congress officially declared war and did not actually participate in the voting. We may only guess how he would have voted. A colleague, Thomas Sammons from Johnstown in the eastern Mohawk region of New York, was present and voted against the war. In January Sammons believed that "nothing but war can bring about a state of things to place our nation in her character of a free people." In May, under the pressure of developments in New York, he had joined the ranks of those pressing for postponement of hostilities and suspension of the embargo and nonimportation laws. Such conduct led John Randolph of Roanoke to note: "Old Sammons has returned from the Mohawk river as decided an advocate for peace as he was a partizan of war, at the commencement of the Session." When the House war resolution came to its initial test on June 4, Sammons voted against it—not because, as he believed, war was any the less necessary, but because "the United States were not prepared to prosecute the war [im]mediately which in my opinion the safety and good of our country required." Surely, a successful beginning to the war was important to sustain public confidence in the Republican party and public support for the war effort.[2]

One other New Yorker followed an apparently inconsistent course that greatly puzzled observers—Dr. Samuel Latham Mitchill of New York City. "It is out of my power to account for the conduct of either P. B. Porter or Doctr Mitchel" wrote the Vermont Federalist Martin Chittenden, in April, "but I doubt whether we shall be invited to [the war] feast this session." Mitchill had told William Plumer in January that we "must" have war. Presumably because of the military situation in New York he pressed for letters of marque to open hostilities. On June 4 he voted against the declaration of war. Despite the fact that at that time he had opposed a Randolph motion to postpone further consideration of war until October, after Senate passage of the war declaration he voted for a brief two-week postponement. This pattern of conduct indicates that he opposed the timing of the war, not the war itself.[3]

For Ohio members of Congress the risks in immediate hostilities argued powerfully against a June declaration of war. Ever since the battle between Harrison and the Prophet at Tippecanoe, Ohioans had feared further trouble from the restless tribes living within their borders and in neighboring Indiana, Illinois, and Michigan territories. In case of war with Great Britain Ohioans expected a full-scale Indian uprising, instigated and supplied by the British in Canada. To meet the danger, responsible leaders believed it imperative to make great exertions. The militia must be furnished with arms and ammunition, mounted rangers must be stationed on the frontier, and regulars must be moved to key points to protect settlers and overcome the Indians. By June, the situation was far from promising. Shortages of arms and ammunition still existed in the state. Some 450 mounted rangers were on duty—strung out thinly along some 700 miles of Indian frontier. To protect the important post at Detroit (and also to strike at Amherstburg) some 1,200 Ohio volunteers and 500 regulars under General William Hull had just left their staging point at Dayton, and were about to cross the 40-mile-wide Black Swamp—an over-all journey requiring bushwacking and roadbuilding of nearly a month.[4]

Under these circumstances Republican leaders believed the state to be in great danger. A former governor of the state, Edward Tiffin of Chillicothe, wrote his brother-in-law, Senator Thomas Worthington, of the grave situation. "I have had awful impressions since it has become too evident we are to be involved in War—we are in Ohio in a helpless unprotected state —Brittish Colonies and faithless Savage foes around our borders." Adequate defensive and offensive preparations would require more time. Senator Alexander Campbell of Ohio, home from Congress to be at the bedside of a sick child, wrote his Senate colleague that everybody he knew in the state believed Congress should adjourn and thereby give longer time for the government to make ready "before the 'Word was given, fire.' "[5]

Ohio's senior senator, Thomas Worthington, was present when the Senate took up the war question, and his voting during the fortnight of consideration accurately reflected the local military situation. On every proposal to limit hostilities to the sea, whether against Britain alone or against both belligerents, he voted in the affirmative. On the Clintonian-Federalist backed proposal to postpone all further consideration of the war bill until November he voted in the negative. Finally, when all possible combinations of limited maritime war had failed, he voted against the declaration of war.[6]

One's sympathies are with this man as one follows him through the session. He certainly believed the nation had no other alternative but to fight. The President's opening message was "strong" and left little doubt "but war must ultimately [be] adopted agst England." In February: "I do not believe there is any good reason to expect England will recede an inch & in that case war must take place." Again, to President Madison in June: "I believe war is unavoidable." [7] Yet he was greatly concerned over the prospect of war with Great Britain. He was critical of presumed irresponsible belligerency in speech-making colleagues; they seemed "insensible of the blessings we enjoy and do not consider the things which belong to our peace." The feeble defenses of Ohio were the main point of his attention. From almost the moment he arrived in Washington he sought arms for the Ohio militia and rangers for frontier patrol. He patched up a quarrel with Governor Return J. Meigs in order that the two might work more effectively in preparing the state for war. He urged Secretary of War Eustis to send a delegation to the Ohio Indians to hear their grievances and work out a peaceful settlement. "I am determined to use every means in my power to provide against the storm in our quarter," he told Governor Meigs. He encouraged the Governor to make all possible haste in ordering Ohio militia to join Hull's army in preparation for a march to Detroit. "Should the Brittish get possession of Detroit I need not tell you that the whole frontier of Ohio would be open to savage & Brittish incursions."

As defense preparations dragged and Hull seemed immobilized at Dayton, his anxieties mounted. By mid-May he was convinced the country lacked the defensive and offensive power to carry on war with effectiveness at the present time, and believed the administration should withdraw from its announced intention of seeking a June declaration. "It will be folly and madness to get into the war for abstract principles when we have not the power to enforce them. To withdraw would be wisdom but I fear this has fled our councils." From the situation in Ohio he projected evils on a national scale. He foresaw a disgraceful opening to the war—with no available offensive force of any strength how could we invade Canada? He foresaw odium to the administration and paralyzing discouragement among the people—all dangerous to party and country. On June 14, in the midst of the see-saw struggle over strategy in the Senate, he called on President Madison and discussed "candidly" Indian affairs and the subject of war. The Ohioan kept a diary record of what he told the President on that day. "My objections candidly stated to him to wit that we are unprepared, that 3 months must elaps before any invasion can take place, that in the mean time the administration will be exposed to the attacks of its enemies, the people will be disheartened." And, "although I may differ with my friends on this question or with him I will be the very last to agree to a disgraceful peace & will rise or sink with my political associates. That I believe war is unavoidable but as we have it compleatly in our power to choose our own time to make it I cannot take the responsibility on me of entering into it in an unprepared [state]." [8]

Nonetheless, local dangers remained an important factor in Worthington's personal equation. Explaining his conduct in an open letter he indicated why he had voted for letters of marque but against a declaration of war. War department enlistment returns had shown the country to be unprepared for immediate war: "war by sea for which I voted was lost and the only alternative was war generally and for this I could not vote without doing that which from the clearest convictions of my own mind I believed wrong." At the time he had thought "we had cause or more than cause of war against England" and that we could successfully maintain the contest with her. But "we were not prepared with an army or armies to carry on the war with effect," and this would give Great Britain "the advantage which would only add to her insolence, protract peace, greatly augment the expences of the war and increase the number opposed to it." Furthermore, he emphasized, the "whole western frontier was unprotected and I was convinced the Brittish would use the influence they possessed over the indians to instigate them to attack and harrass that frontier." Thus both national and local considerations explain Worthington's conduct. For him the safety of party and country, and the safety of Ohio citizens, were in jeopardy from a war that the "abstract principles" at issue did not require the government immediately to fight.[9]

Still other Republicans opposed the declaration of war on grounds of timing. Josiah Bartlett, Jr., was a congressman from Stratham, New Hampshire, representing a constituency which included the seaport of Portsmouth. Bartlett believed, with his party, that there was now no other alternative but force. In April he took a holiday from congressional duties and returned to New Hampshire to get married. There Republican leaders from Portsmouth visited him and urged his immediate return to Washington to press for delay of hostilities. They told him "that they had understood an immediate Declaration of war against G Britain would be made which they & the Republicans generally in Portsmo & its vicinity deemed an extraordinary hasty step considering the immense property in Britain & on the ocean." To Bartlett his visitors "appeared very anxious & warm. they wished if possible that actual hostilities might be commenced by GB which would render the war popular. they fully accorded that war might ultimately ensue if the differences were not adjusted." In response to the pleas of these leaders, Bartlett bid farewell to his bride, and in great haste returned to Washington. When the war resolution came to a vote on June 4 he voted for an October postponement and against the declaration. But once the bill had passed both branches and returned to the House for approval of minor Senate amendments, he reversed himself and voted against all motions to postpone the bill for varying lengths of time. A June declaration was "too hasty," he told his brother, but to postpone after Senate approval would have betrayed weakness in party and government—"it would look like retracing the steps & show a vacillating disposition which the times totally forbid." Still, had he been in the Senate, he would have favored letters of marque instead of an unrestricted declaration: "I did hope the Senate would have so altered the Bill at this time as to give it the character of Reprisals by granting restrictive letters of marque but they did not see fitt." [10]

There was little need for outside pressures to move Richard Cutts of Saco in the District of Maine, the President's brother-in-law. Cutts's own mercantile and shipping interests spoke loudly enough in behalf of merchants whose affairs would suffer from an immediate declaration of war against Great Britain. Cutts had ships and property at sea when war began in June; this made it difficult for him to meet demands on him by a worried creditor after the declaration. Nursing an injured shoulder at his home in Saco during most of the session, Cutts returned to Washington early in June, too late for voting on June 4 but in time for the second round on June 18. At that time his votes showed a wish to postpone the war, but not put it off altogether. On that day he voted against a motion to postpone indefinitely but favored two motions to postpone up to a period of four months. In April, 1812, war seemed to him to be "inevitable," the administration having made "every honorable effort to preserve peace." In June war was still premature. "I was in hopes and did all I could to put off the war for a little time, but in vain," he told his brother shortly after war was declared.[11]

It would be a mistake to attribute Cutts's desire for delay to the sole promptings of personal business interests. His letters indicate keen awareness of the effects of national policy on Republican fortunes in the northeast. In April he told the President that the latest Boston papers "have thrown a gloom over our countenances, as they respect the elections & the proceedings in Washington." Early returns in the gubernatorial contest had shown Federalist gains, probably the result of the reported embargo. "Salem will undoubtedly be federal this year, several other large Towns that sent Republican Representatives last year have given Federal majorities this year." The Massachusetts senate and governorship were probably safe in Republican hands, he believed, but the Federalists would certainly have the house. (Actually, the elections turned out worse than expected—the Republican incumbent, Elbridge Gerry, lost to Caleb Strong, a Federalist.) Surely elections were on Cutts's mind, too, when he wrote his father four months after war had begun: "I am rejoiced that even in the prosecution of the war, no taxes will be required this session. I presume the war can be carried on for any length of time by loans." It may be supposed, therefore, that his votes to postpone the war for varying lengths of time derived from political as well as economic concerns. Premature hostilities might convulse the mercantile world, alienate support essential to victory, bring disgrace on the party, and return the Federalists to control of the northeastern states and even of the nation. These thoughts may have been in his mind when he wrote gloomily the day war began: "The Senate have this day concurred with the House of Representatives in a Bill, the passage of which I fear will be destructive to the best interests of this Country. . . . What will be the consequences of this message it is impossible to foretell." [12]

It is often held that the principal opposition to the War of 1812 came from northeastern mercantile and commercial groups who stood to lose heavily in a war with Great Britain. There was only one Republican against war on these grounds. This was Peleg Tallman, a congressman from Bath in the District of Maine. Tallman was a timber exporter and shipowner who was self-made, and as is sometimes the way with individuals who rise from nothing, was narrowly and single-mindedly devoted to his business affairs. Having lost an arm during service in the American Revolution, he had, despite the handicap, risen through industry and acumen to be a wealthy man. Looking back over his life in 1840, he observed sagely that his career illustrated "how a poor invalid of the Revolution, with one arm, might with hard labor and watching make his way in the world among two-armed people." He seems to have regarded public service as a means of protecting and advancing his own personal interests and those of the maritime business community as he conceived of them. Economic interest, his own and of the merchant community in general, moved this man to oppose the war. He was a "minority man," he told the Maine merchant-politician William King in June, and had voted against war. "You well know," he went on to say, "what my fears have always been, a very few days will show you with what degree of propriety I entertained them. What will this change bring us to!" Months earlier he had warned of the ruinous effect war would have on overseas commerce. The British navy commanded the sea and could have its way with American shipping. With no hope of accommodation between the two nations, "what steps the British will persue, you can Judge as well as I can but it seems clear that our trade must suffer a most Dreadfull eclips.," he wrote to King early in the session. You "can easeyly Figure to yourself what must be the fate of our shiping capital." Indeed, thought Tallman bitterly, the Republicans in their march towards war knew little and cared less about maritime commercial interests. They were all "Law, Phisic & Farmers," and he did not know "a Practical merchant in the house." They all "seeme willing to take a violant stand against england In contempt of the consequences." The "mercantiel & especially the shiping interest has but few admirers, & they amuse themselves at the Folly of men having so long ventered there property on The ocean in such critical times." Tallman paid no attention to the political concepts guiding other Republicans as they sought means to protect American commerce against British depredation. Assured commerce, national independence, national honor, the Republican party, republican government—what mattered to him was business. A lonely figure in the party by his own admission, Tallman is a significant exception that proves a rule.[13]

Other Republicans opposing the war were congressional members of the Clinton faction. The Clintonians were northern anti-administration Republicans headed by the New York leaders George Clinton and his nephew De Witt Clinton. They have not fared well at the hands of American historians. Ever since Henry Adams condemned the Clintons as ambitious place-seekers ready to ally with anyone to promote their selfish ends (he labeled De Witt Clinton as second in ambition and intrigue only to Aaron Burr!), they have found few advocates. Leading national historians have dismissed them as place-seekers and careerists without integrity or concern for national interest. Even more friendly New York State historians, though claiming integrity for these leaders, have found it hard to explain Clintonian policy on grounds other than personal ambition and personal animosity. Nor were contemporary rivals very flattering. Samuel Smith of Maryland in 1805 described the struggle between Burr and George Clinton for control of the party in New York State as entirely a personal and selfish affair. Their quarrel was "in truth without a Political view, but rather a dispute whether you shall worship the Golden Calf I have set up or the one you have, whether a C——— or a b——— shall govern." The view was quite common among Republicans. William H. Crawford of Georgia in 1812 remarked on Clintonian opposition to the coming war. "They are a set of Malcontents, who are more intent upon making De Witt Clinton President, than they are desirous of promoting the public good." [14]

Still, there are difficulties in this interpretation. George Clinton was seven years in the provincial legislature of New York, a delegate to the Continental Congress, seven times governor of his native state, and twice Vice-President of the United States. De Witt Clinton was ten times mayor of New York City, was president of several important learned societies—the New-York Historical Society, the New York Literary and Philosophical Society, the New York Academy of Fine Arts—and four times Governor of New York. When he died in 1828 the outpouring of tributes was so profuse as to take up 200 printed pages in a special volume published to commemorate the unhappy event.

Obviously both men had many devoted admirers and followers and carried great weight with the voters of their state. Could all New York have been utterly blind to their motives for so long? The question is worth consideration.

Both men showed good evidence of stanchly republican sentiments. They believed that in working for the Republican party they were working for republican government. In 1803, when the party seemed firmly in power, George Clinton could write to his nephew that he no longer needed to be active. "The object is happily accomplished and whether my services have contributed to its success or not is immaterial. The cause of Republicanism is now so well established as not to require any new sacrifice on my part." But by 1809 he believed republicanism once more in danger. The party majority, he wrote that year, had unwisely "wedded the Cause of Republicanism to the Measures of the Administration particularly the Embargo, and they [will sink] or swim together." De Witt Clinton considered himself a steadfast defender of republicanism. In early 1809 while Congress vacillated over the question of what to substitute for the embargo he wrote: "The proceedings at Washington have not assumed a decisive complexion— and I am fearful the result will not benefit the republican cause." In the spring of 1812, after Governor Tompkins prorogued the state legislature on a matter involving state politics, and news of the 90-day embargo had reached New York, he wrote: "The promulgation at Albany will not essentially injure our Spring Election: I am fearful of the effects of the Embargo." While traveling in western New York in 1810, looking over possible routes for the New York canal, he crossed into Canada and observed immediately a marked difference in the vigor and enterprise of the inhabitants: in every manner of individual and physical improvement, the Americans had bested their neighbors. The difference was "flattering to our national pride, and to the cause of republican government," he remarked in his journal, a comment that might have been made by a Jefferson contrasting European republics and monarchies.[15]

The conflict between the Clintonians and the Madisonians (or Martling men as they were called after Martling's Tavern, their headquarters in New York City) greatly needs a fresh investigation. Our understanding of early American politics would be greatly enhanced by a new and detailed treatment of the efforts of the Clintonians to win power on the state and national level. One point is fairly certain: the Clintonians thought of their efforts as ruled by necessity, not selfishness. As they saw matters, they must rescue the country and republicanism from an incompetent, popularity-seeking Virginia leadership that was threatening to destroy the party in the northeast and return the nation to the evils of Federalist control. George Clinton put the matter succinctly in April, 1808, to his nephew De Witt Clinton in the midst of discontent over the embargo. "It is in my Opinion impossible that the Cause of republicanism can exist much longer under the present visionary Feeble & I might add Corrupt management of our National Affairs." [16]

The Clintons agreed that depredations on American commerce by the European belligerents were too serious to ignore and that something must be done to end them, but they put little store in the methods actually adopted. Commercial restrictions quickly caused depression and discontent in the commercially oriented northern states without effecting repeal of the British Orders or the French Decrees. An alarming resurgence of Federalist strength took place in New England and New York. By 1808 the Clintons were acting as a rallying point of opposition to continuance of commercial restrictions. In their view these measures merely antagonized the belligerents and injured the United States. Negotiation backed by effective military, naval, and defensive preparations would be far more effective. Once it became clear to the belligerents that the country would fight to defend its rights, they would make the required concessions. The adherence by the Virginia leadership to policies that seemed ineffective and self-destructive, and their refusal to abandon military and naval disarmament, raised deep suspicion in Clintonian minds. Did the Virginians cling to these policies in order to advance their popularity in the south and west while caring little about the well-being of northern commercial states? Perhaps they enjoyed the rewards of office under conditions of crisis and really had little desire to reach a settlement. Nicholas Gilman of New Hampshire, a strong Clinton man, put the matter well in 1810. Britain can have no desire to go to war with us, he wrote; it would be "death to them." Britain's conduct towards us has been exactly graduated by her estimation of what we would bear. Therefore we should adopt measures towards her "better calculated to preserve peace and the rights and fair fame of our nation (according to my own estimation) than anything we have done." But "the love of office—a timid spirit, and the love of popularity strangles every measure calculated to vindicate the fair fame and honor of the nation, in its birth." As time passed, the Clintonians won to their ranks many northern Republicans who believed the nation and party could be saved only by a new administration, headed by a "practical" Republican of ability and integrity who would repeal the restrictive system and negotiate with the belligerents from a position of strength.[17]

To contemporary witnesses, the conduct of Clintonian Republicans during the war session seemed strangely inconsistent. At the beginning of the session they supported the President's program of military preparation. Yet when he proposed a 60-day embargo, they swung into opposition and ultimately voted against war. Certainly, as Samuel Shaw, an administration Republican from Vermont observed in April, "there has been a strange managemt here and at Albany." A "total change of conduct" has taken place with the leading members from New York: "they were amongst the first to support war Measures in the begening but now are hostile to Executive [measures]." A Clintonian might easily have resolved this perplexity. In November, 1811, President Madison recommended preparations for war, but did not entirely shut the door to a settlement. Repeal of the Orders in Council would be welcomed by his administration, he promised, but Congress should put the nation "into an armour and attitude demanded by the crisis." Clintonian Republicans had reacted cautiously to this message. If the President intended military preparation to strengthen his hand for more effective negotiation, then it was a welcome step in the right direction which they would support. Gilman of New Hampshire thus voted for those military measures "best calculated to give effect to negociations or carry on offensive operations, in case of necessity." But Clintonian Republicans could not be certain as to actual administration purposes. Not even Vice-President George Clinton knew the ultimate design. "I dare not hazard an Opinion on a political subject so interesting lest I might Err & unwittingly deceive my Friends. You know I do not belong to the Cabinet Council."

As the session advanced, Clintonian uncertainty intensified. Military preparations lagged. The deadlock-breaking negotiation from a position of strength never took place. Their suspicion grew, as Gilman wrote, that "the highsounding war message was prepared rather with a view to popularity than with any serious intention on the part of the Executive to pursue such measures as would naturally grow out of the recommendations it contained." Then, unexpectedly, even before the nation was half-prepared, the President foolishly recommended a 60-day embargo, and two months later, a declaration of war. Long distrustful of Madison's ability, judgment, and motives, already firmly convinced of the great abilities of De Witt Clinton, Clintonian Republicans felt no personal reason to support these recommendations. Nor did they feel any political reason to do so. Why support the embargo when the country was nowhere near ready for war, and New York merchants and millers were clamoring for relief? Why support a declaration of war when the most promising method for settlement of differences with Great Britain had never been tried? [18]

It is therefore understandable why Obadiah German of New York and Nicholas Gilman of New Hampshire, the leading Clintonians in the Senate, should have supported a motion for postponement of the war question until November, and ultimately voted against war. (They also voted for various limited maritime

war proposals—as less desirable than postponement but preferable to full-scale war.[19]) In their view of the matter, the administration had not yet exhausted all means short of war. Vigorous
military preparation accompanied by an impartial attitude towards the two belligerents would produce repeal of the Orders
in Council, German declared in a June speech against war; if
it did not do so, at least war would be less dangerous than at
the present time. Ever since he had been a senator he had "uniformly" voted appropriations for putting the country into a
state of defense and preparing it for war. "A country well prepared to meet war will scarcely find war necessary, but if it
cannot be avoided, preparation does away half its terrors." This
had not yet been tried, and until it had been, he would not vote
for war. Once an army of 25,000 men had been organized, dis-
ciplined, and made ready for an assault on Canada; once the
navy had been strengthened; once both belligerents had been
placed on an equal footing—"then, I say, if Great Britain will
not do us justice, I will vote at the proper time a declaration
of war against her; and I will use my utmost exertions to make
the war terrible to her." It was on just this ground that Senator
Gilman believed long after war was declared that the Madison
administration might have reached an accommodation with Great
Britain. "As to the great object of our wishes, an adjustment of
differences with Great Britain, I have never en[ter]tained a
doubt that it might have been effected in a satisfactory manner
long before the declaration of war, had our Executive entertained just and proper dispositions in regard to it." [20]

To strengthen the Clintonian case against war were all the
economic and military arguments that had led administration
Republicans from north and east to favor postponement and
limited maritime war. Northern frontiers and the eastern seaboard were dangerously unprotected and vulnerable. Merchants
had millions invested in property afloat or on British soil and in
grain at home awaiting export. Small wonder that Matthias B.
Tallmadge, a New York leader and son-in-law of George Clinton, could write from New York City shortly before the decla-

ration: "The horrible aspect which our Washington news presents is indeed melancholy & as far as I can learn impresses this city with dismay & fear. yet no doubt many of our Martling gentry will glory in the *wise course* till it shall overtake them & then most probably be the first to flee from its calamities." [21]

Why then had the administration recommended war with no justifiable reason for doing so? Perhaps, in Georgia and South Carolina, suggested German, are to be found "the combustibles which have kindled this mighty war flame, and precipitated this nation to the verge of ruin." Crawford in the Senate, Calhoun in the House—these were the leading men in the war movement—had they pressured the President into war measures? Possibly the President was not so unwilling to go to war after all. He might put his little army to use, not against Canada, but "as an enforcement of the restrictive system." [22]

So wretched was the conduct of the Madison administration, that to Clintonian Republicans De Witt Clinton seemed the last sure barrier against a complete Federalist triumph. To prevent this evil the New York *Columbian* called on Republicans to support Clinton in the coming presidential election. The man deserved support "on the broad basis of the honor, independence, and the best interests of the country." The present administration had failed to uphold these objects, and was rapidly losing public confidence. Clinton could "preserve the country from a total change of rulers. . . . We are determined to regain and preserve in this state a republican ascendency, and to exert our influence in preserving to the United States an administration characterized by practical republicanism, rather than countenance or abet its negligent or wilful prostration to the federal party." [23]

Finally, there were antiadministration Republicans of still another sort opposed to the war—Old Republicans. John Randolph of Roanoke and Richard Stanford best illustrate the views of this group. Together with Edwin Gray of Virginia, these orthodox Republican ideologues, or *tertium quids* as they are known to history, stood solidly and bitterly against the war.

Few men in our early national period are more famous and more controversial than John Randolph. This strange, gifted man has evoked and continues to evoke fascination and dispute. In 1801 he had welcomed the incoming administration of Thomas Jefferson and had quickly become a leading supporter in the House of Representatives. By 1806 he was in open rebellion against Jefferson and his policies and remained adamant against Madison during his presidency. Randolph's strange dress and mannerisms, his fierce hates and warm friendships, his apparent hypochondria, above all his distorted but brilliant oratory, raised questions as to his personal stability, even sanity. Admirers saw in him qualities of greatness—constancy of principle, loftiness of view, and brilliance of intellect. More sober estimates stressed his integrity and sincerity, but held him prejudiced and high-handed. Hugh Nelson of Virginia, a first-term member in 1812, lived at the same boarding house as Randolph and saw him on many occasions. "With all his faults, I believe he is as honest as Ld. Chatham and as independent." John Nicholas, a Virginia politician who had moved to New York, also had no doubt of his honesty but believed his principles to be "impracticable" and his prejudices "inveterate." [24]

The more one studies the early career of this lonely Virginian the more one is convinced that the permanent security of republican government in America was of primary concern to him. "Republicanism depends not on a few orators, statesmen and philosophers, but on the diffusion of general information throughout the whole mass of society" he remarked, Jeffersonlike, early in 1801. He backed enthusiastically the reforms and retrenchments of the early Jefferson years—as a good start. But he wanted more. We "have only made a beginning," he told Henry St. George Tucker and "if we procure not a substantial reform in the government, our work will be good for nothing." The state governments must have greater power to make them stronger bulwarks against consolidation. If they "be not invigorated, & that quickly, we shall soon be blended into one mass and find our-selves in the point of monarchy to which our constitution has so strong & so alarming a tendency." (In this same letter Randolph made a characteristically extreme statement that he wished to abandon the present national government and return to one more strictly federal: "Such a government, or any connexion between the states, *not purely federal,* must, in my opinion, *necessarily* eventuate in despotism.") If the memory of William A. Burwell was accurate, Randolph had frequently told him that "certain reforms were indispensable in the [constitution] for its purity, & perpetuation," measures abridging the executive power, purifying the House of Representatives, securing the responsibility of public agents, and punishing violations of civil rights.[25]

By 1804 Randolph was in open disagreement with his Republican colleagues. A Jefferson-appointed commission composed of Madison, Gallatin, and Benjamin Lincoln had recommended a compromise formula to settle the Yazoo land fraud tangle. In 1795 a bribed Georgia legislature had sold a princely domain to several Yazoo land companies for a pittance. In the midst of ensuing public indignation, legislators had repudiated the sale; the federal commissioners recommended purchase of the land from Georgia and distribution to claimants who had purchased land before repudiation. Randolph stood bitterly against all compromise, as a bargain with corruption. Corruption was "the bane of every Republic," and to yield to it was to begin the inevitable march to moral degeneracy and despotism, he warned. "What is the spirit against which we now struggle, and which we have vainly endeavored to stifle? A monster generated by fraud, nursed in corruption, that in grim silence awaits its prey. It is the spirit of Federalism." Again, during the session of 1805–6 he stood out against the administration-backed nonimportation law as inexpedient and dangerous. It was wrong, he vowed, to commit the nation to a contest over unessential matters. "Are you not contented with being free and happy at home? Or will you surrender these blessing that your merchants may tread on Turkish and Persian carpets, and burn the perfumes of the East in their valuted rooms?" To contend for the carrying trade was

to begin the inevitable descent into war and all its evils—an increased debt, a standing army, heavy taxes, increased executive
power, and patronage. The sacrifice was much too great simply
to protect an interest that itself (as his alter-ego James Garnett
of Virginia put it) "must inevitably become deleterious and destructive to the manners, the morals, and the government of the
nation." Instead of nonimportation, the administration should
send a military expedition to the southern border to deal with
recent incursions from Spanish Florida. This would prove to a
contemptuous Europe that America was not to be trifled with
and would afford an incentive for settlement of disputes with
Spain as well as with Great Britain.[26]

Defeated on this policy, it was at this point that Randolph
openly broke with the Jefferson administration and began his
long, lonely, bitter opposition to the Republican leadership.
Republican government, he concluded, was no longer safe in
the hands of the Jeffersonian Republicans. The men who com-
promised with corruption at home and produced embroilments
abroad for the benefit of corrupting interests were themselves, if
not personally corrupt, at least weak, foolish, incompetent, and
not to be trusted with national leadership. But so unsuccessful
were his efforts to rally opposition to the Jeffersonian leaders
that presently he concluded the Republic was nearly beyond
redemption. Power, patronage, and privilege, fostered by the
Federalists, permitted to flourish under Republican executives,
had so eaten away all virtue and independence of mind in both
party and country that nothing but a moral and religious regen-
eration of citizens could avert complete degeneracy and inevitable despotism. The rot had eaten deep into the nation's vital
spirit, he told Garnett. "The world is on the verge of universal
despotism & nothing short of a miracle can arrest it's career. . . .
Without morals & a due sense of religion a free government
cannot stand; be the *form* of it whatever it may. If I could see
something like the old spirit of independence restored amongst
us—open, honest, frank expression of opinion concerning publick measures & publick men too—such as existed before we had

been debauched by Patronage—I should have some hope." Just
how the Republic would fall—whether from a native Cromwell
or Didius, or a foreign Napoleon—Randolph was not altogether
certain. But certain he was that "in whatever manner it be effected, every thing appears to announce the coming of a *master*." [27]

In Randolph's view the nonimportation act embroiled the
country with Great Britain in a policy that would lead ultimately
to war. Over other nonessential interests—the security of American sailors from impressment and the safety of American vessels
engaged in the direct trade—the administration took the nation
further down the road to disaster. Repeal all measures of commercial coercion, Randolph urged time and again. Let trade
shift for itself. Commercial restrictions were impotent threats,
obstructions to settlement. They bore hardest on ourselves, encouraging disrespect for law, corrupting morals, and demoral-
izing the national spirit. Repeal would lay the groundwork for
accommodation. Let the merchants arm in their own self-defense
and repel their molesters. Britain and France would then cease
their depredations. Commerce will protect itself and peace will
be the result.[28]

Unshakeably confident of the rightness of his own thinking,
during the war session of 1811–12 Randolph never accepted the
position that war had become necessary, just, and unavoidable.
For him, significantly, the issue was not war or submission but
"peace or war"; military preparation was "a course not required
by the circumstances of the country"; war was not "absolutely
necessary." Exhortation and oratory would not make the war
palatable, he told war Republicans. "You can neither make the
people go to war, nor keep them at war, unless they be convinced they have no other resource." He "wished the American
people to know what new cause of war had accrued since the
accession of the present President to the Chair—since the return
of Mr. Monroe from his mission to London." It was the Jeffer-
son-Madison leadership, through their foolish commercial restrictions and inept diplomacy, that had created present difficul-

ties and embarrassments. "The nation had been brought into its present alarming and unprecedented situation by means in no wise unaccountable—by steps as direct and successive as Hogarth's celebrated series of prints, 'The Rake's Progress,' beginning at the gaming table and ending in a jail, or in bedlam." Long before, had the men in power entertained proper ideas of national interest and policy, they could have avoided the present impasse.[29]

Why, with the Madison administration so deeply entangled in a net of its own making, was war being urged at this particular time? Randolph's explanation was the logical projection of his own personal view of the world he moved in and the men he knew and despised. Catching at discussions regarding the conquest and annexation of Canada, early in the session he concluded that this war was for "the acquisition of territory and subjects." Republican politicians, many of whom were first-term members eager to make their political fortunes, sought Canada as a way towards popularity and preferment through exploitation of the patronage, profits, plunder, and glory that would come from invasion and conquest. Northern politicians especially had found Canada attractive.

Gentlemen from the North have been taken up to some high mountain and shown all the kingdoms of the earth; and Canada seems tempting in their sight. That rich vein of Gennesee land, which is said to be even better on the other side of the lake than on this. Agrarian cupidity, not maritime right, urges the war. Ever since the report of the Committee of Foreign Relations came into the House, we have heard but one word—like the whip-poor-will, but one eternal monotonous tone—Canada! Canada! Canada!

There were other greedy motives pressing for war. The price of hemp would go up in the event of hostilities with Great Britain. "For a gentleman from Tennessee or Gennessee, or Lake Champlain, there may be some prospect of advantage. Their hemp would bear a great price by the exclusion of foreign supply." There was bound to be profit in a Canadian war for people supplying the army with food and forage. "The upper country on the Hudson and the Lakes would be enriched by the supplies for the troops, which they alone could furnish. They would have the exclusive market: to say nothing of the increased preponderance from the acquisition of Canada and that section of the Union, which the Southern and Western States had already felt so severely in the apportionment bill." All these motives, aided by the pressures of Irish editors, military adventurers, profiteers, contractors, and fugitives from British justice, drove the rest of the party forward. This was not an honorable war, cried Randolph, but a "predatory war." It was not "a war for our homes and firesides—a war that might generate, or call forth manly and honorable sentiment—but, a war of rapine, of privateering, a scuffle and scramble for plunder; when, like the duckers on the Potomac, we should calculate at every discharge, 'so much powder and shot for so much game.'"

Towards spring Randolph thought he could detect a growing aversion to war among Republicans as the costs and difficulties of preparation became known to election-minded congressmen. But there was no turning back. They had committed their personal honor to the invasion of Canada and could not retreat without absolute disgrace. Momentarily, at the end of April, Randolph heard talk of limited maritime war and hypothesized that "a naval, predatory war" was in contemplation but swung back to his original view when war was declared and Canada invaded. Thus, for Randolph, the war for Canada never ceased to derive from motives of the worst kind—ambition and greed. In 1813 he failed to be reelected and began corresponding with the famous Boston Federalist, Josiah Quincy, Jr. The two men saw practically eye to eye on the war. Chiefly responsible for this war were men from the west—Clay, Grundy, and a few others who had maneuvered their colleagues into war to satisfy personal ambition. Even the conduct of the Lord North ministry during the American Revolution sprang from "motives less base than those which prompted the present accursed contest. *That* was a question concerning which honest men might differ. Not so *this*." [30]

During the war session he felt that only evil could come of a war. Under the present irresponsible administration we might well become the allies of the "arch-fiend" now "grasping at the sceptre of the civilized world"—Bonaparte. He wrote Garnett of a dream he had. A war-time inquisition was in process against opponents of the war. His "worthy colleague," the Virginia Federalist John Baker, was on the scaffold about to be executed for treason, the unjust verdict of a packed jury. The commander-in-chief of the attending military force was Robert Smith, the brother of the Baltimore senator, and the grand inquisitor was William Branch Giles. Other horrors haunted his imagination. Rumors of slave unrest in Virginia led to thoughts of the general uprising that would result from a British invasion. The British would probably sack our towns and ravage our coasts; our sons and brothers may die "like rotten sheep at Terre a Boeuf (or some where else) by the gross neglect & incapacity of their officers." How in the name of Heaven could any good come of this contest? "Sadness is now the fixed habit of my mind," he wrote Garnett. "Why should I distress you with my gloomy forebodings." [31]

Small wonder that John Randolph opposed the war! His was a position based on views and prejudices that years of lonely opposition and imagined persecution had frozen into firm conviction. He had moved far from his former associates, so far indeed that he could no longer even understand, much less agree with, old friends now for war—Nathaniel Macon, David R. Williams, Joseph H. Nicholson, and William H. Crawford. "I listen to the wisest of them," he told Garnett, "& to me their talk is as the talk of children. I do not pretend to argue with them, for I speak a language which they cannot understand." The men whom he now could understand were Federalists— Josiah Quincy, Jr., of Massachusetts, Harmanus Bleecker and James Emott of New York, Francis Scott Key of Maryland, James Bayard of Delaware, John Baker and James Breckinridge of Virginia—men with similar views of the war. But fantastic as it may seem, his position was logical in the abstract.

According to his view, there was not the slightest need for war at this time. Ever since 1808 he had known a way to extricate the country from its European entanglements. The men who advocated war were corrupt and evil and irresponsible. Under such leadership how could war for Canada be anything but disastrous to independence, liberty, property, and life. Any one of these counts would have been reason enough to oppose the war.[32]

Standing alongside Randolph was Richard Stanford of North Carolina.[33] Less is known of this man; few of his speeches and letters have survived. He considered himself equally firm in the Old Republican creed. Perhaps his disillusion with men and things was slightly less profound than Randolph's, but he believed the Republican majority to be moved by low enough motives to justify his opposition to the war. The proposed war, he agreed with Randolph, was not defensive—the only legitimate cause according to Old Republican doctrine—but offensive. It was a war not for homes and firesides but for the conquest and annexation of Canada. A war of this kind would prove disastrous to the Republic. To attempt the conquest of Canada "is but to throw aside our pacific character, and put on that of a belligerent military one; in fact, to inflict ruin upon ourselves." We acquire a standing army. We multiply executive patronage. We pass treason and sedition bills. We become imbued with ambition for further military conquests and glory. Thus he wrote gloomily to the Pennsylvania Quaker, George Logan, that the war fever of the present Republican majority had passed all bounds since the memorable years of 1798–99. They intended to invade and conquer the Canadas, and the "seeming spirit of acquisition of those Countries by conquest is not less ardent than it was, when Louisiana was acquired by purchase." He was convinced the majority were in earnest.

[I]f such [a] project, or its attempt, be realized I do most conscientiously believe, we shall be, politically speaking, ruin'd. The character of our government, & all our civil institutions woud, in such event, undergo a radical change, from which it coud never regain itself—for a republic, the very apparatus of war is enough to destroy it—essentially at any rate.

This "war of aggression and of foreign conquest" could in no way be justified. In the year 1798 he had stood with loyal Republican colleagues against the "*quasi* war of Mr. Adams" which had been "founded upon as legitimate causes as the present one, contemplated with G. Britain." He "had opposed the war, and the measures leading to it, as impolitic and unjust, in Mr. Adams's time, and should not feel himself an honest and consistent politician not to oppose the war now contemplated." He had resisted the madness of that period; he would resist the "infatuation of our Councils" now. Indeed:

The rage for war exceeds any time since the memorable years of '98-9. The only difference I can perceive is, that the opposite party have the opposite belligerent to contend with. The war fever is precisely the same, but the mania the more inveterate as the present majority exceeds in numbers, that of the former, over their respective minorities.

In 1798 the Republicans had refused to fight France for commerce; in 1812 he would refuse to do what was even worse— fight Britain for Canada. But as he wrote Logan sadly, he was getting to be almost a "fatalist. My mind is unable to keep up with the political madness of the day without the aid of all the doctrines of fatalism, if I may use the term. We may well implore heaven to forgive us, for it seems literally true, that we know not what we do." Just as with John Randolph, a distorted view of the character of the war and fears of its disastrous consequences on republicanism explain Stanford's opposition.[34]

A variety of motives moved Republicans to oppose the war declaration. No single factor will account for this intraparty opposition. At one with the party majority on the necessity and justice of war, men like Porter, Sammons, Mitchill, Bartlett, Cutts, and Worthington feared baneful effects from a premature declaration on their own states, on their party, and on the nation. Hard facts of economic interest ruled the outlook of Peleg Tallman and produced his determined opposition to war with

Great Britain. Belief that they and their leaders held an unused key to the diplomatic deadlock and that the nation was unprepared for war explains Clintonian opposition. Belief that war was avoidable, that men responsible for this war had base designs, and that nothing but evil and disaster could flow from such a war, explains the opposition of the Old Republicans John Randolph and Dick Stanford. For different reasons, therefore, different Republicans were against the war. Theirs was an ephemeral union produced by the accidental coalition of dissimilar forces.

(8)

THIS WICKED, FOOLISH WAR

Few would deny that at their best the administrations of Washington and Adams were periods of constructive and far-seeing statesmanship. That Federalism, in its heyday of power, created an enduring legacy of accomplishment scarcely needs demonstration. The Federalists funded the state and national Revolutionary war debts, brought into being a reliable revenue system, created a national bank, and established an enviable reputation for sound fiscal management. They set high standards of administrative efficiency and public responsibility. They created a small but effective army and navy. In foreign affairs they set precedents of neutrality and abstention from European affairs. All in all, no matter what Republicans may have said to the contrary, the Federalist period was one of constructive, responsible, and enlightened achievement.

Federalism in its decline contrasted sharply with this bright record. The most ardent admirer will find it difficult to defend the rancorous partisanship, negative obstructionism, and even secessionist plotting that characterized Federalist policy as party fortunes waned after 1798. One can hardly condone, though one can understand, the men who sponsored the notorious Alien and Sedition Laws and opposed President Adams's successful effort to restore peaceful relations with France. The main body of Federalists, after their defeat in the election of 1800, fought the new Republican leaders and their measures at every level of government, national and local, in a bitter, vicious struggle—rarely encountered before or since in our history. They opposed Republican reductions in the military and naval establishments and fiscal reorganization and tax repeal. They fought to prevent removal of colleagues from office, to block repeal of the lame-duck Judiciary Act of 1801, and to obstruct impeachment of judges charged with partisan conduct during the period of the Sedition Law. They uniformly opposed all measures of commercial restriction adopted in the Republican effort to protect American commerce and seamen. They even opposed the Louisiana purchase treaty. Indeed, so consistently and unitedly did they oppose Republican measures that President Jefferson could well complain that Federalists sought to "thwart whatever we may propose," and seemed "drilled to act in phalanx on every question." [1]

The controversy over Louisiana illuminates the obstructionist character of Federalist policy. In 1800 Spain agreed to the conditional cession of Louisiana to France, and in 1803 suspended the right of deposit at New Orleans, a privilege deemed vital to the prosperity of American Mississippi commerce. When reports of these events reached the United States, Federalists and party newspapers clamored for an immediate military expedition to seize New Orleans. Federalist congressmen sponsored resolutions calling on the President to take immediate possession of border territory. To counter these maneuvers, Jefferson sent James Monroe to France to assist Robert Livingston in negotiating the purchase of New Orleans and Florida. When these envoys succeeded beyond wildest dreams, and negotiated a treaty embracing not only New Orleans but the vast expanse of Louisiana, Federalist leaders launched a bitter campaign of criticism against the measure. Practically any argument would do. Why should the United States purchase the area with money— a "mean and despicable" operation—when military conquest would have done the job far more cheaply? The new land would drain citizens from the eastern states and add to the Union a heterogeneous, ignorant, and capricious population. Fifteen million dollars was too much for territory mostly desert anyhow; the title was clouded by a Napoleonic promise to Spain not to cede to a third party; the Constitution granted Congress no authority to acquire territory. Such arguments sounded strange coming from these men, who just a few months previously had been so solicitous in behalf of western interests. Privately, Federalists foresaw great political gains for the administration. It "will encrease the patronage, & enrich the minions, of the Executive," wrote the still-Federalist William Plumer. The Republicans have the west "now fast bound by the ties of gratitude," complained Christopher Gore of Massachusetts.[2]

Following their unsuccessful opposition to the treaty, some Federalist leaders even engaged in secret secessionist plotting. To be sure, their numbers were few—among them, Timothy Pickering of Massachusetts, William Plumer of New Hampshire, Uriah Tracy, Roger Griswold, James Hillhouse, Benjamin Tallmadge, and Chauncey Goodrich of Connecticut. The plan was to separate from the Union and establish a northern confederacy composed of the New England states and New York. Even Canada and Nova Scotia might join. To obtain New York's adherence, these leaders approached Aaron Burr, a candidate for governor in that state in 1804. The Vice-President would give no commitment, and since Rufus King and Alexander Hamilton and the great mass of the Federalist rank and file opposed these plans, the scheme got nowhere.[3]

Federalist leaders presumed their Republican counterparts to be unprincipled demagogues—animated by class hatred, sectional rivalry, personal jealousy, and cynical ambition. With the possible exception of a few statesmanlike figures of the Rufus King type, the active Federalist leadership believed the opposition to be irresponsible and unscrupulous in method and base and corrupt in motive. It was logical, therefore, for these men to suspect Republican policies as defective, as politically motivated, without concern for the national interest. Republicans, to attain their selfish objects, single-mindedly sought power for themselves; they must have framed their policies solely to this end. The famous Boston Federalist, Josiah Quincy, Jr., put the point well in reference to the Federalist case against the Louisiana treaty: "Nothing, it seems to me, can be politically good whose root springs on the other side of the political Equator. . . . A pure stream cannot issue from a corrupt fountain." The only possible ground for supporting the purchase was if "upon examination it shall be found so wonderfully excellent (of which I have no belief) as to counterbalance all the evil of putting a shore much wanted under the rotting popularity of a corrupt party." Instinctively, Federalists presumed Republican measures to be detrimental to the public welfare. Some southern Federalists eventually supported the Louisiana treaty—its advantages were too obvious and compelling to be ignored. Significantly, their support came slowly and after much weighing of consequences, a measure of their reluctance to believe that anything good could come from Republicans. As Quincy said: some Federalists "have half a mind to support this treaty" and say "what shall we do if we think it upon the whole good?" The typical response to Republican measures was epitomized by Samuel Taggart who confessed in 1808 that the basis of his opposition was distrust of the opposing party. In Congress he was "almost a sullen spectator of what is going on," and since he did not "place much confidence in the administration" could "do little else than vote against almost every measure which is brought to view." [4]

Integrity, intelligence, and devotion to public interest—these were the personal attributes needed for able, responsible leadership at home and abroad. There was no room for these qualities in the Federalist view of their opponents. How could an administration devoted principally to perpetuating its own power deal competently with pressing national problems? One could pretty well predict Federalist reaction when Republicans undertook to protect American commerce during the wars of Napoleon.

When British seizure of American merchantmen began after the *Essex* decision in 1805 the Federalists castigated their Republican opponents for failure to protect American shipping. It was an easy matter to put the blame on Republican demagoguery, incompetence, and weakness. Presumably to court popularity at home, the administration had slashed military, naval, and defense establishments, and had repealed all taxes, but had never given a thought to the invitation thus held out to foreign nations to plunder our commerce. Not even the most anglophile Federalist would deny that British seizures could not be permitted to continue. But to bring seizures to an end, a special mission composed of men of ability and character—who else but Federalists?—should be named to negotiate with Great Britain. Certainly the current American negotiator, James Monroe, a despicable pro-French Virginia politician, was neither qualified nor competent to carry out such a task.[5]

The Federalists characteristically opposed nonimportation, the embargo, and subsequent restrictive measures. The fact that these were measures of despised and suspected party adversaries does more to explain the instantaneous and united opposition of Federalism than do all the theories hypothesizing Federalists as the champions of commerce or of Britain's fight against Napoleon. Thus Federalists looked upon the Republican nonimportation proposals of 1806 as chiefly designed to court popularity in a country angry at British aggressions. The disadvantages in such legislation were easy to find—once one set out to look for them. Federalists soon built up the case that commercial restrictions were irritating and provocative, obstacles rather than inducements to settlement. They argued that restrictions hurt American commercial interests far more than British interests.[6] Their reaction to the embargo was even more extreme. They considered the measure deliberately framed to destroy commerce in order ultimately to desolate the northeast and perpetuate southern dominance of the nation.[7] They even believed that Napoleon himself was behind the new policy. Either the French dictator had bullied or cajoled the American President into support of his anti-British Continental System. Everyone knew, of course, that Jefferson manipulated American anglophobia to suit his own political ambition. Until now few suspected him of such weakness as to permit a foreign potentate to dictate American foreign policy.[8] No wonder men were gloomy at the prospect of continued Republican rule, and could write as did one Federalist: "The sky is lowering. What it will produce no one can tell. That the Administration is bent on checking the spirit of Commerce, and gradually undermining it I have no doubt. That it is favorably disposed towards the French Government I more than Suspect." [9] Federalists ignored all arguments in behalf of the preventive and coercive functions of the embargo, but seized on its presumed foreign origin, its destructive effect on commerce, its corrupting influence on public morality, and its probable impeding effect on negotiation. [10]

The Republicans argued that Great Britain was to blame for the continued controversy over neutral rights. Federalists took the contrary position that nothing stood in the way of friendly relations with Great Britain except Republican hostility, aggressiveness, and refusal to settle outstanding issues. Was not Jefferson's demand for an end to impressment made in the knowledge that Britain, who needed sailors to man her wooden walls against Napoleon, could not agree? Were not our periodic warnings and preparations for war deliberately made to gall her? Were not restrictive measures irritating to her statesmen? A Federalist congressman from Connecticut, James Hillhouse, spoke for many when he said that he believed it possible to resolve issues between the two nations "provided our Government are sincere in their wishes to preserve peace, and a good understanding with that nation. [Of] that I have my doubts, judging from the irritating measures adopted, and the unfriendly disposition manifested on every occasion which offers." Federalists came to believe settlement attainable only through repeal of all commercial restrictions, a strengthening of military and naval forces, and friendly, firm, able negotiation. A prominent Federalist senator from Connecticut, Chauncey Goodrich, affirmed in 1810: "Our course is to use our endeavours to free our commerce from the fangs of the Law, to fortify our most prominant harbours, to equip and man our navy—to provide means of defence—and there to pause." He was confident, as he made clear on another occasion, that we could then adjust all points at issue—"I mean," he qualified, "if the negociation was ably conducted [!]" This, of course, was a plan that administration Republicans regarded as submission.[11]

As the controversy continued, Federalists began to feel confident that Jefferson and his party were playing an evil and sinister game with the international situation. These Republicans had no intention of coming to terms with Great Britain at all. They intended to keep relations with her in a state of exacerbation. Confidence became obsession as more evidences accumulated. Repeated warnings of war seemed calculated to anger British public opinion and prevent concessions to the United States. The nonintercourse law, opening commerce with all nations except the two European belligerents, bolstered Republican popularity by easing the hardships of the embargo, but at the same time it kept up the quarrel. Madison's interpretation of the ambiguous Cadore letter, which led to resumption of the nonimportation act, was an open revelation of his desire to avoid an accommodation.[12]

Then did the Republican leaders want war? Federalists did not think so. War, with all its hardships and sacrifices, was bound to prove unpopular, and would end in disgrace under such incompetent leadership. On the other hand, a state of continued controversy enabled the Republicans to pose as defenders of American rights and honor against British aggression. This would win them popularity among the unthinking anti-British masses. At the same time, they could placate Napoleon by supporting his Continental System with commercial restrictions. Chauncey Goodrich stated the view of many colleagues when he wrote:

Our administration will not treat with England;—that would offend Bonaparte & their friends; they will not fight, because that will shake them from their seats. The present irritable state of things answers the purposes of party at home, & keeps up the public passions to such a point as follows after the Administration in their restrictions on British commerce.

Another New England Federalist, Timothy Pickering, reemphasized this opinion:

Mr Jefferson & Mr Madison, amidst numberless fair professions, have never seriously intended an adjustment of our differences with G. B. While they have ascribed the failure of all their negotiations to her injustice and inadmissible claims Villifying, at the same time, the whole body of the federalists, as the friends of G. B., as under her influence, and willing to sacrifice our just rights to her unwarrantable pretensions.

Thus viewing their French connection to be essential to their existence as the dominant party; & fearing also the power of Bonaparte, at whose feet ere this time Mr. Jefferson confidently pronounced that proud Britain was to have fallen—the administration have not dared to come to any settlement with her on any one point: for the adjustment of that single point would remove one cause of popular irritation, and loosen one cord by which they hold the people. By such management they hope to preserve their power, avoiding a war with G. B. so long as Bonaparte will be contented with a *neutrality* so *hostile* towards that nation.

Even Madison's brief agreement with the British minister, David Erskine, made in April, 1809, and repudiated by Foreign Secretary Canning two months later, could fit this view. The Federalists would not consider the agreement to be evidence of administration willingness to terminate disputes, but deemed it a consequence of their own efforts to force the administration to settle. As the Federalist Rufus King wrote: "One side rejoice because they think that the Embargo &cᵃ. has brought England to terms, and the other side rejoice because they believe that the opposition to the late Measures of Congress has obliged the administration to abandon their system, and to accept a Reconciliation with England." [13]

The 12th Congress that voted war included 43 Federalist members. Of the 40 Federalist congressmen and senators actually voting, all cast votes against war. Nor do the figures sustain a sectional interpretation of this vote. True, 31 Federalists against war came from northern constituencies. But it is seldom noted that 9 Federalists who voted against war came from south of the Mason-Dixon line. Twenty-three percent of the Federalist vote against war came from southern members of the party. Outside Congress Federalists condemned the measure. Federalist newspapers denounced it. Federalist-controlled town meetings and state legislatures passed condemnatory resolutions. Federalist merchants and shopkeepers closed places of business when they heard the news, Federalist deacons tolled church bells, and Federalist ship captains lowered their colors to half-mast. Everywhere, north and south, Federalism stood against the war. Was this typical Federalist negativism to all things Republican? The private letters of congressional Federalists reveal that it was so.

Republican senators and congressmen voted for war because they believed there was no other acceptable alternative. President Madison had taken the position that everything possible short of war had been tried and failed. Britain would persist in her Orders in Council until forced to retract by measures of force. Republicans believed the President and voted for war when the time came to do so.

No Federalist would accept these views. The very idea that the administration had tried everything in its power was absurd. How could anyone accept this argument when everyone knew that the Republican leaders had done their utmost to avoid settlement with Great Britain? Unneutral and unfriendly commercial restrictions, rejection of the Monroe-Pinkney treaty, threats and menaces of war, unfair and extreme demands—all these heightened the controversy, as Republicans intended they should do. Most Federalists agreed with Republicans in condemning the Orders in Council as unacceptable infringements on American commerce and sovereignty.[14] This certainly did not mean that the time had finally come to go to war. There had yet to take place a sincere and unprejudiced effort to obtain repeal of the Orders. "Certain it is," wrote Samuel Taggart of Massachusetts, "that no fair attempt has been made on the principles of candid negotiation to obtain a redress of our wrongs; especially since our disputes began to assume a serious aspect in the years 1805, 6." The Republicans have sought consistently to frighten Great Britain into concessions, to extort them from her fears. The nonimportation act of 1806, the embargo, the nonintercourse law, the late nonimportation policy, and the present threat of war "are all of this complexion and all have been equally abortive and probably have been so intended by the American government." [15] Therefore, repeal all commercial restrictions and appeal to that power in a firm and friendly manner to do us justice.

Neither would Federalists believe that Republicans seriously meant war. No one with any knowledge of Republicans and their past behavior could doubt that war was anything but bluff. All the war talk and military preparations were a cheap political trick to court popularity and discredit the Federalist party. A war declared by these cynical demagogues would prove politically disastrous, as they well knew, for with no good cause for war, the people would soon tire of sacrifice and topple those responsible from power. But by threatening war the Republicans, in the forthcoming spring and fall elections, could exploit expected Federalist opposition. When the American public saw Federalists oppose Republican military measures they would identify the Federalists with "Toryism" and vote for the party that stood up manfully to a life-long enemy. Meanwhile the Republicans would have backed out of the war and returned to commercial restrictions, anticipating Federalist relief from escape from war and acquiescence in continuation of peace.

Wild views certainly, but Federalists believed them. Private letters are plentiful in confirming this point. The leading Federalist in the House of Representatives was Josiah Quincy, Jr., the Massachusetts congressman. In reference to the war program, the future mayor of Boston and future president of Harvard College wrote that the intention of the Madison administration was "to identify federalists with British antipathies, predominating in the country, and to render even federalists content with those embarrassments of commerce." The Federalist leader in the Senate, James A. Bayard of Delaware, a man Madison appointed to the peace commission in 1813 as a loyal minority member, declared that Republican "swaggering and blustering about England has served their purpose long enough" and that Federalists, through support of military preparations, intended "to go far enough to convince the country that we have no British partialities." [16]

On this basis Federalists could confidently assure colleagues and constituents that the war was a fraud. The North Carolina Federalist congressman, Joseph Pearson, told a constituent that the administration knew "too well" the costs and liabilities of war "to have systamatically resolved on that event." The junior senator from Delaware, Outerbridge Horsey, stated the matter even more bluntly when he wrote in January that as to war "I have no idea it is meant by the administration," and again, that war "is all in my eye, orders off or on." With equal assurance did Elijah Brigham of Massachusetts affirm that "the spirit of war, so much vociferated—is spurious." [17]

To evade the Republican trap some Federalists resorted to devious countertactics. They would support the Republican war program on the announced basis of a need for peacetime military and naval preparedness. In this way they would not be vulnerable to charges of British partisanship. Nor would there be a chance for their opponents to slip out of war pleading Federalist obstructionism. In the face of united support for their program the Republicans could not hold Federalism responsible for inadequate measures of military preparation and national disunity. Advancing to the brink of war, they would have no plausible excuse for avoiding war and consequently would face the dilemma of disgraceful retreat or advance to disaster.[18] The presumed fraudulence of the war program also led Federalists, as we have seen, into treasonable communication with the British government. Two unidentified Federalists in February, 1812, called on the British minister, Augustus Foster, to urge firm adherence to the Orders in Council and no concessions that would enable the Madison administration to save itself from a disgraceful retreat or a demonstration of wartime incompetence. Alexander Hanson of the Baltimore *Federal Republican* similarly appealed to Francis James Jackson and argued that the "only way to dislodge the prevailing party from the post of power" was to stand firm and force the Republicans to war or disgrace.[19]

As the session wore on, it became gradually apparent to Federalists that the Republicans intended to go forward. Presumably Republicans had chosen this course rather than risk political disgrace. To escape the contempt of voters these demagogues would now plunge the nation into an unnecessary and avoidable conflict. So Senator Bayard had in mind when he wrote at the moment of decision in June: "You have thought the thing all along a jest, & I have no doubt in the commencement it was so, but jests sometimes become serious and end in earnest." Frustrated rage and childish revenge seemed to reinforce political motivation. A congressman from Connecticut, John Davenport, revealed this point of view when he wrote that the war advocates "seem enraged at the defeat of the loan, and the fate of the Eastern elections. [B]y these events they are stimulated to pursue their mad course— Their honor is to be supported & they cannot retreat without disgrace." Indeed, continued the Connecticut congressman indignantly:

Ignorant of the true policy to be adopted by this country, and destitute of every right principle, they are influenced by selfish considerations & the gratification of willful & obstinate passion not to be subdued, even with extreme suffering—Milton's speech in Satans' mouth applies to their feelings
  Better to reign in Hell
  Than serve in Heaven.[20]

More familiar to students of this period was the Federalist hypothesis that pitted Republican "war hawks" against "peace men" in an intraparty struggle over future policy. A conflict of this kind seemed plausible enough. Belligerent speeches from freshman Republican congressmen contrasted sharply with vague warnings from the President and members seeking to leave Great Britain a path of escape. The presumed struggle was at its peak when Quincy informed Oliver Wolcott, Jr., in April that the Executive had utterly failed to prepare the country for war but congressmen were insisting that " 'war must & will be declared' —now—before the end of ninety days." The scene seemed "absolutely incomprehensible" except on the "hypothesis that administration have no policy, except Embargo—that there is in the house of Representatives a strong party for war—that they counteract each other, and that the result is wholly problematical."

Taking note of the western origin of belligerent-sounding congressmen, Samuel Taggart found war party motivation explainable in terms of sectional politics. War men from the west knew that war "would bring distress and ruin incalculable upon the maritime frontier," thus forcing eastern inhabitants to seek safety in the interior and enriching and populating western states. Catching at Republican discussion regarding the conquest and possible annexation of Canada, other Federalists attributed "war hawk" policy to imperialist ambitions. "These backwoodsmen mean that a predatory invasion of Canada shall avenge our commercial rights," avowed Quincy. Elijah Brigham charged that we are engaged in "a war of invasion to get possession of the Canadas on the north . . . a war of Ambition a war of conquest—having no other specific object but the conquest of the Canadas," a war of "rapine & plunder." Building on statements and legislation connecting Canada with Florida for invasion purposes, Federalists even presumed a bargain between northern and southern expansionists to annex both territories. The Federalist senator from Rhode Island, William Hunter, in 1813 publicly made such a charge:

Last year the propositions to seize East Florida and to conquer Canada were associated. The inducements then held out were, an enlargement and arrondissement of the territory at the two extremeties; a fair division of the spoil. We consent that you may conquer Canada, permit us to conquer Florida. The declaration that Canada should be conquered and retained was the exacted pledge of the Northern men who voted for war.[21]

What of the Republicans who did not want war, notably President Madison and his immediate supporters? The answer was plain: the "war hawks" had blackmailed them into support of their plan. In memoirs written long after the war was over, Josiah Quincy recalled the incident as well as if it had happened the day before. President Madison "was heart and soul a convert to Jefferson's policy, and held to the commercial restrictive system with the grasp of death." A war, he thought, would put an end to chances of reelection. Nor did he "quit this grasp till waited upon by a committee of which Henry Clay was the Chairman, and was plainly told that his being supported as the party candidate for the next Presidency depended upon his screwing his courage to a declaration of war." Reluctantly, the Virginian had acceded, made a formal war recommendation to Congress, and won a second term. "On this combination of violence with individual interest and ambition was laid the foundation of the war of 1812 with Great Britain." [22]

But no Federalist statement could match the fantastic *mélange* composed just ten days after the Republicans had launched their war by the distinguished member from Vermont, Martin Chittenden. Chittenden's composition had practically everything Federalist imaginations had thus far been able to concoct. There were the pro-French prejudices that originally had brought about commercial restrictions. There were the fears of political disaster after commitment had made retreat a matter of public disgrace. The Vermont congressman included section-based motives of territorial expansionism. There was even the "war hawk" blackmail of President Madison capping this remarkable synthesis of the "many causes" contributing to war.

In addition to the strong French [partia]lities & the desire to save the sincking party, the Southern people are determined on the acquisition of the Floridas &c & the Western people covet the Indian possessions. Some few of the Northern & Eastern Men are flattered with the prospect of making their fortunes in Canada & poor Madison was threatened with abandonment in the Presidential election; unless he would aid their views— Nothing [sh]ort of a positive recommendation of the President would have secured a Majority in either branch of the Legis[lature] in favor of a Measure calculated to pro[duce] disstress & ruin— Thus by action & reaction they have many of them been forced I believe reluctantly to take this fatal step. We are now in a state of war unable to give satisfactory reasons, why or wherefore & destitute of the means to produce either a speedy or a favorable issue.[23]

Republican assertions to the contrary, Federalists condemned this war as utterly unjustified. No Federalist ever accepted the Republican argument that no other course remained. How could anyone do so when the most promising solution of all had not yet been tried? And when, as everybody knew, the Republican administration had deliberately avoided settlement since Great Britain first began her depredations? Spurning Republican contrary assertions, the Federalists conjured up various alternative hypotheses, all presuming corrupt and unconscionable motives. Not that these Federalist myths lacked semblances of truth. Republicans, as we have seen, did feel as the session wore on that party honor demanded war. Republicans did discuss Canada and Florida as the twin targets of offensive operations, they did talk about annexing Canada, and they did couple measures to establish temporary government and assure protection to inhabitants in both these areas. Clay did visit the President—but not to threaten him.

Some Federalists were not altogether content with these explanations, but looked for other motives. In September, 1812, Benjamin Stoddert of Maryland, formerly secretary of the navy in John Adams's cabinet, sought the views of a prominent North Carolina Federalist on the matter. "Do you not see clearly, that not one of the pretences for War, was the real cause[?]" he asked. "Where is the real cause to be found? I wish I could answer with proofs, that question." Just one day later Stoddert wrote to another Federalist, in whose discretion he felt more confidence, that Napoleonic pressure was the cause of war. Federalists who believed that Republican "war hawks" had dragooned the President were wrong, he declared. All evidence that Madison and his advisers had opposed the war had actually been "contrived with a view to make it," and "Congress were made to act the part they did, during the last session, by his & Gallatin's, and Jefferson's contrivances." This remarkable feat of legislative prestidigitation had been performed on orders from the French Emperor. Either Napoleon had bribed these men to carry out his plans, or had blackmailed them. "The war, I have no doubt, is in subserviency to the views of France. Whether these men are actually sold to France—or whether Bonaparte has secrets of theirs which must not be disclosed, if the ruin of this Country will prevent it, I cannot determine— But this War, is entirely for French objects." [24]

Did Federalists fear the consequences from such a war as this? Almost unanimously historians attribute Federalist opposition to concern for the safety of commerce and shipping. On the contrary, many Federalists predicted ultimate benefits to themselves and the country from this war. Its corrupt basis, the heavy American losses in goods and produce at home and abroad, the unprepared state of the nation, and the Republican incompetence in managing the war—all these circumstances would surely bring eventual political disaster to their opponents. There might be lives lost, shipping destroyed, and commerce disrupted; the British navy might bombard a seaport or two. But these were of less consequence than the benefit war would bring. At long last America would awaken to the real nature of present leadership and return the Federalists to power.

Thus Josiah Quincy, Jr., urged colleagues to "look definitely, to the fact of a possibly resulting war and analise its fair consequences and see, whether in truth, much of the evils are not those of imagination; and whether the fact of such a war would not crush the political influence of those, who should induce it." Abijah Bigelow of Massachusetts, foreseeing that war might be "the means of putting down an administration unfit, both in talents and integrity," remarked when war was declared that if the people failed to entrust national leadership "to more able hands our case is rather desperate, but I trust a proper remedy will be applied, before it is too late." A notable letter from Governor Roger Griswold of Connecticut carried the firm assurance of the benefit war would bring. "But if the event really happens, I make no doubt that it will produce a better state of things than the present." Outerbridge Horsey showed little fear of the impending decision: "Never did I till now so much rejoice that the people are sovereign, They must speak—and no doubt will speak with the celerity of lightening & the voice of thunder." Even James Bayard doubted that Britain would seek to make the war "active and destructive" against the country, and "probably a change of sentiment among the People may render it a war of no great duration." Indeed, Benjamin Tallmadge of Connecticut reported that "many" Federalists thought war would drive the Republicans from power. A Federalist sympathizer visiting Washington in June reported that the "federalists think this measure likely to produce an ultimate benefit to the country; as it will, in all probability, be the means of pulling down the present unprincipled administration." Small wonder that Federalists could report "high spirits" and "a good degree of composure" among colleagues on the eve of war.[25]

Did any Federalists hold a contrary view, that there were more adversities than benefits in war? Some, a minority, did look upon war with genuine fear of the consequences. Tallmadge of Connecticut did not anticipate the revolution in public sentiment so strongly counted on by colleagues. Such a complete reversal seemed unlikely—he was "not so sanguine as many, who fully believe that such an Event would change the whole political face of our Country." His mood when war began was one of unrelieved gloom and foreboding. With Republican defeat at the polls unlikely, there was reason to fear much from the continued leadership of such unprincipled and irresponsible men—most of all, an independence-ending alliance with the European tyrant, Bonaparte: "Heaven only knows what our Destiny is to be; but my fears forebode every Evil— As the Cap to the Climax, I dread that above all, which Shall link us to the fortunes, & chain us to the Carr of the French Emperor." Joseph Pearson of North Carolina feared ultimate disaster. Announcing the commencement of hostilities to a party colleague, he forecast an eventual French alliance. "France is our loving friend & will no doubt soon be our ally— In what those dreadful measures will end—God only knows—If the people do not interpose their constitutional power—I fear all is lost." And Leonard White of Massachusetts, three days after passage of the war bill, voiced dread of "the current which is hurrying us to destruction. The situation in which the Country is now placed causes the mind to shudder at the thought of." Great Britain has the power to bring destruction to our defenseless coastal cities and towns and capture our vessels in her ports and on the ocean. She can seize American property of great value in her warehouses. Lacking credit to borrow or funds to carry on war without resort to taxes, driven to the ruinous expedient of paper money, having neither a navy to protect our coasts nor an army to defend our northern and western frontiers—"in this deplorable situation we are plunged into a war with a nation who has in her power to do us every injury, & all to gratify the malice & revenge of a few men who see & know the people are not with them." But "what is more than all to be dreaded & feared is an alliance with the Emperor of France which must naturally & most assuredly will be the consequence of this measure, unless the people rise in the majesty of their strength & at the approaching elections put it out of the power of those now in office to consummate the total wretchedness & misery of the Country." [26]

Thus, when Federalists voted against the Republican war they did so out of a curious mixture of motives. On the one hand, while some gloomily prophesied disastrous consequences, others anticipated great political advantages from this war. They believed the temporary evils of war a price well worth paying when it meant defeat of political adversaries and restoral of the country to responsible, able, and high-minded Federalist leadership. But to reap the benefits war would bring, Federalists must of course go on record as opposed to the conflict. On the other hand, all believed war to be avoidable, unnecessary, and founded in unconscionable motives. The integrity of this moral disapproval is revealed in private correspondence. Pearson of North Carolina denounced the war to a party colleague as "Democratic folly & wikedness." Quincy castigated war as "unnecessary and wicked," and vowed that administration men "cannot justify the principle of such [a] war." William Reed of Massachusetts called war "an Act, I could not vote for, believing it inexpedient & wicked." Brigham referred to it as "this wicked and foolish war." Chittenden termed it a decision for which Republicans were "unable to give satisfactory reasons, why or wherefore." [27] Though divided among themselves as to the relative benefits and evils in war, Federalists were united in a common spirit of genuine moral disapproval.

(9)

A LONG STRIDE
TOWARDS PERMANENCY

Deeply and bitterly divided we went to war in 1812. Public demonstrations across the nation showed the split in opinion. Illuminations, parades, and cannon-firing welcomed the decision; tolling church bells, flags at half-mast, and empty shops and counting houses bore witness to condemnation. Federalists in the city of Providence, Rhode Island, set church bells slowly ringing, and Republicans countered with cannon and recruiting drums. Sailors in Boston harbor fought off a Federalist boarding party after their Republican captain refused demands to lower his flag to half-mast. Republican "huzzas and acclamations" at a Philadelphia coffee house greeted a public reading of the war resolution; Federalist "hissers" were told to take their business elsewhere, "that they must not *now* consider this as a *British* Coffee-house; henceforth it must be and shall be, an *American* Coffee house." Editorial opinion was also divided along party lines. Federalist journals denounced the "dreadful tidings," and reported: "Dissatisfaction, disgust, and apprehensions of the most alarming nature have seized on every mind." This "overwhelming calamity—so much dreaded by many—so little expected by the community at large" had at last taken place. Republican editors were exultant. "*War,* long expected, long demanded by an indignant nation, comes now, gloriously, in place of *base, infamous, abject* submission." No "true American" could read the President's summons to war "without feeling an honest and implicit confidence in the truth and justice of the great cause in which his country is engaged." Were these fellow citizens of a common country? [1]

Experienced observers would not have been surprised at such responses. Ever since the early 1790s when Republicans first organized against the Hamiltonian program the two parties had clashed on practically every measure brought forward. The constant conflict evoked gloomy predictions from contemporaries. "The pregudices and self will of parties and party men to support principles and measures right or wrong if it is brought forward by their political freinds has appeared to me for some time verry dangerous," warned the New York Republican, Thomas Sammons. Federalists and Republicans "have each in turn supported and opposed the same acts and measures with but few exceptions—no reformation appears to take place, every one is just, all parties are right at Least in their own opinion." Would this not lead to ultimate disaster? The "internal heat of parties may raise to burn—as by a continual rubing of two peaces of timber the heat encrescis till fire proceeds and often consumes the timber." So profound was the division between parties that members could not even live in common boarding houses when Congress was in session. Landlords rented exclusively to Republicans or Federalists—a welcome practice to tired legislators seeking nightly relief from day-long squabbles. The letter of a New York Federalist sympathizer, Clement C. Moore, visiting the nation's capital for the first time, spoke volumes:

I have hitherto associated almost entirely with federalists. To day I am to dine among some democrats. The opposite parties live separate from each other; and have but little intercourse, except on business. I once asked Mr Potter [a Rhode Island Federalist] if it would not be better for the members of different parties to live more together, and become more sociable with each other. He said they could not live in peace together; and that, after the contentions which they continually had in the hall, they required some rest and quiet when they got home. He said also, that some of the democrats are men of such unruly minds that it is extremely difficult to be upon good terms with them; "There is that Willis Alston," said he, "why he is as clear a brute as ever wore a tail." [2]

Party suspicion and animosity cut deep into local affairs. Federalists and Republicans in Newburyport, Massachusetts, libeled each other in party newspapers, organized separate marine insurance companies, and avoided all possible social contact; their ladies even refused to call on the wives of rival partisans. Federalist and Republican householders in nearby Salem had homes in different neighborhoods, and their rival news sheets and banking corporations reflected deep-grained suspicions that barred men from common enterprises. Feeling in this town ran so high that in 1799 the Republican Crowninshields boycotted the funeral of a relative who had married the famous Federalist merchant, Elias Hasket Derby. In 1802 Federalists officially excluded leading Republican families from the dancing assembly, that "crowning glory of the social season." Time had not played tricks on the memory of New Hampshire's William Plumer when he recalled in 1818 how in the former era the "spirit of party ran high, divided families, neighborhoods, towns & states; &, blind to public interest, embittered the sweets of social life, & hazarded the rights of the nation." [3]

This party conflict is a very different phenomenon from today's political contests between Democrats and Republicans. No one doubts the firm loyalty of contemporary politicians to basic political institutions and processes. No responsible twentieth-century Republican or Democrat believes that rival leaders would plunge the nation into a major war, or sell out to a foreign power, for personal or partisan benefit. But this is just what the best men in the Federalist-Jeffersonian era believed of their opponents. Such beliefs produced bitter feeling between parties, constant quarrelling over legislation, self-imposed social segregation, and a nearly unbroken record of party-line division on major national and state issues.

Was there any truth in these conceptions, or were they wholly mistaken? Some Federalists remained skeptical of republicanism. Alexander Hamilton, as we have seen, harbored life-long doubts on this score: "It is yet to be determined by experience whether [republicanism] be consistent with that stability and order in government which are essential to public strength and private

security and happiness." George Cabot of Massachusetts deemed
it impossible to have good government in America because any
"government *altogether popular* in form tends irresistibly to
place in power the levellers of public authority, order, and law." [4]
But this does not necessarily prove that these men plotted to
subvert the state. It has never been established that Hamilton
conspired at any time to destroy the government. As late as 1802
he could write to Gouverneur Morris of his continuing efforts
"to prop the frail and worthless fabric." Charles Carroll of
Carrollton, a Maryland Federalist leader, in 1800 denied that
anyone in his party plotted monarchy and declared that these
Republican "declaimers in favor of freedom & equality act in
such a questionable shape I cannot help suspecting their sincerety." [5]

True, after 1800 a few Federalists conspired to bring about
secession and establishment of a northern confederacy. But they
had a scant following. As Stephen Higginson who desired disunion wrote dejectedly from Boston in 1804: "It is impossible to
alarm, much less to convince, a large portion of the Federal
party here of their danger." But a Federalist leader avowed that
"the project was not, and could not be, abandoned." The embargo probably added to the ranks of Federalist secessionists.
By 1809 Harrison Gray Otis believed that secession was a possibility, but only after southern states had turned down Federalist demands for constitutional revision. Not until 1814 did
Federalist leaders convene at Hartford to air grievances and
formally draft a program for reform. It is difficult to determine
just what kind of government Federalist secessionists would
have established had they been able to have their way—suffrage
limited to substantial property holders, possibly a senate and
executive for life. No one ever actually sought to establish hereditary forms, much less the Hanoverian restoration that Governor
Elbridge Gerry of Massachusetts feared. [6]

When Republicans charged that Federalist leaders plotted
with Great Britain they came closer to the truth. The John
Henry documents, accepted by all Republicans as authentic

proof of Federalist guilt, did not establish the fact of an Anglo-American conspiracy to destroy the Republic. But Foster's dispatches and the Hanson missive to Francis James Jackson revealed a plan to gain Britain's aid in bringing down the Madison administration. Federalists by their own statements denied England the right to her Orders in Council; some now encouraged her to maintain her edicts and drive the Republicans from power.

What of the Republican leaders whom the Federalists believed to be irresponsible, ambitious demagogues? No important leader, except for Aaron Burr, comes close to this stereotype. If either Jefferson or Madison were cynical self-servers, then an entire generation of historians and biographers have totally misread the record. The Clintons, Samuel Smith, William Branch Giles, and Michael Leib have traditionally worn the label, but much evidence points to their integrity of motive. William Plumer, a candidate for governor of New Hampshire in 1812, probably spoke for most Republican leaders when he claimed a higher commitment than mere personal ambition: "The result of the election, to me, appears doubtful & uncertain—& if I could separate myself from the *cause* I should feel little anxiety on the subject." The New Hampshire politician had ambition, but it was to serve an interest larger than himself. Wilson Cary Nicholas in 1808 put the matter in a nutshell: "Our sole object is the public good, the greater the pressure the more merit in saving the republic, let us my friend do our duty & I have no doubt all will be right. At all events we shall have the satisfaction of knowing that any disaster that may befall our Country cannot be ascribed to us or our measures." [7]

Republican and Federalist views of party opposites are largely false. Both parties grossly distorted rival intentions and motives into wild parodies of the truth. Why? How does one explain this blindness and misunderstanding? Why, when the majority of men in each party sought to preserve the Republic against foreign and domestic foes, should there have persisted such deep-seated suspicion and distrust? Part of the answer lies in irrational motives of fear. Federalists harbored deep fears of mass dis-

orders led by unscrupulous demagogues. Republicans feared
the propensity of men in office to grasp greater and more permanent power for themselves. When these men saw others acting
in ways identifiable with these fears, they concluded the worst.
Anxiety also freezes perception into a more permanent form.
Adversaries readily accepted whatever men did as evidence of
evil. Republicans and Federalists found themselves caught in
an endless round of suspicion and conflict from which they could
not break free, not even long after the controversy had passed
into memory. As late as 1840 survivors of these party struggles
remained convinced of the correctness of their suspicions. "We
still know aged men," wrote an historian in that year, "who
firmly believe that all the federal party were identical with the
Tories of the revolution, and others who associate their democratic opponents with the Jacobins of France." Occasionally
party men caught glimpses of loyalty and integrity in opponents. Senator Thomas Worthington of Ohio, after conversing
with a Federalist in November, 1811, found it so striking an
experience that he noted in his diary that he had become "more
convinced that the party spirit which [exists has] no foundation
in propriety & that all upright men mean the same." But eight
months later, after a bitter and divided session, he had slipped
back into partisanship. He "candidly" warned President Madison that "the administration will be exposed to the attacks of its
enemies" from a premature war declaration; and that "although
I may differ with my friends on this question or with him I will
be the very last to agree to a disgraceful peace & will rise or sink
with my political associates." Such revelations as came to Worthington were brief and rare.[8]

More fundamental was a personal inexperience with political parties that encouraged men to identify opponents with their
fears. There was no personal knowledge of parties such as we
know them today—organizations that seek to gain political
power but also remain firmly committed to the national welfare
and institutions. Eighteenth-century political thought extolled
the blessings of the harmonious commonwealth and condemned

sustained, organized party activity. A generation reared in this tradition instinctively presumed prolonged opposition to rest on selfish, even traitorous, motives. Furthermore, as the history of former republics revealed, parties in their pursuit of power had characteristically ignored the common good. Their paralyzing squabbles and treasonable intrigues had led to the downfall of these republics. It was against the evil of party activity that Washington, in the famous Farewell Address, had warned his countrymen against "the spirit of party." In governments "of the popular character, in Governments purely elective, it is a spirit not to be encouraged." Distrust of parties explained Jefferson's remark that it would be the "bitterest" day of his life when he became convinced of the permanence of political parties. If Republicans and Federalists had lived through and witnessed an epoch in which parties had proven themselves equally devoted to the national welfare and institutions, they would have been far less susceptible to such wild distortions. But their experience, derived as it was from history and the factional contests of the colonial period, gave them no reason to believe in the high-mindedness of opponents; if anything, it gave them positive reason to believe the contrary.[9]

Republicans in 1812 feared that submission would gravely weaken public confidence in republicanism. Repeated negotiation and commercial restrictions caused, as Calhoun put it, "distrust at home and contempt abroad." Was it true that Americans had actually begun to mistrust their republican government? Faith clearly waned during the period of the Articles of Confederation. At that time, even men like Washington, Adams, and Marshall expressed a doubt as to whether republican government would do. Hamilton remained consistently skeptical, and, by the end of the 1790s when Federalists found themselves challenged by the Republican mob, others joined him. In the Jeffersonian period Republicans began to have doubts. William Jarvis, a Boston leader, admitted in 1808 that if the American people did not support the administration and obey the embargo, then "we must with reluctance admit a doubt of the stability of republican institutions." John McKim, Jr., the Baltimore leader, wrote Henry Clay in 1812 that if the government now gave way to the Orders in Council "we may as well give up our Republican Government & have a Despot to rule over us." Joseph Nicholson, the Maryland Republican leader, dismayed at the feeble public response to the war loan, wrote despairingly to his brother-in-law Albert Gallatin in the spring of 1812: "The Apathy of the Nation is not yet thrown off and never will be. The small Subscription to the Loan is an Evidence, and a most mortifying one, that we have no public Virtue left. The first man of Talents and ambition who can press himself into the presidential Chair, will enslave us."

True, one can also find brave avowals of confidence in the future destiny of republicanism. Nathaniel Macon of North Carolina, warning his congressional colleagues in January, 1812, that failure to fight now would bring down the administration, presumed a steady American affection for their form of government.

Much has been said about the strength of this Government. Some think it is not strong enough; but if there be any strong Government in the world it must be this Government, and what gives it this strength is the attachment of the people to it; and it is as strong under an unpopular as a popular Administration, because the people know there is a time approaching when they can change the Administration, if they do not like it.

But it is doubtful that Macon's optimism was as great as this passage would suggest. He did, after all, allow in the very same speech for the fact that we might not be able to declare war and if we could not do so that it was time to put ourselves "under the protection of some other Power." He had, too, in 1809, deplored the retreat from the embargo and confessed that this demonstration of weakness made him "fear we are undone as a nation." Again, in 1812, when presumed Executive inefficiency and weakness seemed responsible for lagging military preparations, he did allow himself to be "sick to the heart." John C. Calhoun was optimistic on the subject of the strength of the government and in 1813 affirmed his resolve to advance the war effort, despite Federalist menaces and threats of disunion. "I speak personally. I by no means dispair of the destiny of our nation or government. National greatness and perfection are of slow growth, often checked often to appearance destroied. The intelligence, the virtue and the tone of publick sentiment are too great in this country to permit its freedom to be destroied by either domestick or foreign foes."

Calhoun's faith, however, had not always been so high. After all, he had worried in the spring of 1812 that the war might fail and that failure would cause "the greatest injury to the character of the government." Edward Fox, the Philadelphia Republican, took a very gloomy view of the future of republicanism. Continued factional strife would surely lead men to agree to "any change" that "will promise quiet and tranquillity." Still, he knew that others were less pessimistic. "I know it is a maxim with you," he wrote to Jonathan Roberts, the Pennsylvania congressman, "not to dispair of the Commonwealth." Confidence obviously varied among individuals and rose and fell with passing events.[10]

It is difficult to estimate the extent to which the public at large had come to doubt the efficacy of their government. There are occasional letters from citizens which suggest the beginning of a trend. An obscure Virginian told James Monroe that "the Predictions of the Tories, seems as Tho they were now coming to Pass, towit, that our republic could endure, for a short time only; for want of Internal stability, or virtue amongst our Rulers." An unknown New Yorker who gave thanks to God for placing him "on the Land of Liberty, where Kings nor Tyrants cannot controll me" warned of "unhappy events" should Federalists continue to obstruct government operations. The Philadelphia *Aurora*, an outspoken critic of Republican pusillanimity since 1809, in 1812 warned that "the national reputation has been sinking ever since, and the people are daily losing confidence in the justice and fidelity of their government." Had effective measures been taken three years ago "the nation would have obtained the respect of the world, and the government the confidence of the people." Clement C. Moore, visiting the capitol in 1812, disparaged the low prestige of the government: "The famous capitol is a dusky coloured building: the centre of it, as you know, is not built up yet; and the whole, at a little distance, has the appearance of a ruined castle. It appears to me an emblem of our political state, ruined before it is completely reared." A Virginian wrote Monroe in December, 1812, when the war was going badly: "Still I hope:—But I confess I fear That our Republic is on the Toter." It is not beyond possibility that failure to fight in 1812 would have swung public opinion towards constitutional reforms such as Hamilton had proposed at the Constitutional Convention—a president and senate for life, or at least for good behavior. A division of the union into separate republics possessing more social and economic uniformity is also conceivable. It is doubtful that given the deep commitment of the American people to representative institutions of self-government there would have been appreciable sentiment for hereditary monarchy or aristocracy. To say this, however, is not to deny the importance of widespread fears that the Republic was in danger.[11]

The Jefferson administration took office in 1801 determined to check a presumed swing towards monarchy and preserve the government from Federalist control. Facing the problem of commercial depredation and impressment brought on by the Napoleonic wars, Jefferson and his advisers determined they must protect commerce if reputation was to be preserved abroad and public confidence upheld at home. Commercial restriction and negotiation afforded the means by which he and his successor sought to attain these ends. By mid-1811 it became clear that these weapons were useless in the contest with Great Britain. The inducements of nonimportation, embargo, nonintercourse, the Macon law, and possible conflict with France had failed; the presumed repeal of the French Decrees as they affected American neutral rights had produced no comparable British action; Britain continued her seizures and not only refused to repeal her Orders as they affected American neutral commerce, but made

demands that revealed determination to make them codetermi-
nate with her struggle with France. The Madison administration
saw that no course remained but war or submission. Madison,
Monroe, and their party associates in Congress and in the country at large believed submission would gravely imperil the very
objects they had long sought. Aside from economic privation,
infringement of national sovereignty, and the loss of national
honor and morale, submission would work grave injury to the
party and to the prestige of republicanism. Republicans rejected
submission and reluctantly took the other alternative. Preparing
for war they endeavored to use the threat of military force in a
final effort to induce repeal. When this too failed the President
recommended war—a war that now would put an end to impressment as well.

Sentiment in Congress on the question of war divided closely
along party lines, Republican and Federalist. The great majority
of Republicans supported war because they, like the President,
saw no other option. They concurred with the reasoning which
led the President and secretary of state to this conclusion. They
were able to agree because they trusted the good faith and integrity of all past efforts to achieve settlement. They could agree
to Henry Clay's avowal that: "Not a man in the nation could
really doubt the sincerity with which those in power have sought,
by all honorable pacific means, to protect the interests of the
country." [12] Had these policies and negotiations been the work
of Federalists they would doubtless have opposed them. But they
were not; they were the work of fellow Republicans, men who
could be trusted.

Within the limits set by this consensus there developed sharp
disagreements among Republicans as to when and how hostilities should begin. Should not war delay until the country was
better prepared? Should it not begin in a limited way, confined
to the sea? The safety of the persons and property of constituents in northern and eastern localities made strong cases for an
affirmative to both these propositions. In the final days of peace,
men already at odds with administration leadership openly chal-

lenged the agreed-upon strategy in an unsuccessful bid for limited belligerency against one or both belligerents. Opposing these efforts were a hard core of southern and western members championing a strategy that would better satisfy the needs of the country and their own constituents as they conceived them to be.

Not all Republicans could support the declaration of war. A few from northern and eastern constituencies, after defeat of the limited war strategy, voted against war because they feared ruinous effects from a war inadequately prepared for on the lives and property of constituents and on the party. Clintonians joined them out of conviction that they and their leaders held an unused key to accommodation with Great Britain and fearing Federalist resurgence from a premature war. Economic interest and distorted views of the evil character of the war and fear of its results account for other scattered opposition.

The Federalists furnished the greatest number of votes against the war. A united and determined band, they could not agree to the reasoning which led to the position that war was just and unavoidably necessary. The Republicans had never tried seriously to negotiate with Great Britain; they had deliberately created and protracted the embroilment for their own nefarious purposes. Federalists at the outset had scoffed at Republican war pronouncements and military legislation as more political maneuvering. When the Republicans took the nation into war, the Federalists attributed this unexpected move to such apparent causes as French partialities, the disgrace of retreat, a corrupt presidential bargain, and base territorial ambitions. It was an unnecessary and immoral war, clearly avoidable and fully justifying righteous and determined opposition—an opposition which many expected would eventually return them to power.

President Madison in the years 1811–12 faced the difficult task of arousing the country and warning Great Britain that war would take place if she did not repeal her Orders. Striving to give his adversary an avenue of retreat and to prevent possible preemptive attack before the country was adequately prepared, he failed on both these counts. Owing to his ambiguous pronouncements, their discrepancy with those of congressional colleagues, and Federalist propaganda, much of the country and the British government remained throughout most of the session unaware of administration intentions. The complexity of the issue and the presence of men who doubted the willingness of the administration to make war made it vital for the President to make clear, bold policy statements in order to arouse the country and convey warning to the adversary. There was some sense to the effort to respect British pride. There was less logic in the effort to convey a determination to fight and yet give no motive at all for prior attack. Madison had few illusions that Britain would yield without actual war, and his main task should have been to prepare the country as quickly and effectively as possible for military action against this formidable adversary. In the face of the consequent unpreparedness, Republicans from different areas of the country divided among themselves as to when and how force should be applied. Sectional and interest-group pressures are natural to our form of government: all the more reason for efforts to remove the conditions that generated these forces. Americans adequately warned of impending hostilities would have had sufficient opportunity to prepare for conflict. Madison was an able, astute negotiator, highly accomplished in the ways of traditional eighteenth-century European diplomacy. He was beyond his depth, however, in managing the affairs of an unruly, fractious nineteenth-century republic as it moved towards war.

The year 1812 for the student of our early history bears an heretofore unperceived meaning. The waning prestige of republicanism in 1787 had given deep urgency to the movement that produced a new blueprint of republican government—the Constitution. By 1812 republicanism seemed again in peril. Contemporaries perceived the parallel between the two periods. The present moment, exclaimed Calhoun of South Carolina, "is a period of the greatest moment to our country. No period since the formation of our constitution has been equally important."

Once again men felt that a momentous outcome hung in balance. We must consider our actions with great care, urged William King of North Carolina, "when the destinies of the country are about to be launched on an untried ocean, and when the doubt is about to be solved, whether our Republican Government is alike calculated to support us through the trials and difficulties of war, and guide us in safety down the gentle current of peace." [13]

Nor did the sense of urgency concerning republicanism and the party dissipate after war began. The nation had shown it could declare war. It must now show that it could wage war. A letter from Secretary Monroe to Senator William H. Crawford reveals a continuing concern. Would the Senator call to discuss candidates to head a confused and leaderless War Department, asked the Secretary, at a particularly low point in American fortunes? "This is the time when the arrangements that are to insure success to the republican party & to free government for our country, are to be made, or which will lay the foundation for their overthrow." From the Virginia son-in-law of the Secretary of State, George Hay, a state party leader, came this warning. "According to my limited views of the state of things in the UStates, this is the crisis of the republican cause. If it sustains the present shock, it will prevail and flourish for many years. The undivided strength of its friends ought therefore to be exerted with the utmost vigilance and circumspection." A speedy recruitment of an efficient military force, wrote William W. Bibb of Georgia in 1814, involved "the safety, if not the very existence of this free government." Only with news of the Peace of Ghent did there come relief from the sense of crisis. There had been disasters in this war, but also triumphs. Jonathan Roberts spoke for many when in 1815 in a letter to his brother he appraised the war. It had not been a defeat or even a stalemate but a victory—for the party and for republicanism.

We have not got a stipulation about impressments & orders in council nor about indemnity— But victory perches on our banner & the talisman of invincibility no longer pertains to the tyrants of the

Ocean— But the triumph over the Aristocrats & Monarchists is equally glorious with that over the enemy— It is the triumph of virtue over vice of republican men & republican principles over the advocates & doctrines of Tyranny.[14]

There would be future crises which would call into doubt the energy and staying power of the American Republic. But to many Americans like Roberts the War of 1812 was one long stride in the march towards permanency.

APPENDIX

Bibliographical Note; Letter of Royall Tyler
to James Fisk, May 13, 1812

In the period which has elapsed since 1964 when this book was first published, it has been heartening to note how much new work has helped to confirm its most controversial themes. The thesis that the division over the war was primarily an issue between parties rather than between the representatives of geographical sections or interest-groups is one that has been sharply challenged. Addressing itself immediately to this problem, a quantitative study of roll-call voting in the House of Representatives during the war session, recently completed by Ronald L. Hatzenbuehler of Kent State University, decisively establishes the war's party basis ("Party Unity and the Decision for War in the House of Representatives, 1812," unpublished seminar paper, 1970, Department of History, Kent State University). Using cohesion, scaling, and cluster-bloc analyses, Mr. Hatzenbuehler concludes that both parties maintained a high degree of unity throughout the session, that their attitudes were highly polarized, and that a party voting pattern was much more consistent and pervasive than a factional or sectional one. In addition, three fine studies of the Federalists demonstrate the primacy of party values and party activity during this troubled era. Specifically, the books by David H. Fischer (*The Revolution of American Conservatism: the Federalist Party in the Era of Jeffersonian Democracy*, New York, 1965), Lisle A. Rose (*Prologue to Democracy: the Federalists in the South 1789–1800*, Lexington, 1968), and James M. Banner (*To the Hartford Convention: the Federalists and the Origins of Party Politics in Massachusetts 1789–1815*, New York, 1970) show how the Federalists built a nation-wide grass-roots political organization, engaged in electioneering against their Republican adversaries, and identified the nation's security and well-being with their party's success at the polls.

One notable exception to this emphasis on parties and their role as the primary units of political behavior is James Sterling Young's important study of politics in the nation's capital during the Jeffersonian era (*The Washington Community: 1800–1828*, New York, 1966). Describing Congress at this time as highly fragmented into particularistic boarding-house blocs, Mr. Young affirms that its members were hardly conscious of formal party affiliations and acted according to what they thought would best serve the special interests of their own local constituents. But contemporary letters and party listings, not consulted for the period 1809–1815 by Mr. Young, indicate that men were very aware of party ties, and knew quite precisely Congressional party strength and membership (see, for example, the remarkably accurate list of Republican and Federalist members of the new Twelfth Congress published in Niles' *Weekly Register*, 30 November, 1811). Mr. Young's generalizations would seem much more valid for the period which began with the dissolution of the Federalist party after the Ghent Treaty and ended with the rise of the second American party system in the 1830s.

As for the thesis that concern for the success of the Republic motivated Republicans to rally behind the administration, reject submission, and press forward to war, this too has had its share of critics. The recent books by Gordon S. Wood (*The Creation of the American Republic 1776–1787*, Chapel Hill, 1969) and James M. Banner (*To the Hartford Convention: the Federalists and the Origins of Party Politics in Massachusetts 1789–1815*), as well as Pauline Maier's forthcoming study of the Revolutionary origins of republicanism (*From Resistance to Revolution: 1765–1776*, to be published by Alfred A. Knopf), make clear the preoccupation of this generation with building a successful republic that would earn the confidence and loyalty of the American people. A most personally satisfying confirmation of this thesis was the discovery of an important letter, not available at the time this book was first published, which sets forth in the most detailed fashion of any evidence yet found the Republican case against submission. Written by Royall Tyler, the author of the patriotic drama, *The Contrast*, and in 1812 the Republican Chief Justice of the Vermont Supreme Court, the letter spells out the belief that to remain at peace any longer would threaten the Republic by undermining the confidence of even the staunchest Republicans in its ability to carry on war. Describing a growing mood of disenchantment at the grass-roots with the Republic's stability and functional cohesiveness, the letter suggests that Republican fears about the loss of popular support for republican government had more than an imaginary basis.

Addressed to James Fisk, a Republican congressman in the Twelfth Congress from Barre, Vermont, Tyler's letter appears in a manuscript volume entitled "Memoirs of Hon. Royall Tyler, late Chief Justice of Vermont," 1873, 301–4, into which it was copied by his son, Thomas P. Tyler; the volume is part of the Royall Tyler Collection, gift of Helen Tyler Brown, Vermont Historical Society, Montpelier. The letter was first published with descriptive comment in my article, "A Vermont Republican Urges War: Royall Tyler, 1812, and the Safety of Republican Government," *Vermont History*, XXXVI, number 1 (winter, 1968), and is printed in full below with the permission of the Director.

Your estimable favor of the 2d inst. was received last evening. It was doubly welcome, first because it contained information calculated in some degree to dissipate the dense clouds which overshadow our political horizon, the sombre influence of which the firmest of our Republican brethren feel in common with myself; and secondly that it assures me that you are, where you ought to be, at your post in the hour of national peril.—. . . .

Since my return from the curcuit I can give you but little more than the opinion of a retired man but from what I can obtain from conversation with the Republicans in my vicinity, and from some letters from various parts of the State, I am led to conclude that the only safety for the Republican interest is to declare war immediately, or at least to take some decided & progressive step towards it;—ex gratiā, by issuing letters of Marque & Reprisal. I do not fear the exertions of the Federalists simply considered, although I expect that our Washingtonian Society will bring every party vote to the poles, and their energies will be stimulated by Atlantic influence, but what I sincerely apprehend is the loss of Republican confidence in our government,—I mean in the very form & essence of our government. In Republican circles I hear it frequently observed: "Well, if Congress does sneak out:—if they have put us to all this expense for nothing: if they have not resolution sufficient to maintain the national rights: if they will not crush our domestic enemies: if we must be always exposed to have our rights sacrificed to the contentions and private views of our leading men, we shall be led to believe that the Federalists are right, and there is not virtue in the people to support a republican government. Why will not Congress put this great point in dispute in issue? We are ready to support the Government as it is; but if it is inherently defective, give us a government that is worth supporting."—Conversations of this kind are but too common, and are exceedingly alarming. If an Administration does wrong in any particular point we can displace it & elect another. What Republicans are in office is of little comparative importance, but that measure which tends to diminish our confidence not in men but in our republican institutions is of the highest import and ought to be avoided. We should all recollect that our Government is in a train of experiment. Those of Europe are opposed to it from principle and have no belief in its durability. Every attempt will be made to embarrass, & eventually to destroy it. Its weak spots will be successively attacked, and they will find aid from the avaricious, the ambitious, the discontented, and the feeble minded of our own citizens. The freedom of the press has long presented an inviting occasion to pervert public opinion. The Merchantile interest, weighing public good by private profit, has in all countries hung like a dead weight on the hands of Government.—Another weak spot is the arraying the Administration of one or more states against the General Government. This is next to be tried. A small exertion of this nature was evinced by the Executive of Connecticut refusing to draft their quota of the 100,000 men called for by the Genl. Govt. some years past; and should the Administration of Massachusetts be completely Federal—which, blessed be *God* cannot be this present year—you will have to contend with their Legislature—for they know that a state cannot be hung for a rebel, and they are wrought up to all opposition. If this state of things is to be apprehended,—if the Legislative opposition of [a] single large state is to be feared, much more is to be dreaded the combined opposition of the New-England states, aided perhaps by New-York. The governing principles of some at least of their statesmen seems to be to set a high value on their state influence, & carry it to the best market.—Do not conclude, my friend, from this melancholly view of our affairs that I despond. Indeed I do not. I believe you will meet all these impediments to National prosperity with firmness. I notice these things merely to introduce an opinion that these difficulties can be avoided by a corresponding energy on the side of the Government.—If for instance Massachusetts should have a complete federalist Administration, and should pass Resolutions, and even make Laws hostile to the General Government, let the question be immediately put to issue, which shall recede: *for this question in the course of our history is one day to be tried,* if not by that state, yet in some one of the states. Men of local influence will array their particular state against the Genl. Govt. And where or when could it be tried with more favorable auspices for the National authorities? When may we expect a greater union on the floor of your House or the Senate; and when can any state be expected by the division of her political numbers to be worse prepared to contend than Massachusetts? If unhappily this state or any other should attempt such opposition, meet them boldly & instantly. If you parly the Government is lost, for your friends will believe that you have not power, or lack resolution to defend the Constitution.—Indeed I view the diminishing of Republican confidence in the National Govt. as the most to be dreaded, and I consider that it can only be secured by a Declaration of war, or at least by issuing letters of Marque & Reprisal. A declaration of war will confound the Federalists; it [will] derange their present plans which are calculated only for political campaigns; introduce new topics of conversation; invite many Federalists into the army—and soldiers are always patriotic in time of war; it will relieve commerce from the embargo, and by opening new sources of risk or gain will break the mercantile phalanx; and above all it will place the opposition on slippery ground, and drive them to silence or rebellion. I do not fear the latter.—

Yours truly   *R. Tyler*

MANUSCRIPT SOURCES

The manuscript sources cited in this study come from many depositories in states east of the Mississippi River. A brief listing here of the most useful collections may help others interested in the domestic political background of the War of 1812. Many of these collections will also serve researchers in other aspects of early American history. Extensive quotations from these materials and a more specific discussion of individual collections may be found in my "A Republic in Peril: the Crisis of 1812" (M.S. dissertation, 1959, Harvard Archives). A useful listing of American, British, and French sources is Bradford Perkins, *Prologue to War: England and the United States, 1805–1812* (Berkeley, Calif., 1961), pp. 439–46.

The most useful collection of sources for this period belongs to the Manuscript Division, Library of Congress. The papers of Thomas Jefferson and James Madison, rich in incoming and outgoing correspondence, are of fundamental importance. The Library has the papers of many other political figures of the period that can be used with profit. They include Josiah Bartlett, Jr., William A. Burwell, George Washington Campbell, William H. Crawford, Gideon Granger, Andrew Jackson, William Lowndes, James McHenry, James Monroe, Hugh Nelson, Wilson Cary Nicholas, Joseph H. Nicholson, William Plumer, John Randolph, William C. Rives, Caesar Rodney, Samuel Smith, Joseph Story, Martin Van Buren, and Thomas Worthington. The papers of Henry Clay and John C. Calhoun no longer require such careful search as formerly inasmuch as *The Papers of Henry Clay*, ed. by James F. Hopkins (Lexington, Ky., 1959), Vol. I, and *The Papers of John C. Calhoun*, ed. by Robert L. Meriwether (Columbia, S.C., 1959), Vol. I, bring together available material. The journal of Augustus J. Foster reveals the observations and comments of a British diplomat in Washington as do the diplomatic dispatches reproduced in photostat copies of the Foreign Office Series 5. The Personal Miscellany Collection has an important letter of John Sevier and will yield other letters to the careful searcher.

The National Archives is another storehouse of material in the Washington area. Correspondence received by the Secretaries of War and Navy relating to military and naval affairs may be consulted in the War and Navy Department Branches; the Legislative Branch has a revealing collection of petitions on the 90-day embargo and war.

Southern manuscript holdings are extensive and of great value. The Georgia Historical Society, Savannah, has the papers of William Jones, an important Georgia Republican. The University of Georgia, Athens, has the very useful Thomas Carr, Telamon Cuyler, and Keith Read collections of manuscripts. In the South Caroliniana Collection of the University of South Carolina, Columbia, are letters written by Secretary of the Navy Paul Hamilton. In the Southern Historical Collection of the University of North Carolina, Chapel Hill, are the valuable papers of William S. Burwell, William Gaston, W. S. Hamilton (microfilm), William Lenoir, William Lowndes, John Randolph (microfilm), Thomas Ruffin, John Steele, and John Rutledge, Jr. At the North Carolina Department of Archives and History, Raleigh, are the papers of the merchant-politician, John Gray Blount. Duke University, Durham, has the very useful papers of David Campbell and John Clopton; the William Bolling MS also has a few relevant letters. The library of the University of Virginia, Charlottesville, holds important materials: the papers of Joseph Cabell, John Cocke, Wilson Cary Nicholas, and Creed Taylor, as well as the Samuel Smith-Robert Carter and John Randolph-William Garnett collections. At the Maryland Historical Society, Baltimore, the Harper-Pennington MS has correspondence to and from Robert G. Harper and the miscellaneous collection in the vertical file has a letter of Stevenson Archer.

Collections in the North are strong in contemporary sources. The Historical Society of Pennsylvania, Philadelphia, has superb holdings: the Dreer and Gratz Collections contain much material and the papers of Charles Jared Ingersoll, William Jones, George Logan, Thomas R. Gold, and Jonathan Roberts are very important. The holdings of the Delaware Historical Society were not personally consulted, but the James Canby MS has letters of Federalists. The Roberts Collection at Haverford College has one or two useful letters. At the New-York Historical Society the papers of Albert Gallatin are valuable; there are also letters of De Witt Clinton, William H. Crawford, Samuel Hambleton, and the editorials of James Monroe written for the *National Intelligencer*. The New York Public Library has a small but important James Monroe Collection, letters of Pierre Van Cortlandt, and the Emmett and Meyers autograph collections, which contain relevant letters. Columbia University has the De Witt Clinton MS, and the Museum of the City of New York possesses letters of Clement Clarke Moore and Samuel L. Mitchill. At the New York State Library, Albany, are to be found miscellaneous letters of George Clinton and the Daniel Tompkins MS; in the Stevens Collection, the papers of Jonathan Hubbard, recipient of Federalist letters, are revealing. In the Sir William Johnson Mansion, Fort Johnson, New York, are the little-known letters of Thomas Sammons.

The Connecticut Historical Society, Hartford, is a leading New England depository of the letters of Federalist leaders: the John Treadwell MS and the papers of Oliver Wolcott and Oliver Wolcott, Jr., are most useful. Letters of Chauncey Goodrich and Samuel Dana may be found at the Yale University Library. The papers of their Federalist colleagues, Harrison Gray Otis and Timothy Pickering, belong to the Massachusetts Historical Society, Boston, as do the Henry Dearborn and Levi Lincoln MS. The Chamberlain Collection at the Boston Public Library has a few letters of Federalists. The Essex Institute, Salem, has the papers of William Bentley, a Republican, and Daniel White, a Federalist. The American Antiquarian Society, Worcester, has some Elijah Brigham MS. The Vermont Historical Society, Montpelier, has James Fisk MS; the New Hampshire State Library, Concord, has William Plumer, Jr. MS; and the Maine Historical Society, Portland, has the important William King MS and several individual letters in the J. S. H. Fogg autograph collection.

The kind assistance of librarians has made it possible to draw upon several collections in depositories west of the Alleghenies without a personal search. At the Ross County Historical Society, Chillicothe, Ohio, are the very revealing papers of Thomas Worthington. At the Filson Club, Louisville, Kentucky, are Joseph Daviess MS. At the Mississippi Department of Archives and History, Jackson, are important letters written by George Poindexter.

This book rests heavily on manuscript sources to which many references are made. Abbreviated citations of manuscript depositories referred to in notes are as follows.

CHS: Connecticut Historical Society, Hartford
Delaware HS: Delaware Historical Society, Wilmington
Ft. Johnson, NY: Sir William Johnson Mansion, Fort Johnson, New York
GaHS: Georgia Historical Society, Savannah
GaU: University of Georgia, Athens
HSP: Historical Society of Pennsylvania, Philadelphia
LC: Library of Congress, Washington, D.C.
Maine HS: Maine Historical Society, Portland
MdHS: Maryland Historical Society, Baltimore
MHS: Massachusetts Historical Society, Boston
Mississippi Dept. Archives and History: Mississippi Department of Archives and History, Jackson
NA: National Archives, Washington, D.C.
NC Dept. Archives and History: North Carolina Department of Archives and History, Raleigh
NYHS: New-York Historical Society, New York City
NYPL: New York Public Library, New York City
NYSL: New York State Library, Albany

RCHS: Ross County Historical Society, Chillicothe, Ohio
UNC: University of North Carolina, Chapel Hill
USC: University of South Carolina, Columbia
VaU: University of Virginia, Charlottesville

NOTES

Chapter 1. Will Republicanism Prevail?

1. John Winthrop, "A Modell of Christian Charity," in S. E. Morison, ed., *Old South Leaflets*, No. 207, p. 20; Frederick Merk, *Manifest Destiny and Mission in American History* (New York, 1963); Benjamin Thomas, *Abraham Lincoln* (New York, 1952), pp. 266–69, 314, 396–403; John F. Kennedy, "Inaugural Address," in *Public Papers of the Presidents of the United States, John F. Kennedy, 1961* (Washington, D.C., 1962), pp. 1–3.

2. For republicanism and the American Revolution, see the suggestive and ground-breaking discussion in Cecelia Kenyon, "Republicanism and Radicalism in the American Revolution: an Old Fashioned Interpretation," *William and Mary Quarterly*, XIX (1962), 153–62. Also see John Marshall to James Wilkinson, 5 Ja 87, quoted in Charles Warren, *The Making of the Constitution* (Boston, 1929), pp. 31–32; Thomas Jefferson to Spencer Roane, 6 S 19, *Writings of Thomas Jefferson*, ed. by P. L. Ford (New York, 1892–99), X, 140; Page Smith, *John Adams* (New York, 1962), I, 225–35, 242–49, 258–64, 267–74, 291, 296; and "General View of the Work," *The Papers of Thomas Jefferson*, ed. by Julian P. Boyd (Princeton, N.J., 1950–), I, vii–xi.

For contemporary definition and meaning of republicanism, see John C. Miller, *Alexander Hamilton: Portrait in Paradox* (New York, 1959), p. 164; Washington to John Jay, 1 Ag 86, Department of State, *Documentary History of the Constitution* (Washington, D.C., 1905), IV, 20, and the suggestive paragraphs in R. R. Palmer, "The World Revolution of the West: 1763–1801," *Political Science Quarterly*, LXIX (1954), 4–5. On this point and others I have profited greatly from discussion with Richard Buel, Jr., whose "Studies in the Political Ideas of the American Revolution, 1760–1776" (M.S. dissertation, 1962, Harvard Archives) deals with the problems of interest, liberty, and consensus in a republic.

3. Tocqueville elaborated on this theme as follows: "But a democracy can only with great difficulty regulate the details of an important undertaking, persevere in a fixed design, and work out its execution in spite of serious obstacles. It cannot combine its measures with secrecy or await their consequences with patience." Alexis de Tocqueville,

Democracy in America, ed. by Philips Bradley (New York, 1945), I, 235–36, 243.

4. James Madison, "Address to the States," agreed to by Congress, 24 Ap 83, quoted in Adrienne Koch, *Jefferson and Madison: the Great Collaboration* (New York, 1950), pp. 8–9.

5. Esmond Wright, *Fabric of Freedom, 1763–1800* (New York, 1961), pp. 157–60; Edmund Morgan, *Birth of the Republic* (Chicago, 1956), pp. 113–28.

6. Washington to John Jay, 1 Ag 86, *Documentary History of the Constitution,* IV, 20; Madison to Jefferson, 19 Mr 87, quoted in Warren, *Making of the Constitution,* p. 47.

7. Madison, Notes on Congress Proceedings, 21 F 87, *Documentary History of the Constitution,* IV, 81. The newspaper essays are quoted in Warren, *Making of the Constitution,* pp. 29–30. Benjamin Tupper to Henry Knox, April, 1787, quoted in Louise B. Dunbar, "A Study of 'Monarchical' Tendencies in the United States from 1776 to 1801," *University of Illinois Studies in the Social Sciences,* X (1922), 73; John Adams to Benjamin Rush, 5 Jl 89, quoted in Smith, *John Adams,* II, 755–57; Marshall to Wilkinson, 5 Ja 87, quoted in Warren, *Making of the Constitution,* pp. 31–32; Washington to Madison, 31 Mr 87, *The Writings of George Washington,* ed. by J. C. Fitzpatrick (Washington, D.C., 1931–44), XXIX, 190.

8. Madison to Edmund Pendleton, 22 Ap 87, quoted in Warren, *Making of the Constitution,* p. 50. The statements by Randolph, Morris, Gerry, and Madison are quoted in Warren, *Making of the Constitution,* pp. 82, 273.

Warren, *Making of the Constitution,* and Neal Riemer, "The Republicanism of James Madison," *Political Science Quarterly,* LXIX (1954), 45–64, stress the importance of concern for republicanism in the thought of the fathers of the Constitution. In giving emphasis to this aspect of the constitutional reform movement of 1787, I do not mean to imply that all members of the Convention feared for republicanism, or that opponents of the Constitution were necessarily antirepublican. Not all participants in the Convention were ardent republicans, and many critics of the Constitution expressed concern that the new instrument provided inadequate means of representation and insufficient safeguards against subversion by the one or the few.

9. Hamilton's speeches, 26 Je 87, 18 Je 87, *The Basic Ideas of Alexander Hamilton,* ed. by Richard B. Morris (New York, 1957), pp. 122, 128. Hamilton's most recent biographers, Broadus Mitchell and John C. Miller, accept his preference for a British-type monarchy, but affirm his loyalty and commitment to republicanism. Broadus Mitchell, *Alexander Hamilton: Youth to Maturity, 1755–1788* (New York, 1957), pp. 394–400, and Miller, *Hamilton: Portrait in Paradox,* pp. 182–83.

10. Hamilton to James McHenry, 18 Mr 99, Hamilton, *Basic Ideas,* p. 369; Hamilton to Edward Carrington, 26 My 92, *The Works of*

Alexander Hamilton, ed. by Henry C. Lodge (New York, 1903), IX, 533–35; Hamilton to Gouverneur Morris, 27 F 02, Hamilton, *Basic Ideas,* p. 440. Broadus Mitchell and John C. Miller believe that Hamilton's central purpose was to build an enduring, vigorous, and powerful nation. Both authors note also Hamilton's desire to make the new government a success. Broadus Mitchell, *Alexander Hamilton: the National Adventure, 1788–1804* (New York, 1962), pp. 206, 354–56, 508–14, and Mitchell, *Hamilton: Youth to Maturity,* p. 400; Miller, *Hamilton: Portrait in Paradox,* pp. 163, 219–20, 232, 235, 284–85, 318.

11. Jefferson to George Washington, 23 My 92, *The Life and Selected Writings of Thomas Jefferson,* ed. by Adrienne Koch and William Peden (New York, 1944), p. 512.

12. Many historians have treated Republican and Federalist distortions of rival motivation as sincere expressions of actual belief. Marshall Smelser has pinpointed the matter in two articles, "The Federalist Period as an Age of Passion," *American Quarterly,* X (1958), 391–419 and "The Jacobin Phrenzy: the Menace of Monarchy, Plutocracy, and Anglophilia, 1789–1798," *Review of Politics,* XXI (1959), 239–58. Among others are Henry Adams, *History of the United States* (New York, 1930), I, 209–11, 224; Broadus Mitchell, *Heritage from Hamilton* (New York, 1957), p. 67; John C. Miller, *Hamilton: Portrait in Paradox,* pp. 352, 371, 384, 575; Dumas Malone, *Jefferson and the Rights of Man* (Boston, 1951), pp. 287–88, 349 59, 367, 437, 451–77, and *Jefferson and the Ordeal of Liberty* (Boston, 1962), 7–8, 55–56, 264–69, 364–66, 408–9.

13. Jefferson to Phillip Mazzei, 24 Ap 96, *Life and Writings of Jefferson,* p. 537. For a detailed description of Federalist policies, language, manners, and ideas that aroused suspicion of their subversive purposes, see Smelser, "The Jacobin Phrenzy: the Menace of Monarchy, Plutocracy, and Anglophilia." On this point there is the revealing statement in 1812 of John Taylor of Caroline, a Virginia planter who during the 1790s had helped organize the Republican party. Here Taylor criticizes President Madison for making public letters which purportedly linked unnamed Federalist leaders with a British spy, John Henry, in a plot to lead New England out of the Union into the British empire. "As to the part in the drama assigned to the northern federalists, it is only a repitition of a known fact also. It has been always known that many of them were monarchists. It was the policy of twisting our government round to monarchy by law, whilst the monarchical federalists guided it, or a desire for the loaves and fishes, which created the republican party. Allowing it the honourable motive, we must allow it a knowledge of the facts producing that motive. It accused its adversary of attempting to change the government, in power, by law, out of it, by intriguing with England, or by dividing the union. Would Mr. Jefferson or Mr. Madison have better known that Mr. King and the Adams's were monarchists, if Henry had told them so? Or would his telling them what they knew, have caused them to persecute as traytors, the

men whom they trusted as patriots? If not, ought the nation to be plunged into a war, because a spy has told it, that which the republican party has been telling it these twenty years?" John Taylor to James Monroe, 12 Mr 12, Monroe MS, LC.

14. Joseph Charles, *The Origins of the American Party System* (New York, 1961), pp. 91–140; Noble Cunningham, Jr., *The Jeffersonian Republicans: the Formation of Party Organization, 1789–1801* (Chapel Hill, N.C., 1957); William N. Chambers, *Political Parties in a New Nation: the American Experience, 1776–1809* (New York, 1963).

15. Paul Goodman, "The Democratic-Republicans of Massachusetts, Politics in a Young Republic" (M.S. dissertation, 1961, Harvard Archives), portrays well the social backgrounds of the Federalist and Republican leadership. A recent grass-roots study, Benjamin W. Labaree, *Patriots and Partisans: the Merchants of Newburyport, 1764–1815* (Cambridge, Mass., 1962) confirms the point for one town where "almost all of the prominent merchants and professional men supported the Federalist cause" while newcomers—ship captains and lately arrived "esquires"— went Republican. "The line between the office-seekers was rather one between established merchants, lawyers, and their associates, and those still working their way up from the quarterdeck to the countinghouse," p. 140. Also, William T. Whitney, Jr., "The Crowninshields of Salem, 1800–1808," *Essex Institute Historical Collections*, XCIV (1958), pp. 13–18, 29; and Norman L. Stamps, "Political Parties in Connecticut, 1789–1819" (M.S. dissertation, 1950, Yale University), pp. 21, 77, 83, 94, 129, 156, 160.

For the landlord-tenant division, see Staughton Lynd, "Who Should Rule at Home? Dutchess County, New York, in the American Revolution," *William and Mary Quarterly*, XVIII (1961), 330–59.

Southern Federalists in commercial areas and northern colleagues were of similar background. See Larkin Smith to Wilson Cary Nicholas, 30 Ag 08, Nicholas MS, LC; Walter Leake to Nicholas, 15 D 07, Smith-Carter MS, VaU; Peter Freneau to Jefferson, 18 S 08, Jefferson MS, LC; John H. Wolfe, "Jeffersonian Democracy in South Carolina," *James Sprunt Studies in History and Political Science*, XXIV (1940), 155–56, 162, 165, 169, 182, 186–87, 232n.105. For an account of the organization of the Republican party in a southern state, see Harry Ammon, "The Republican Party in Virginia, 1789 to 1824" (M.S. dissertation, 1948, University of Virginia).

16. Jefferson to William Branch Giles, 31 D 95, *The Works of Thomas Jefferson*, ed. by P. L. Ford (New York, 1904–5), VIII, 201–4; James Ross to George Washington, February, 1798, quoted in Stephen G. Kurtz, *The Presidency of John Adams: the Collapse of Federalism, 1795–1800* (Philadelphia, 1957), p. 293; Jefferson to Edward Rutledge, 24 Je 97, *Life and Writings of Jefferson*, p. 544.

17. Jefferson to Albert Gallatin, 1 Ap 02; Annual Message, 8 D 01; Jefferson to John Dickinson, 23 Jl 01, to Elbridge Gerry, 28 Ag 02, to

Dupont de Nemours, 18 Ja 02, Jefferson, *Writings*, VIII, 139–41, 120–23, 76, 169, 125–27. Adams, *History of the United States*, I, 223–28, 238–43. Adams writes in a striking passage that when Jefferson entered the presidency in 1801 "his mind was filled with the conviction that he had wrung power from monarchy, and that in this sense he was the founder of a new republic. Henceforward, as he hoped, republicanism was forever safe; he had but to conciliate the misguided, and give an example to the world, for centralization was only a monarchical principle." *History of the United States*, I, 209–10.

18. Jefferson to Joseph Priestley, 21 Mr 01, Jefferson, *Works*, IX, 216–19; Jefferson to Pierce Butler, 26 Ag 01, to Dupont de Nemours, 18 Ja 02, Jefferson, *Works*, VIII, 83, 125–27.

19. Jefferson to Lyman Hall, 6 Jl 02, to Gallatin, 12 Jl 03, to Thomas McKean, 19 F 03, Jefferson, *Writings*, VIII, 156–57, 251–52, 218–19; Jefferson to Gallatin, 13 D 03, Jefferson, *Works*, X, 56–58. For further evidence of Jefferson's preoccupation with the safety of republicanism, see Jefferson to Thomas Mann Randolph, 2 F 00, to General E. Meabe, 8 Ap 00, to John Langdon, 22 D 06, to Isaac Weaver, Jr., 7 Je 07, to William Wirt, 10 Ja 08, Jefferson MS, LC.

20. Jefferson to Boston citizens, 26 Ag 08, to Thomas Lehré, 8 N 08, Jefferson MS, LC; Madison to George Joy, 22 My 07, Madison MS, LC; Madison to James Monroe and William Pinkney, 20 My 07, *American State Papers Foreign Relations* (Washington, D.C., 1832), III, 166; Samuel Smith to Mrs. Mansfield, 8 Je 10, Smith-Carter MS (copies), VaU; Jefferson to Thomas Cooper, 18 F 06, Jefferson MS, LC.

21. Gerry to Madison, 19 F 06, 13 Mr 06, Madison MS, LC; Monroe to Jefferson, 26 S 05, Jefferson MS, LC.

22. Jefferson to Thomas Cooper, 18 F 06, Jefferson MS, LC; Jefferson to Gallatin, 13 D 03, Jefferson, *Works*, X, 56–58; Jefferson to Michael Leib, 23 Je 08, Jefferson MS, LC. Jefferson wrote a day later: "That the embargo is approved by the body of republicans throughout the Union cannot be doubted. [It] is equally known that a great proportion of the Federalists approve of it; but as they think it an engine which may be used advantageously against the Republican system, they countenance the clamours against it." Jefferson to Daniel Brent, 24 Je 08, Jefferson MS, LC; Jefferson to Thomas Lehré, 8 N 08, Jefferson MS, LC.

23. Ezekiel Bacon to Joseph Story, 4 N 08, also 5 N 08, Story MS, LC; Elbridge Gerry to Madison, 20 F 09, Rives MS, LC; Joseph Varnum to George Washington Campbell, 19 Mr 10, Campbell MS, LC. Republicans like Gerry believed the Federalist leaders to be divided in their strategy for restoring monarchy. Some Federalists presumably favored an American king and nobility; others, a British king. Thus he wrote in 1811 while governor of Massachusetts: "[My] policy is directed to this point, a discrimination & as far as it can be effected, a seperation, between the revolutional, & anti revolutional federalists. the former, altho some of them may pant for a monarchy, in order to be nobles, are

generally disposed to preserve our Union & independence; the latter
with some disappointed expectants, & visionary Burrites were decidedly
for a secession of the northern states & the erection over them of an
Hanoverian monarchy." Gerry to Henry Dearborn, 2 S 11, J. S. H.
Fogg Collection, Maine HS. That this was a widely held view is seen
in John Taylor to Monroe, 12 Mr 12, Monroe MS, LC, quoted in note
13 above.

Italics in text quotation are in the original. Hereafter, only my own
emphases in a quoted source are explicitly noted; emphases in the original
are not indicated as such.

Chapter 2. No Other Option

1. Madison to Jefferson, 14 S 05, Jefferson MS, LC; Jefferson to
Thomas Paine, 18 Mr 01, to Robert R. Livingston, 9 S 01, quoted in
Henry Adams, *History of the United States* (New York, 1930), I,
214–15; Jefferson to Albert Gallatin, 1 S 04, *The Works of Thomas
Jefferson*, ed. by P. L. Ford (New York, 1904), X, 99–100. Also articles
in *National Intelligencer*, 13 N 05, 18 N 05, 20 N 05.

2. Bradford Perkins, *Prologue to War: England and the United States
1805–1812* (Berkeley, Calif., 1961), pp. 84–95. This is the best recent
discussion of the maritime issues.

3. Bradford Perkins, *The First Rapprochement: England and the
United States 1795–1805* (Philadelphia, 1955), pp. 86–89, 177–80.

4. Perkins, *Prologue to War*, pp. 104–6, 147–48, 198–210.

5. Perkins, *Prologue to War*, pp. 69–70.

6. Perkins, *Prologue to War*, pp. 71–72. From 1803 to 1807 the British
seized 528 vessels while the French seized 206. Thus British seizures
over a nine-year period totaled 917, Napoleonic, 675.

7. Irving Brant, *James Madison: Secretary of State, 1800–1809* (Indianapolis, Ind., 1953), pp. 160–62, 171–76, 254–56.

8. Jefferson to John Minor, 2 Mr 06, to Monroe, 16 Mr 06, Jefferson
MS, LC; John Randolph to James Garnett, 27 Ap 06, 11 My 06, Garnett-
Randolph MS, VaU; Herbert Heaton, "Non-Importation, 1806–1812,"
Journal of Economic History, I (1941), 178–98.

9. For more detailed discussion of these events, see Perkins, *Prologue
to War*, pp. 101–83 and Reginald Horsman, *The Causes of the War of
1812* (Philadelphia, 1962), pp. 83–143. See documents in *American State
Papers Foreign Relations* (Washington, D.C., 1832), III, 230–32, 247–49,
255–56, for the British and French answers to the American effort. For
the preventive and coercive purposes of the embargo, see Jefferson to
Gideon Granger, 22 Ja 08, to Joseph Eggleston, 7 Mr 08, to Benjamin
Smith, 20 My 08, to Thomas Leiper, 25 My 08, Jefferson MS, LC;
Jefferson to Benjamin Rush, 3 Mr 08, Jefferson MS (photostats), VaU;
Jefferson to Levi Lincoln, 22 Je 08, Lincoln MS, MHS; *National Intelli-
gencer*, 23 D 07.

10. For letters that illuminate Republican sensitivity to Federalist

political gains and threats of secession, see William H. Crawford to Thomas Carr, 31 D 08, Carr Collection, GaU; Ezekiel Bacon to Joseph Story, 4 N 08, 5 N 08, 22 Ja 09, 5 F 09, 15 F 09, 26 F 09, Story MS, LC; Elbridge Gerry to Madison, 20 F 08, Madison MS, LC; Jefferson to Thomas Mann Randolph, 2 Ja 09, 31 Ja 09, Jefferson MS, LC.

11. *Annals of Congress,* 10th Cong., 2d Sess., pp. 1824–30; Irving Brant, *James Madison: the President, 1809–12* (Indianapolis, Ind., 1956), pp. 39–42.

12. For the deemphasis of the impressment issue, details on the *Chesapeake,* and the eclipse of the Rule of 1756 issue, see Perkins, *Prologue to War,* pp. 69, 95, 191–97, 104–5, 202, 207. Both Jefferson and Madison were optimistic that the British would agree to cease impressment if the United States barred British sailors from employment on American vessels. Jefferson to Thomas Mann Randolph, 26 O 07, Jefferson MS, LC. Indeed, Jefferson records that he told the British minister, David Erskine, on November 9, 1808, that "altho' the question of impressmts was difficult on their side & insuperable with us yet had that been the sole question, we might have shoved along, in the hope of some compromise [without resort to the embargo]." Jefferson, Notes of Conversation with Erskine, 9 N 08, Jefferson MS, LC. In contrast, Jefferson had written in January, 1808, concerning the Orders and Decrees: "I think the British order of Nov. 14. which was known to be intended, declaring they will take every thing which France does not take, can leave no doubt of the propriety of the embargo. If we had suffered our vessels, cargoes and seamen to have gone out, all would have been taken by England or it's enemies, and we must have gone to war to avenge the wrong. it was certainly a better alternative to discontinue all intercourse with these nations till they shall return again to some sense of moral right" Jefferson to Gideon Granger, 22 Ja 08, Jefferson MS, LC. And again: "The decrees & orders of the belligerent nations having amounted nearly to declarations that they would take our vessels wherever found, Congress thought it best in the first instance to break off all intercourse with them." Jefferson to William Lyman, 30 Ap 08, Jefferson MS, LC. Also Jefferson to John Taylor, 6 Ja 08, to Benjamin Smith, 20 My 08, Jefferson MS, LC.

13. Brant, *Madison the President,* pp. 34–50, 66–101; Perkins, *Prologue to War,* pp. 234–38.

14. *Annals,* 11th Cong., 2d Sess., pp. 2582–83; Brant, *Madison the President,* pp. 117–20; Perkins, *Prologue to War,* pp. 238–44.

15. Madison to Jefferson, 7 My 10, Jefferson MS, LC; Jefferson to Caesar Rodney, 30 S 10, Rodney MS, LC.

16. Champagny, Duc de Cadore to John Armstrong (translation), 5 Ag 10, *ASPFR,* III, 387; Brant, *Madison the President,* pp. 208–10.

17. Presidential Proclamation, 2 N 10, Cadore to Louis Turreau, 23 Ag 10, quoted in Perkins, *Prologue to War,* pp. 249, 246–47.

18. Madison to William Pinkney, 30 O 10, *The Writings of James*

Madison, ed. by Gaillard Hunt (New York, 1900–10), VIII, 120; Robert Smith to John Armstrong, 2 N 10, quoted in Perkins, *Prologue to War*, pp. 249–50. Irving Brant has made clear the technical basis for the decision to announce repeal. Brant, *Madison the President*, pp. 212–21.

19. Madison to Caesar Rodney, 30 S 10, Rodney MS, LC. Also, Madison to Monroe, 26 Mr 11, Madison MS, LC; Madison to Jefferson, 19 O 10, Madison, *Writings*, VIII, 109.

20. A. J. Foster to Marquis Wellesley, 2 Jl 11, 5 Ag 11, Foreign Office Series 5, LXXVI (photostats), LC; Brant, *Madison the President*, p. 331.

21. Marquis Wellesley to A. J. Foster, 10 Ap 11, "Instructions to the British Ministers, 1790–1812," *Annual Report of the American Historical Association for the Year 1936*, III, 310–19.

22. A. J. Foster to Monroe, 3, 14, 16, 24, 26 Jl 11, *ASPFR*, III, 435–45; Monroe to Foster, 15, 23 Jl 11, *ASPFR*, III, 438–42. The negotiation may be followed also in Foster to Wellesley, 7, 12, 18 Jl 11, 5 A 11, Foreign Office Series 5, LXXVI (photostats), LC. Madison to Henry Dearborn, July, 1811, Roberts Collection, Haverford College. The Jefferson and Madison administrations had made the distinction between the municipal and antineutral features of the Decrees since April, 1808. Perkins, *Prologue to War*, pp. 175, 177, 215.

23. Monroe to Foster, 23, 26 Jl 11, *ASPFR*, III, 439–42; Foster to Wellesley, 5 Ag 11, Foreign Office Series 5, LXXVI (photostats), LC. On July 18 Foster reported that Monroe had told him, explaining the American delay in conducting an inquiry on the recent *President-Little Belt* encounter, "that since it was discovered that I had no power to satisfy this Government in regard to His Majesty's Orders in Council, there was no use in settling any other points." Again: "In the conversation which I had yesterday with the American Secretary on these subjects, after our discussion upon the affair of the Little Belt, he frankly owned to me that unless I had power to declare His Majesty's Orders in Council at an end nothing could be effected towards a reconcilement of any of our differences." Foster to Wellesley, 18 Jl 11, Foreign Office Series 5, LXXVI (photostats), LC.

24. Monroe to John Taylor, 13 Je 12, Monroe MS, LC; Foster to Wellesley, 2, 12 Jl 11, Foreign Office Series 5, LXXVI (photostats), LC.

25. Monroe to Foster, 23 Jl 11, *ASPFR*, III, 441; Madison to Jefferson, 18 Mr 11, 3 My 11, 7 Je 11, to Joel Barlow, 17 N 11, Madison, *Writings*, VIII, 133–35, 151, 157, 169.

26. Madison to Henry Dearborn, July, 1811, Roberts Collection, Haverford College.

27. Madison to Henry Dearborn, July, 1811, Roberts Collection, Haverford College; Madison to Monroe, 23 Ag 11 (mistakenly endorsed and arranged chronologically under date 23 Ag 12), Monroe MS, LC; Monroe to Madison, 15 Ag 11, 7 S 11, 13 S 11, Rives MS, LC.

28. Joseph Gales, "Recollections of the Civil History of the War of

1812 by a Contemporary," *National Intelligencer*, 12 S 57. For other articles in the series, see *National Intelligencer*, 9, 16, 25 Je 57, 14, 30 Jl 57, 8, 15, 29 Ag 57. For a full discussion of these articles, and of Gales's relation to the Madison administration, see Howard F. Mahan, "Joseph Gales, The National Intelligencer and the War of 1812" (M.S. dissertation, 1958, Columbia University).

29. Brant, *Madison the President*, pp. 340–483; Theodore Clarke Smith, "War Guilt in 1812," *Proceedings of the Massachusetts Historical Society*, LXIV (1930–32), 319–45.

30. Madison to John Quincy Adams, 15 N 11, Madison, *Writings*, VIII, 166–67; Madison to Governor Willie Blount (no date), Madison MS, LC, printed in *National Intelligencer*, 14 Ja 12; Madison to Jefferson, 3 Ap 12, Madison, *Writings*, VIII, 185.

31. Monroe to Joseph J. Monroe, 6 D 11, *The Writings of James Monroe*, ed. by S. M. Hamilton (New York, 1898–1903), V, 196; Monroe to John Taylor, 13 Je 12, Monroe MS, LC.

32. Gallatin, Notes on Madison's Message Sent 5 N 11, Rives MS, LC; Gallatin to Jefferson, 10 Mr 12, Jefferson MS, LC. The letters of other cabinet members—Secretary of the Navy, Paul Hamilton, and Secretary of War, William Eustis—show Madison firm in resolution to fight for repeal of the Orders. Paul Hamilton to Morton Waring, 4 N 11, 11 My 12, 19 My 12, Hamilton MS, USC; William Eustis to George Logan, 14 My 12, Logan MS, HSP.

33. Madison to Jefferson, 18 Mr 11, Madison, *Writings*, VIII, 135.

34. Monroe to John Taylor, 13 Je 12, Monroe MS, LC; Madison to J. Q. Adams, Madison, *Writings*, VIII, 166–67; Dolley Madison to Anna Cutts, 20 D 11, quoted in Allen C. Clark, *Life and Letters of Dolly Madison* (Washington, D.C., 1914), p. 124.

35 The use of war preparations to force British repeal of the Orders in Council is described in Monroe to John Taylor, 13 Je 12, Monroe MS, LC, and in Chapter 5 of this book.

36. Madison, Message, 5 N 11, Madison, *Writings*, VIII, 158–65.

37. A. L. Burt, *The United States, Great Britain, and British North America* (New Haven, Conn., 1940), pp. 297–316; Horsman, *Causes of the War of 1812*, pp. 259–60, 267.

38. Madison, Message, 1 Je 12, Madison, *Writings*, VIII, 192–200.

39. Monroe to Jonathan Russell, 26 Je 12, *ASPFR*, III, 585.

40. Monroe to ? on Administration Policy (undated; from internal evidence written after declaration of war, in folder marked "Decr, 1812"), Monroe MS, NYPL.

41. John A. Harper to William Plumer, 13 My 12, Plumer MS, LC; Madison, Message, 1 Je 12, Madison, *Writings*, VIII, 192–200.

42. Madison to Henry Wheaton, 26–27 F 27, Madison, *Writings*, IX, 273–74. Mr. Perkins believes that had the British conditional repeal of the Orders become known in time in the United States it "would have prevented war," and that at the very moment of beginning war,

the Americans "raised their terms" to include impressment. Perkins, *Prologue to War*, p. 421. I think this is a correct judgment.

43. Jonathan Russell to Joel Barlow, 14 Ja 12, to Monroe, 19 F 12, 9 My 12, quoted in Perkins, *Prologue to War*, pp. 317, 323, 333.

44. Timothy Pitkin, *A Statistical View of the Commerce of the United States* (Hartford, Conn., 1816), pp. 158, 167–68. Pitkin calculated the average annual imports from all countries in 1802, 1803, and 1804 to be $75,316,000; from Great Britain and her dependencies, $35,970,000. He calculated the value of imports from Great Britain and Ireland to be $32,877,059 in 1800, $39,516,218 in 1801, and $35,779,245 in 1806.

45. See Perkins, *Prologue to War*, pp. 138–39, 201, 206. Pitkin, *A Statistical View*, pp. 160, 190. Pitkin calculated the average annual exports of domestic products to the northern powers, Germany, and Prussia for 1802, 1803, and 1804 to be $2,918,000; to the dominions of Holland, France, Spain, and Italy to be $12,183,000. Since Spanish ports were no longer under blockade as they came under the control of Wellington's army, exports to Spain, computed to be $2,304,193 in 1804, have been excluded from the comparison. The $2,918,000 to the German and Baltic countries is roughly one-third of $9,878,807 sent to the dominions of Holland, France, and Italy. Thus American exports to countries still under blockade by the Order of 1809 were ordinarily much more substantial than to those countries opened by the Order to her trade.

46. Auckland to Charles Grey, 27 Ja 09, quoted in Perkins, *Prologue to War*, pp. 205–6, 315–17. Mr. Perkins shows persuasively that the depression began in 1810 at a time when the Macon law had actually opened American trade with Great Britain.

Chapter 3. A Reluctant Majority

1. The most recent discussions which stress the role of "war hawks," though with differences as to precise motivation, relative strength, and exact influence, are Bradford Perkins, *Prologue to War: England and the United States, 1805–1812* (Berkeley, Calif., 1961), pp. 344, 347, 391–92, and Reginald Horsman, *The Causes of the War of 1812* (Philadelphia, 1962), pp. 181, 217–18, 226, 228, 254. Also, Julius Pratt, *The Expansionists of 1812* (New York, 1925) and Bernard Mayo, *Henry Clay* (Boston, 1937). Most textbooks share this view. Among them are Harry J. Carman, Harold C. Syrett, and Bernard W. Wishy, *A History of the American People* (New York, 1960); T. Harry Williams, Richard N. Current, and Frank Freidel, *A History of the United States* (New York, 1960); and Samuel E. Morison and Henry S. Commager, *The Growth of the American Republic* (New York, 1962).

The term "war hawk" appears in Josiah Quincy to Harrison Gray Otis, 26 N 11, Otis MS, MHS; William Reed to Timothy Pickering, 25 Ap 12, Pickering MS, MHS; Benjamin Tallmadge to James McHenry, 11 Ap 12, McHenry MS, LC.

2. *Annals of Congress,* 12th Cong., 1st Sess., pp. 297, 1637. The *Annals* reports the Senate vote as 19 to 13. The roll call actually shows only 12 negative votes, but Pope of Kentucky, missing on the roll call, voted against war. Josiah Bartlett, Jr., to Ezra Bartlett, 18 Je 12, Bartlett MS, LC; Thomas D. Clark, "Kentucky in the Northwest Campaign," in William T. Utter and others, *After Tippecanoe: Some Aspects of the War of 1812* (East Lansing, Mich., 1963), pp. 84–85.

3. Margaret K. Latimer, "South Carolina—A Protagonist of the War of 1812," *American Historical Review,* LXI (1955–56), 914–29, and George R. Taylor, "Agrarian Discontent in the Mississippi Valley Preceding the War of 1812," *Journal of Political Economy,* XXXIX (1931), 471–505, stress southern and western economic distress. Julius Pratt, *Expansionists of 1812,* makes the classic statement of the expansionist thesis. A. L. Burt, *The United States, Great Britain, and British North America* (New Haven, Conn., 1940), pp. 306–10, and Reginald Horsman, *Causes of the War of 1812,* pp. 175–76, argue the case for northeastern opposition. Leading textbooks follow, with minor variations, the sectional approach.

4. Jonathan Roberts to Matthew Roberts, 4 Ap 12, Roberts MS, HSP; Jonathan Roberts to William Jones, 7 Je 12, Jones MS, HSP; Henry Dearborn to Madison, 12 Je 12, Madison MS; John Sevier to George W. Sevier, 13 Ja 12, 26 Ap 12, "Some Unpublished Letters of John Sevier to His Son, George Washington Sevier," *Tennessee Historical Magazine,* VI (1920), 62–68.

5. For a convenient listing of members according to party affiliation, see Niles's *Weekly Register,* 30 N 11. I have taken the Mason-Dixon line east to Delaware as dividing south from north and the Appalachian barrier as demarcating the west.

Bradford Perkins in *Prologue to War,* pp. 407–17, has perceived the party basis of voting.

6. Monroe to John Taylor, 13 Je 12, Monroe MS, LC.

7. Franklin to William Lenoir, 15 F 12, Lenoir MS, UNC; Franklin to Thomas Ruffin, 14 N 13, Ruffin MS, UNC; Sevier to G. W. Sevier, 13 Ja 12, 26 Ap 12, "Some Unpublished Letters of John Sevier," pp. 62–68.

8. Hall to William Jones, 11 Ja 12, Jones MS, GaHS; Roberts to Matthew Roberts, 12 N 11, 8 D 11, Roberts MS, HSP; Roberts to William Jones, 7 Je 12, Jones MS, HSP; Bibb to Governor Charles Scott, 23 F 12, in Lexington *Reporter,* 7 Mr 12; Thomas Gholson to Constituents, 4 Jl 12, William S. Burwell MS, UNC; Porter to William Eustis, 19 Ap 12, Letters Received, War Department Branch, NA. For full quotations and similar statements of twenty additional members, see Roger H. Brown, "A Republic in Peril: the Crisis of 1812" (M.S. dissertation, 1959, Harvard Archives).

9. Norman K. Risjord, "1812: Conservatives, War Hawks, and the Nation's Honor," *William and Mary Quarterly,* XVIII (1961), pp. 196–210, especially 205–7; Horsman, *Causes of the War of 1812,* pp.

156–57, 177, 182–87, 222–23, 266–67; Perkins, *Prologue to War*, pp. 267, 343–50, 373–74, 392, 406–7, 415–16, 432–37.

10. Campbell to Governor Willie Blount, 24 F 12, Campbell MS, LC; Crawford to Thomas Carr, 20 F 09, Carr Collection, GaU; Nicholas to Jefferson, 22 D 09, Nicholas MS, VaU; Desha to Joseph Daveiss, 17 F 10, Daveiss MS, Filson Club, Louisville; Madison to William Pinkney, 20 Ja 10, *The Writings of James Madison*, ed. by Gaillard Hunt (New York, 1900–10), VIII, 90–91.

11. Clay to Monroe, 15 Mr 12, to Caesar Rodney, 17 Ag 11, *The Papers of Henry Clay*, ed. by James F. Hopkins (Lexington, Ky., 1959), I, 637, 574; Joseph C. Cabell to John H. Cocke, 31 N 11, Cabell MS, VaU; Clay Speech, 31 D 11, Clay to ?, 28 F 12, to Thomas Bodley, 12 My 12, Clay, *Papers*, I, 609, 633, 653.

12. Calhoun Speech, 12 D 11, Calhoun to Virgil Maxcy, 2 My 12, *The Papers of John C. Calhoun*, ed. by Robert L. Meriwether (Columbia, S.C., 1959), I, 76–77, 101.

13. Clay Speeches, 22 F 10, 28 D 10; Clay to Caesar Rodney, 11 Ja 11, 7 Mr 11, 17 Ag 11; Clay Speech, 31 D 11, Clay to ?, 28 F 12, to Thomas Bodley, 12 My 12, Clay, *Papers*, I, 448–52, 515, 522, 546, 574, 609, 633, 653.

14. Charles M. Wiltse, *John C. Calhoun, Nationalist, 1782–1828* (New York, 1944), pp. 51–53. Mr. Wiltse's evidence for his statement that Calhoun campaigned for Congress in 1810 on a war platform is, in my judgment, inconclusive. I can find no supporting evidence in the cited *Correspondence*. Other evidence cited by Mr. Wiltse consists of personal reminiscences, an anonymous campaign biography, and a personal memoir. But neither Ebenezer Smith Thomas's *Reminiscences*, the *Life of John C. Calhoun*, nor Colonel W. Pinkney Starke's *Account of Calhoun's Early Life* states explicitly that the campaign of 1810 turned on the issue of war, or that Calhoun at that time advocated war. The most these sources suggest is that South Carolina voters were disgusted with members of the 10th Congress who had voted to repeal the embargo.

15. Calhoun to Patrick Calhoun, 24 Ja 12, to Patrick Noble, 22 Mr 12, 17 Je 12, to James Macbride, 17 F 12, to Virgil Maxcy, 2 My 12, Calhoun Speech, 12 D 11, Calhoun, *Papers*, I, 89–90, 95–96, 126, 91, 76.

16. Roberts, Macon, and Grundy in *Annals*, 12th Cong., 1st Sess., pp. 502, 505, 493, 661, 1139; Perkins, *Prologue to War*, p. 267.

17. Madison's Third Annual Message, 5 N 11, Madison, *Writings*, VIII, 158–65; Thomas Rodgers to Jonathan Roberts, 17 N 11, Roberts MS, HSP; John Sevier to George W. Sevier, 13 Ja 12, "Some Letters of John Sevier," pp. 62–63; George Poindexter to Cowles Mead, 11 N 11, Poindexter MS, Mississippi Dept. Archives and History; Grundy to Willie Blount, 18 N 11, quoted in Joseph H. Parks, *Felix Grundy: Champion of Democracy* (Baton Rouge, La., 1940), p. 37.

18. Thomas B. Cooke to Governor Daniel B. Tompkins, 6 N 11,

Tompkins MS, Box 7, Package 1, NYSL; Macon to Nicholson, 21 N 11, Nicholson MS, LC; Peleg Tallman to William King, 18 N 11, King MS, Maine HS; Clay to Caesar Rodney, 17 Ag 11, Clay, *Papers*, I, 574; Joseph C. Cabell to John H. Cocke, 31 N 11, Cabell MS, VaU; *Annals*, 12th Cong., 1st Sess., p. 343.

19. Lowndes to Wife, 7 N 11, Lowndes MS (copies), UNC; Calhoun to Patrick Calhoun, 14 N 11, Calhoun, *Papers*, I, 63; Tait to Governor David Mitchell, 10 Ja 12, Gratz Collection, HSP; John A. Harper to William Plumer, 2 D 11, Plumer MS, LC.

20. *Annals*, 12th Cong., 1st Sess., pp. 373–77, 414. The committee may also have stressed impressment to satisfy members who considered that the United States should fight over impressment alone even if Britain repealed the Orders in Council. But few Republicans, if any, would have pressed for war until after further negotiation on this issue. Otherwise why should leaders like Clay, Roberts, and William Lowndes have anticipated that repeal of the Orders would save the peace, and why should Madison have written years later that had repeal of the Orders in Council occurred a few weeks earlier "our declaration of war as proceeding from that cause would have been stayed, and negociations on the subject of [impressment], the other great cause, would have been pursued with fresh vigor & hopes, under the auspices of success in the case of the orders in council." Clay to James Morrison, 21 D 11, to Monroe, 25 Mr 12, Clay, *Papers*, I, 600, 637; Jonathan Roberts to Matthew Roberts, 25 Ja 12, Roberts MS, HSP; William Lowndes to Wife, 7 D 11, Lowndes MS (copies), UNC; Madison to Henry Wheaton, 26 F 27, Madison, *Writings*, IX, 273–74.

Since 1807 when the Orders in Council became their chief preoccupation, neither the President nor his predecessor had made a strong effort to negotiate the impressment issue. Actually, Madison had a plan that he believed might solve the problem to the mutual satisfaction of both countries: an American pledge not to employ British seamen, an end to British impressment on the high seas. He did not, however, press the point. Madison to Jefferson, 17 Ap 07, 4 My 07, Jefferson MS, LC; Madison to Jefferson, 1 My 09, Madison, *Writings*, VIII, 54–55; Perkins, *Prologue to War*, pp. 64, 95.

21. Tallman to William King, 21 N 11, Maine HS.

22. W. W. Bibb to William Jones, 1 D 11, Jones MS, GaHS; Stevenson Archer to Elijah Davis, 4 D 11 (photostats, vertical file), MdHS; Hugh Nelson to Joseph Cabell, 28 D 11, Cabell MS, VaU.

23. Roberts to Matthew Roberts, 12 N 11, 19 N 11, 30 N 11, 8 D 11, Roberts MS, HSP; Harper to William Plumer, 2 D 11, Plumer MS, LC; Clay to James Morrison, 21 D 11, Clay, *Papers*, I, 600; Poindexter to Mead, 12 D 11, Poindexter MS, Mississippi Dept. Archives and History. Also, Poindexter to Mead, 25 Ja 12, 10 Ap 12, Poindexter MS, Mississippi Dept. Archives and History; Calhoun to Mrs. Floride Colhoun, Sr., 21 D 11, Calhoun, *Papers*, I, 87; Peleg Tallman to William King, 22 D 11,

King MS, Maine HS; W. W. Bibb to William Jones, 1 D 11, Jones MS,
GaHS; Isaac Coles to John Cocke, 7 D 11, Cocke MS, VaU, to Joseph
Cabell, 9 D 11, Cabell MS, VaU; John Sevier to George W. Sevier, 13
Ja 12, "Some Unpublished Letters of John Sevier," pp. 62–63. Compare
Nathaniel Macon's letter of November 21 ("it is however probable, that
there is not more than five or six opinions amongst us") with his letter
of January 2, 1812 ("I still think we shall have war with G. B.—unless
our affairs are settled with her, before Congress adjourn") and letters
of January 9, March 23, 28, and 30 reiterating this view. Nicholson
MS, LC.

24. Smilie in *Annals*, 12th Cong., 1st Sess., p. 1592; Calhoun to Virgil
Maxcy, 2 My 12, Calhoun, *Papers*, I, 101; Findley in *Annals*, 12th Cong.,
1st Sess., pp. 501–2; Manuel Eyre to William Findley, 12 Ja 12, Gallatin
MS, NYHS; Nelson to Joseph C. Cabell, 28 D 11, Cabell MS, VaU.

25. Macon and Harper in *Annals*, 12th Cong., 1st Sess., pp. 661, 655;
Roberts to Matthew Roberts, 25 Ja 12, Roberts MS, HSP.

26. W. W. Bibb to William Jones, 1 D 11, Jones MS, GaHS; Charles
Tait to Governor David Mitchell, 10 Ja 12, Gratz Collection, HSP, to
Thomas Carr, 1 Mr 12, Carr Collection, GaU; Hugh Nelson to Charles
Everette, 16 D 11, Nelson MS, LC; Gideon Granger to John Tod, 26
D 11, Granger MS, LC; Paul Hamilton to Morton A. Waring, 4 N 11,
25 Jl 12, Hamilton MS, USC; William Eustis to Henry Dearborn, 28 Ja
12, Dearborn MS, MHS; Richard Rush to Charles Jared Ingersoll, 10
My 12, Ingersoll MS, HSP.

27. Calhoun to Patrick Calhoun, 24 Ja 12, to Patrick Noble, 22 Mr 12,
17 Je 12, to James Macbride, 16 Mr 12, 18 Ap 12, Calhoun, *Papers*, I,
89–90, 95, 126, 93, 99–100.

28. Clay to John Parker, 7 D 11, Speech, 31 D 11, Clay to Monroe, 15
Mr 12, Speech, 22 Ja 12, Clay to Thomas Bodley, 12 My 12, to Monroe,
15 Mr 12, Clay, *Papers*, I, 599, 602–4, 637, 621, 653, 637.

29. Tait to Thomas Carr, 1 Mr 12, Carr Collection, GaU; Bibb to
William Jones, 1 D 11, Jones MS, GaHS; Lowndes to Wife, 7 N 11,
Lowndes MS (copies), UNC; Pickens to ?, 6 Mr 12, Personal Miscellany
MS, LC; Franklin to William Lenoir, 15 F 12, Lenoir MS, UNC; Archer
to Elijah Davis, 4 D 11 (vertical file), MdHS; Mitchill to William
Plumer, 17 Ja 12, Plumer MS, LC; Turner to William Bentley, 3 Ap 12,
Bentley MS, Essex Institute, Salem, Mass.; Grundy to Andrew Jackson,
12 F 12, *Correspondence of Andrew Jackson*, ed. by J. S. Bassett (Wash-
ington, D.C., 1926–35), I, 215–16, and Jackson MS, LC; Campbell to
Jackson, 24 D 11, Jackson, *Correspondence*, I, 212, to Jackson, 10 Ap 12,
Jackson MS, LC.

30. For Federalists, see Chapter 8 of this work. Grundy to Jackson,
28 N 11, 12 F 12, Jackson, *Correspondence*, I, 208, 215; Clay to Monroe,
15 Mr 12, Clay, *Papers*, I, 637.

31. Roberts to Matthew Roberts, 25 Ja 12, 20 D 11, Roberts MS, HSP.
Also, Roberts to Matthew Roberts, 12 N 11, 17 N 11, 25 N 11, 30 N 11,

Roberts MS, HSP. Levi Bartlett to Josiah Bartlett, Jr., 12 Ja 12, Bartlett MS, LC. In May, this same Roberts could boast fatuously of his part in bringing to publication a wretched song praising war and the President.

> The measure of our wrongs is filld
> For violated laws
> A nation's arm must 'strike redress'
> Nerv'd by a righteous cause
> The word will soon be warrior's march
> The brave will follow on
> Huzza-huzza-huzza-huzza
> For war & Madison.

Roberts to Matthew Roberts, 31 My 12, Roberts MS, HSP.

32. John Clopton to Son, 11 My 12, Public Letter, 20 Ap 12, Notes of a Speech on War, 1812, Clopton MS, Duke. Clopton was anxious to know of the effect of his letter on constituents; towards the end of June he sent off a whole batch of addresses to constituents. Clopton to Son, 8 Je 12, 29 Je 12, Clopton MS, Duke. Compare Grundy to Jackson, 4 D 11, Jackson MS, LC, and Grundy to Citizens of West Tennessee, 19 Je 12 in *Carthage Gazette* (Tenn.), 11 Jl 12, with Grundy to Jackson, 12 F 12, Jackson MS, LC.

33. George Poindexter to Cowles Mead, 12 D 11, Poindexter MS, Mississippi Dept. Archives and History; Abijah Bigelow to Jonathan Hubbard, 30 Ja 12, Hubbard MS, Stevens Collection, NYSL; Grundy in *Annals*, 12th Cong., 1st Sess., p. 1139.

34. Plumer to Charles Cutts, 30 D 11, Plumer MS, LC.

35. *Annals*, 12th Cong., 1st Sess., pp. 564, 617, 1003, 1069, 1353; Grundy to Jackson, 28 N 11, 12 F 12, Jackson, *Correspondence*, I, 208, 215; Charles Cutts to William Plumer, 11 D 11, Plumer MS, LC.

36. Clay Speech, 31 D 11, Clay, *Papers*, I, 609; Sevier to George W. Sevier, 13 Ja 12, "Some Unpublished Letters of Sevier," pp. 62–63.

37. Jonathan Roberts to Matthew Roberts, 20 My 12, Roberts MS, HSP; John A. Harper to William Plumer, 2 D 11, Plumer MS, LC; William Reed to Timothy Pickering, 18 F 12, Pickering MS, MHS.

Chapter 4. The Republic in Peril

1. Roberts to Matthew Roberts, 25 Ja 12, Roberts MS, HSP; Macon in *Annals of Congress*, 12th Cong., 1st Sess., p. 661; Harper in *Annals*, 12th Cong., 1st Sess., p. 655.

2. Bibb to William Jones, 1 D 11, Jones MS, GaHS; Tait to David B. Mitchell, 1 Ja 12, Gratz Collection, HSP, to Thomas Carr, 1 Mr 12, Carr Collection, GaU; Gallatin, Notes on Madison's Message of 5 N 11, Rives MS, LC.

3. Gallatin, Notes on Madison's Message of 5 N 11, Rives MS, LC; Gallatin to Jefferson, 10 Mr 12, Jefferson MS, LC; Nelson to Charles

Everette, 16 D 11, Nelson MS, LC; Gideon Granger to John Tod, 26 D 11, Granger MS, LC.

4. Paul Hamilton to Morton Waring, 4 N 11, 25 Jl 12, Hamilton MS, USC; William Eustis to Henry Dearborn, 28 Ja 12, Dearborn MS, MHS; Clay to John Parker, 7 D 11, *The Papers of Henry Clay*, ed. by James F. Hopkins (Lexington, Ky., 1959), I, 599; Calhoun to Patrick Calhoun, 24 Ja 12, to James Macbride, 18 Ap 12, to Patrick Noble, 17 Je 12, *The Papers of John C. Calhoun*, ed. by Robert L. Meriwether (Columbia, S.C., 1959), I, 89–90, 99–100, 126. See Chapters 5 and 6 of this book for further discussion of the military danger.

5. Bibb to Jones, 1 D 11, Jones MS, GaHS; Desha, Pickens, and Williams in *Annals*, 12th Cong., 1st Sess., pp. 489, 643, 678–80; Franklin to Edmund Ruffin, 14 N 13, Thomas Ruffin MS, UNC; Augustus J. Foster to Marquis Wellesley, 21 N 11, Foreign Office Series 5, LXXVII, LC.

6. Grundy to Andrew Jackson, 12 F 12, Jackson MS, LC; William Blackledge to John G. Blount, 18 Mr 12, Blount MS, NC Dept. Archives and History; Roberts to Matthew Roberts, 17 Je 12, Roberts MS, HSP; Clay to William W. Worsley, 9 F 12, Clay, *Papers*, I, 630.

7. Gerry to Madison, 12 Je 12, Madison MS, LC; Dearborn to Madison, 12 Je 12, Madison MS, LC; Rodgers to Jonathan Roberts, 20 Ap 12, Roberts MS, HSP; Binns to Jonathan Roberts, 19 Je 12, Roberts MS, HSP; Richard Rush to Charles Jared Ingersoll, 16 My 12, 24 My 12, Ingersoll MS, HSP, to Jonathan Roberts, 9 Je 12, Roberts MS, HSP.

8. Calhoun, Williams, and Cheves in *Annals*, 12th Cong., 1st Sess., pp. 479, 482, 682, 686, 805–6; Calhoun to James Macbride, 17 F 12, Calhoun, *Papers*, I, 90–91.

9. King, Roberts, Clay in *Annals*, 12th Cong., 1st Sess., pp. 518, 503, 599–600, also Richard M. Johnson and Joseph Desha in *Annals*, 12th Cong., 1st Sess., pp. 464, 489.

10. Calhoun to James Macbride, 17 F 12, Calhoun, *Papers*, I, 90–91; Williams in *Annals*, 12th Cong., 1st Sess., p. 682; Franklin to William Lenoir, 15 F 12, Lenoir MS, UNC. See also the remarks of Joseph Desha of Kentucky and William King of North Carolina in *Annals*, 12th Cong., 1st Sess., pp. 489, 518. Others sharing Franklin's small interest in uninterrupted commerce were William H. Crawford of Georgia, Willis Alston of North Carolina, and Thomas Worthington of Ohio. See Crawford to Thomas Carr, 20 F 09, Carr Collection, GaU; Augustus J. Foster, 18 Mr 12, 24 Mr 12, Journal in America, 1811–12, LC; Thomas Worthington, 12 Mr 12, Diary, Worthington MS, LC. Obviously, other motives governed their decision for war.

11. Williams and Pickens in *Annals*, 12th Cong., 1st Sess., pp. 679, 646; Grundy to Andrew Jackson, 4 D 11, Jackson MS, LC.

12. Tait to Thomas Carr, 1 Mr 12, Carr Collection, GaU; Clay and Pickens in *Annals*, 12th Cong., 1st Sess., pp. 601, 645; John Sevier to George W. Sevier, 31 My 12, Personal Misc. MS, LC.

13. Foster, 24 My 12, Journal, LC; Eustis to Logan, 14 My 12, Logan

MS, HSP; Grundy to Willie Blount, 18 N 11, quoted in Joseph Parks, *Felix Grundy: Champion of Democracy* (Baton Rouge, La., 1940), p. 37; Dearborn to Monroe, 12 Je 12, Monroe MS, NYPL.

14. Gallatin, Notes on Madison's Message of 5 N 11, Rives MS, LC; Binns to Jonathan Roberts, 3 My 12, Roberts MS, HSP; Jackson to Madison, 13 Ap 12, Madison MS, LC; Crawford to Madison, 28 Mr 12, Madison MS, LC; Sevier to George W. Sevier, 31 My 12, Personal Misc. MS, LC. Sevier identified the Federalists with "the old Tory party," presumably allied with monarchical-aristocratical Britain in a plot to put an end to republicanism. Sevier to Isaac Shelby, 17 Ja 10, NYPL Emmett Collection (transcripts in NC Dept. Archives and History); Sevier to George W. Sevier, 26 Ap 12, "Some Unpublished Letters of John Sevier to His Son, George Washington Sevier," *Tennessee Historical Magazine,* VI (1920), 64–66.

15. Gerry to Madison, 14 My 12, Madison MS, LC; Harper to William Plumer, 13 Ap 12, 29 Ap 12, Plumer MS, LC; Roberts to Matthew Roberts, 27 Ap 12, 20 My 12, 20 Je 12, Roberts MS, HSP. On this point also, consider the revealing letter of Charles Turner, Jr., a Massachusetts congressman. Turner affirmed his opposition to a recess. At the same time he noted that Augustus J. Foster, the British minister, had desired the measure and after its rejection had expressed very great dissatisfaction and met with "the British partizans of both Houses" the next evening. This led Turner to observe: "It is not easy for me to suppress my feelings, excited by the wicked acts, intrigues, and machinations of the enemies of *heaven-born Liberty,* to extirpate it from the Earth, but supported by a steady trust in the God of *Our Fathers I cannot dispair of the Commonwealth;* even if we should be severely chastized for our *ingratitude.*" Turner interpreted the actions of Foster and the Federalists as steps in a campaign to eliminate *"heaven-born Liberty,"* i.e., republicanism, from the earth. Turner to William Bentley, 27 Ap 12, Bentley MS, Essex Institute, Salem, Mass.

16. Washington to John Jay, 1 Ag 86, Department of State, *Documentary History of the Constitution* (Washington, D.C., 1905), IV, 20; Clay in *Annals,* 11th Cong., 3d Sess., pp. 63–64.

17. Granger to John Tod, 26 D 11, Granger MS, LC; Washington, D.C. *National Intelligencer,* 7 N 11; Pleasants to William Bolling, 5 Mr 12, Bolling MS, Duke; Pleasants in *Annals,* 12th Cong., 1st Sess., p. 1299; Nelson to Constituents, 7 Jl 12, Joseph Cabell MS, VaU.

18. McKim to Henry Clay, 13 My 12, Clay, *Papers,* I, 654; Calhoun to Virgil Maxcy, 2 My 12, Calhoun, *Papers,* I, 101; Bassett in *Annals,* 12th Cong., 1st Sess., p. 1315.

19. John Roberts to Jonathan Roberts, 12 Ap 12, Roberts MS, HSP; Calhoun in *Annals,* 12th Cong., 1st Sess., p. 479; Foster, 15 Ap 12, Journal, LC; Calhoun to James Macbride, 17 F 12, Calhoun, *Papers,* I, 90–91.

20. Calhoun Speech, 14 Ja 13, Calhoun, *Papers,* I, 160–61; see also, Calhoun Speech, 15 Ja 14, Calhoun, *Papers,* I, 191–92. See also speeches of

William Blackledge and David R. Williams in *Annals*, 12th Cong., 1st Sess., pp. 924, 682.

21. Leech to Jonathan Roberts, 14 Je 12, Roberts MS, HSP; Campbell to David Campbell, 17 O 12, Campbell MS, Duke; Macon in *Annals*, 12th Cong., 1st Sess., p. 661.

22. Jackson to Madison, 5 Jl 07, Madison MS, LC; Roberts in *Annals*, 12th Cong., 1st Sess., p. 503.

23. Jackson to Madison, 5 Jl 07, Madison MS, LC; Campbell to Alexander Smyth, 12 My 12, Campbell MS, Duke; Fox to Jonathan Roberts, 16 Je 12, Roberts MS, HSP; Nicholas to William B. Giles, 30 Ja 13, Nicholas MS, LC; Plumer to John A. Harper, 27 Ap 12, 11 My 12, Plumer MS, LC. For the belief that some northern Federalists sought reunion with Great Britain under the Hanoverians, see Elbridge Gerry to Henry Dearborn, 2 S 11, J. S. H. Fogg Collection, Maine HS., and John Taylor to Monroe, 12 Mr 12, Monroe MS, LC. These important letters are quoted in Chapter 1, notes 23 and 13 of this work.

24. Madison to South Carolina House of Representatives, 8 Ja 12, *The Writings of James Madison*, ed. by Gaillard Hunt (New York, 1900–10), VIII, 174–75; Rush to Charles J. Ingersoll, 29 Ap 12, Ingersoll MS, HSP; Madison, Annual Message, 4 N 12, Second Inaugural Address, 4 Mr 13, Madison, *Writings*, VIII, 230, 236; Dolley Payne Madison to Mrs. Richard Cutts, May, 1812, Madison-Cutts MS (microfilm), LC.

25. Monroe to John Taylor, 13 Je 12, Monroe MS, LC; Monroe to ? (no date, copy and endorsed as follows: "Written in the fall of 1811, and addressed to some person high in influence in England"), Monroe MS, LC; Foster to Marquis Wellesley, 3 My 12, Foreign Office Series 5, LXXXV, LC.

26. Rodgers to Jonathan Roberts, 21 Je 12, Roberts MS, HSP; "War Song" in New York *Columbian*, 1 Jl 12; *National Intelligencer*, 27 Je 12 on response in Richmond, 30 Je 12 on response in New York; Boston *Independent Chronicle*, 29 Je 12, on responses in Philadelphia, Frederickstown, and Annapolis; Lexington, Ky. *Reporter*, 27 Je 12, on responses in Lexington, Frankfort, Winchester, Richmond, and Nicholasville; Gerry to Madison, 5 Jl 12, Madison MS, LC.

27. Clay in *Annals*, 11th Cong., 3d Sess., pp. 63–64; Clay to Caesar Rodney, 27 My 10, Clay to William Worsley, 9 F 12, Clay, *Papers*, I, 472, 630; Clay in *Annals*, 12th Cong., 1st Sess., p. 600; Clay to Thomas Bodley, 12 My 12, Clay, *Papers*, I, 653; Clay in *Annals*, 14th Cong., 1st Sess., p. 783.

Chapter 5. The Trials of Preparation

1. Madison to Jefferson, 14 S 05, Jefferson MS, LC.

2. Charles Tait to Governor David Mitchell, 10 Ja 12, Gratz Collection, HSP; Nathaniel Macon to ?, 2 Ja 12, Personal Misc. MS, LC; John A. Harper to William Plumer, 2 D 11, Plumer MS, LC; Felix Grundy to Andrew Jackson, 28 N 11, *The Correspondence of Andrew Jackson*, ed.

by J. S. Bassett (Washington, D.C., 1926–35), I, 208; Monroe to John Taylor, 13 Je 12, Monroe MS, LC.

3. Gallatin, Notes on President's Draft Message of November 5, 1811, Rives MS, LC; Coles to Joseph C. Cabell, 9 D 11, Cabell MS, VaU; Coles to John Cocke, 7 D 11, Cocke MS, VaU.

4. Madison to Congress, 5 N 11, *The Writings of James Madison*, ed. by Gaillard Hunt (New York, 1900–10), VIII, 158–65; Gallatin, Notes on President's Draft Message of November 5, 1811, Rives MS, LC; Madison to Governor Willie Blount, in Reply to Letter of 23 N 11 Enclosing Tennessee Legislative Address, *National Intelligencer*, 14 Ja 12, original in Madison MS, LC.

5. The *National Intelligencer* on 18 Ja 12 gave the first clear statement of presidential intentions. The Monroe drafts of editorials of April 7, as well as other dates, are in the Monroe MS, NYHS. See also Irving Brant, *James Madison: the President, 1809–1812* (Indianapolis, Ind., 1956), pp. 435–36, plate opposite p. 416.

6. Foster to Marquis Wellesley, 21 N 11, 29 N 11, 25 N 11, 18 D 11, Foreign Office Series 5, LXXVII (photostats), LC.

7. Foster to Wellesley, 12 Mr 12, Foreign Office Series 5, LXXXIV (photostats), LC; Foster to Wellesley, 13 Mr 12, Foreign Office Series 5, LXXXV (photostats), LC.

8. Poindexter to Cowles Mead, 12 D 11, Poindexter MS, Mississippi Dept. Archives and History; Nelson to Charles Everette, 16 D 11, Nelson MS, LC; Nelson to Joseph C. Cabell, 28 D 11, Cabell MS, VaU; Nelson in *Annals*, 12th Cong., 1st Sess., pp. 497–99.

9. Foster to Wellesley, 25 N 11, 11 D 11, 18 D 11, 28 D 11, Foreign Office Series 5, LXXVII (photostats), LC; Foster to Wellesley, 16 Ja 12, 30 Ja 12, 31 Ja 12, 13 F 12, Foreign Office Series 5, LXXXIV (photostats), LC.

10. Leonard White to Daniel White (?), 11 Ap 12, Daniel White MS, Essex Institute, Salem, Mass.

11. William Reed to Timothy Pickering, 18 F 12, 25 Ap 12, Pickering MS, MHS; Joseph Pearson to John Steele, 2 Mr 12, Steele MS, UNC; Martin Chittenden to Jonathan Hubbard, 1 Je 12, Hubbard MS, Stevens Collection, NYSL.

12. Madison to Jefferson, 7 F 12, Madison, *Writings*, VIII, 175–77; Monroe to John Taylor, 13 Je 12, Monroe MS, LC; Tench Coxe to William Eustis, 8 Mr 12, 18 Mr 12, Letters Received, War Department Branch, NA; Thomas Porter to Eustis, 13 Ap 12, P. P. Schuyler to Eustis, 25 Ap 12, James Wellborn to Eustis, 7 My 12, Register of Letters Received, War Department Branch, NA. The *National Intelligencer* on March 19 admitted that recruiting for the new army had just begun. On April 18 the *Intelligencer* stated that recruiting instructions and money for bounties had been sent out between March 15 and 30. The newly appointed officers, assigned the task of recruiting, did not receive Senate confirmation until mid-March. William Reed to Timothy Pickering, 18

F 12, Pickering MS, MHS; Joseph Pearson to John Steele, 2 Mr 12, Steele MS, UNC.

13. Foster to Wellesley, 2 F 12 ("Separate and Secret" in cipher), Foreign Office Series 5, LXXXIV (photostats), LC; Hanson to Jackson, 7 Mr 12, quoted in Bradford Perkins, *Prologue to War: England and the United States 1805–1812* (Berkeley, Calif., 1961), pp. 352–53.

14. Outerbridge Horsey to Thomas Bradford, 4 F 12, Gratz Collection, HSP; Hartford, Conn. *Courant*, 22 Ja 12; Baltimore *Federal Republican and Commercial Gazette*, 31 Ja 12; *Alexandria Gazette*, 22 Ja 12, quoted in Perkins, *Prologue to War*, p. 353.

15. William Montgomery to James Monroe, 7 D 11, Misc. Letters, Foreign Affairs Branch, NA; John Binns to Jonathan Roberts, 11 Ap 12, Roberts MS, HSP; William Plumer to John A. Harper, 11 My 12, Plumer MS, LC.

16. Thomas Rodgers to Jonathan Roberts, 5 Ap 12, Roberts MS, HSP; see memorials on this subject in Memorials to Senate and House, Legislative Branch, NA.

17. See Memorials to Senate and House, 12 Congress, Legislative Branch, NA; Josiah Bartlett, Jr., to Ezra Bartlett, 30 My 12, Bartlett MS, LC; Manuel Eyre to Jonathan Roberts, 19 Ap 12, Roberts MS, HSP; John McKim, Jr., to Henry Clay, 13 My 12, *The Papers of Henry Clay*, ed. by James F. Hopkins (Lexington, Ky., 1959), I, 654.

18. William Eustis to Henry Dearborn, 28 Ja 12, Dearborn MS, MHS; Richard Rush to Charles Jared Ingersoll, 1 F 12, Ingersoll MS, HSP; Nelson Luckett to Eustis, 15 Ap 12, Letters Received, War Department Branch, NA; L. Hakell to W. S. Hamilton (?), 9 Ja 12, W. S. Hamilton MS (microfilm, reel 1), UNC; Coxe to Eustis, 18 Mr 12, Letters Received, War Department Branch, NA.

19. Thomas Worthington, Notes on Senate Speech, June, 1812, Worthington MS, RCHS; William A. Burwell to Wilson C. Nicholas, 23 My 12, Nicholas MS, VaU. Worthington's figures on the number of regular soldiers under arms came from a War Department report made in June, 1812. See Alfred B. Sears, *Thomas Worthington: Father of Ohio Statehood* (Columbus, Ohio, 1958), p. 168. Nelson Luckett to Eustis, 15 Ap 12, Letters Received, War Department Branch, NA; Jacquiline Howie to Paul Hamilton, 23 Ap 12, Misc. Letters, III, 1812, Navy Department Branch, NA; Dearborn to Eustis, 27 Ap 12, Letters Received, War Department Branch, NA.

20. Worthington, Notes on Senate Speech, June, 1812, Worthington MS, RCHS; Return J. Meigs to Worthington, 23 Ja 12, 5 Ap 12, Roswell Mills to Worthington, 3 F 12, William Perry to Worthington, 17 Je 12, "Thomas Worthington and the War of 1812," *Document Transcriptions of the War of 1812 in the Northwest*, ed. by Richard C. Knopf (Columbus, Ohio, 1957), III, 45, 75, 49, 97; Timothy Dix to William Plumer, 27 Je 12, Plumer MS, LC; John Montgomery to Albert Gallatin, 1 Jl 12, John J. Astor to Gallatin, 30 My 12, Peter Sailly to John Smith,

19 Je 12, Gallatin MS, NYHS. Details regarding Dearborn's and Hull's armies, and the situation at Calais and other points may be found in Register of Letters Received, War Department Branch, NA. The Inspector-General's report is cited in Sears, *Worthington*, p. 168.

21. William Lowndes to Wife, 23 Mr 12, Lowndes MS (copies), UNC; Clay to Monroe, 15 Mr 12, Clay, *Papers*, I, 637; *Annals*, 12th Cong., 1st Sess., pp. 187–90; *National Intelligencer*, 9 Ap 12, 11 Ap 12, 14 Ap 12, 18 Ap 12, 23 Ap 12, 28 Ap 12.

22. Thomas Rodgers to Jonathan Roberts, 26 Ap 12, Roberts MS, HSP; Albany merchants to Congress, 16 Ap 12, Mass., N.Y., Maryland Petitions on Embargo and War, 12 Congress, Legislative Branch, NA.

23. Boston merchants to Congress, 24 Ap 12, Portsmouth merchants to Congress, 15 Ap 12, New York merchants to Congress, 16 Ap 12, and others, Committee of the Whole to Authorize Importations from G. B., Legislative Branch, NA.

24. Josiah Bartlett, Jr., to Ezra Bartlett, 30 My 12, Bartlett MS, LC; Edward Fox to Jonathan Roberts, 8 Ap 12, Roberts MS, HSP; Return J. Meigs to Thomas Worthington, 23 Ja 12, 5 Ap 12, Roswell Mills to Worthington, 3 F 12, William Perry to Worthington, 17 Je 12, "Thomas Worthington and the War of 1812," pp. 45, 75, 49, 97; Peter B. Porter to Eustis, 19 Ap 12, 20 Ap 12, Letters Received, War Department Branch, NA; Manuel Eyre to Jonathan Roberts, 19 Ap 12, Roberts MS, HSP; Peter Sailly to John Smith, 19 Je 12, Gallatin MS, NYHS.

25. Monroe to Joel Barlow, 26 Jl 11, *American State Papers Foreign Relations* (Washington, D.C., 1832), III, 509–12; Brant, *Madison the President*, pp. 337–38; Barlow to Monroe, 21 N 11, 19 D 11, 31 D 11, *ASPFR*, III, 513, 515–16; Madison to Barlow, 24 F 12, Madison, *Writings*, VIII, 177–82.

26. Madison to Barlow, 24 F 12, Madison, *Writings*, VIII, 177–82; Edward Fox to Jonathan Roberts, 10 Mr 12, Roberts MS, HSP; Brant, *Madison the President*, pp. 423–24.

27. Senate Petitions and Memorials, 12 Congress, Legislative Branch, NA; Roberts to William Jones, 7 Je 12, Jones MS, HSP.

28. Boston Town Meeting, 11 Je 12, Petitions to Senate, Legislative Branch, NA; Rhode Island Legislative Resolutions, May, 1812, Massachusetts Legislative Resolutions, 2 Je 12, *Annals*, 12th Cong., 1st Sess., pp. 253–54, 260–61.

Chapter 6. By Land or by Sea?

1. For suggestive discussion of these ideas, see Thomas Worthington, Notes on Senate Speech and Notes on Senate Debate, June, 1812, Worthington to ?, November, 1812, Worthington MS, RCHS; Worthington, Diary, 14 Je 12, Worthington MS, LC; Wilson C. Nicholas to William B. Giles, 30 Ja 13, Nicholas MS, LC; Thomas Sammons to James Lansing, 8 My 12, Sammons MS, Ft. Johnson, N.Y.; Josiah Bartlett, Jr., to Ezra Bartlett, 30 My 12, 18 Je 12, Bartlett MS, LC.

2. Thomas Worthington, Notes on Senate Speech, June, 1812, Worthington to ?, November, 1812, Worthington MS, RCHS; Worthington, Diary, 14 Je 12, Worthington MS, LC; Wilson C. Nicholas to William B. Giles, 30 Ja 13, Nicholas MS, LC; Jefferson to Levi Lincoln, 13 N 08, Lincoln MS, MHS; John Pope Address, New York *Evening Post*, 22 S 13; Andrew Gregg to ?, 4 Je 12, Philadelphia *United States Gazette*, 15 Je 12; Madison to Jefferson, 24 Ap 12, 25 My 12, *The Writings of James Madison*, ed. by Gaillard Hunt (New York, 1900–10), VIII, 187–92.

3. Manuel Eyre to Jonathan Roberts, 19 Ap 12, Roberts MS, HSP; John J. Astor to Gallatin, 30 My 12, Gallatin MS, NYHS. Astor wrote again after news of the declaration of war had reached New York City: "You will be pleased to Learn that pepol here are more reasonable about the war measure than what I exspected & altho many Disapprove of the manner and time it was Declared all agree that we have plenty cause—and the most Speeke in favour of Suporting the Administration. even Mr Clintons friends find that the othr will not Do." Astor to Gallatin, 27 Je 12, Gallatin MS, NYHS.

4. Thomas Sammons to James Lansing, 8 My 12, Sammons MS, Ft. Johnson, NY; Sammons to Governor Daniel Tompkins, 18 Je 12, Tompkins MS, Box 3, Package 3, NYSL; Nathaniel Macon to Joseph H. Nicholson, 30 Ap 12, Nicholson MS, LC; Josiah Bartlett, Jr., to Ezra Bartlett, 18 Je 12, Bartlett MS, LC; *Annals*, 12th Cong., 1st Sess., pp. 1609, 1635.

5. *Annals*, 12th Cong., 1st Sess., pp. 1630–38; William Eustis to Henry Dearborn, 4 Je 12, J. S. H. Fogg Collection, Maine HS. On June 4 Eustis appraised congressional sentiment as follows: "And now my Dear Sir, let me give you in confidence our prospects & the results which may within a very short time be expected. A large & decided Majority of the house are for an unqualified & immediate declaration of war—a part of the majority would be satisfied with Letters of Marque & Reprisal in the first instance—some few are for coupling both nations in this last measure. Of the Senate less is known & understood. A majority of that body would it is presumed prefer Letters of Marque to open total unqualified war."

6. This paragraph rests on sources too numerous to cite fully. For Smith, see Smith-Carter MS, VaU, Smith MS, and Nicholas MS, LC, and John S. Pancake, "The General from Baltimore: a Biography of Samuel Smith" (M.S. dissertation, 1949, University of Virginia). For Giles, see Nicholas MS, Creed Taylor MS, James Barbour MS, VaU, Rives MS, LC, William Jones MS, HSP, and Dice R. Anderson, *William Branch Giles: A Biography* (Menasha, Wisc., 1915). For Gregg, see Gregg MS, LC, and Jones MS, HSP. Leib and Pope letters are few and scattered. For specific references, see Roger H. Brown, "A Republic in Peril: the Crisis of 1812" (M.S. dissertation, 1959, Harvard Archives), pp. 168–72. Key items on the attitudes of these five senators are: Philip

Nicholas to Wilson C. Nicholas, 13 D 11, Nicholas MS, LC; Samuel Smith, Notes on Foreign Relations Committee Hearing, 30 Mr 12, Smith MS, LC; Smith to Michael Leib, 14 O 12, Personal Misc. MS, LC; William Branch Giles to Wilson C. Nicholas, 19 Mr 12, Nicholas MS, VaU; Nicholas to Giles, 30 Ja 13, Nicholas MS, LC; Giles in *Annals*, 12th Cong., 1st Sess., pp. 35–54; Michael Leib to Callender Irvine, 11 F 12, Roberts Collection, Haverford; John Pope Address, New York *Evening Post*, 22 S 13; Andrew Gregg to ?, 4 Je 12, *United States Gazette*, 15 Je 12.

7. *Annals*, 12th Cong., 1st Sess., pp. 268–98.

8. Jonathan Roberts to Matthew Roberts, 17 Je 12, 20 Je 12, Roberts MS, HSP; Monroe to John Taylor, 13 Je 12, Monroe MS, LC.

9. The concern of these senators over domestic and foreign developments is reflected in actions reported in the *Annals*, 12th Cong., 1st Sess. This is what lay behind motions to extend the administration-recommended embargo (p. 189), the motions to recess for a short period (pp. 212–16), the requests for more evidence regarding the authenticity of French repeal of the Decrees (pp. 161, 229–31), the examination of merchant petitions requesting measures to permit the securing of property (pp. 197, 200, 238), and the votes and motions to repeal the nonimportation law (pp. 237–39). On friendly views of their motives, see Wilson C. Nicholas to William B. Giles, 30 Ja 13, Nicholas MS, LC; John A. Harper to William Plumer, 14 Je 12, Plumer MS, LC. On their own views of themselves, see Samuel Smith to Michael Leib, 14 O 12, Personal Misc. MS, LC; William B. Giles to James Barbour, 31 Ja 13, Barbour MS, VaU; Andrew Gregg to William Jones, 8 Ap 10, Jones MS, HSP; Michael Leib to Madison, 3 My 09, Madison MS, LC; Leib to Caesar Rodney, 19 My 08, Gratz Collection, HSP; John Pope Address, New York *Evening Post*, 22 S 13.

10. Madison to Jefferson, 25 My 12, Madison, *Writings*, VIII, 190–92; Monroe to ? on Administration Policy (undated, from internal evidence written after declaration of war, in folder marked "Decr, 1812"), Monroe MS, NYPL.

11. Monroe to Gallatin, 1 Je 12, Gallatin MS, NYHS. The top portion of this letter, perhaps explaining Monroe's reasons for desiring the strategy change, has been carefully torn off and cannot be found. William Lowndes, Commonplace Book, Lowndes-Pinckney MS, LC. For a different view, one that holds President Madison responsible for a rejection of maritime war, see Irving Brant, *James Madison: the President* (Indianapolis, Ind., 1956), pp. 476–77.

12. William Lowndes, Commonplace Book, Lowndes-Pinckney MS, LC; Thomas Worthington, Notes on the Senate Debate, June, 1812, Worthington MS, RCHS. Worthington took notes of points made in debate by Republican opponents of letters of marque. In view of the space and emphasis given by him to the arguments of Crawford, Bibb,

and Campbell, these senators must have led the opposition. Aside from speeches of Obadiah German and James Bayard the Senate journal gives little indication of the nature of this debate. This is not surprising; the June sessions were secret and reporters and observers could not attend. Our best available source as to the arguments advanced against limited maritime war are the Worthington notes, unfortunately brief enough themselves. See also Worthington, Notes on Senate Speech, June, 1812, Worthington MS, RCHS.

13. Significantly, Crawford wrote to Monroe three months after war began: "The only difficulty I had in declaring war, arose from the incompetency of the men, to whom the principal management of it was to be confided." William H. Crawford to Monroe, 9 S 12, Monroe MS, LC.

14. This paragraph rests on my own interpretation of the basic logic behind points made by Bibb and Crawford as recorded by Worthington. Thomas Worthington, Notes on Senate Debate, June, 1812, Worthington MS, RCHS.

15. William Henry Harrison to William Eustis, 4 D 11, Samuel Goode Hopkins to Governor Charles Scott, 9 My 12, "The National Intelligencer Reports the War of 1812 in the Northwest," *Document Transcriptions of the War of 1812 in the Northwest*, ed. by Richard C. Knopf (Columbus, Ohio, 1958), V, 30, 86, and *passim*. Thomas Worthington, Notes on Senate Debate, June, 1812, Worthington MS, RCHS. The British government actually wished to restrain the Indians, but irresponsible officials like Elliott were probably trying to incite them. Reginald Horsman, *The Causes of the War of 1812* (Philadelphia, 1962), pp. 204-16.

16. Clay to Adam Beatty, 21 Je 12, *The Papers of Henry Clay*, ed. by James F. Hopkins (Lexington, Ky., 1959), I, 677.

17. Julius W. Pratt, *The Expansionists of 1812* (New York, 1925); Thomas A. Bailey, *A Diplomatic History of the American People* (New York, 1950), pp. 129-39.

18. Monroe to John Taylor, 13 Je 12, Monroe MS, LC; Henry Clay to Thomas Bodley, 18 D 13, Clay, *Papers*, I, 842.

19. Tench Coxe to Jonathan Roberts, 12 D 11, Roberts MS, HSP; Gideon Granger to John Tod, 26 D 11, Granger MS, LC; Hugh Nelson to Charles Everette, 16 D 11, Nelson MS, LC; Felix Grundy, Richard M. Johnson, and John A. Harper in *Annals*, 12th Cong., 1st Sess., pp. 426-27, 457, 657; Concord *New Hampshire Patriot*, 4 F 12; Windsor *Vermont Republican*, 27 Ap 12.

20. Grundy and Harper in *Annals*, 12th Cong., 1st Sess., pp. 426-27, 657; Granger to John Tod, 26 D 11, Granger MS, LC.

21. John A. Harper to William Plumer, 13 My 12, Plumer MS, LC.

22. Harper in *National Intelligencer*, 18 Ja 12; Harper to Plumer, 29 Ap 12, 13 Ap 12, Plumer MS, LC. See also, Harper to Plumer, 2 D 11, 2 Ap 12, 7 Ap 12, 14 Je 12, Plumer MS, LC; and Harper to Plumer, 24 Mr 12, Plumer MS, NYHS.

23. William Plumer to John A. Harper, 7 Ap 12, Plumer MS, NYHS; Harper to Plumer, 9 My 12, 21 My 12, 14 Je 12, Plumer MS, LC.

24. *Annals*, 12th Cong., 1st Sess., pp. 322–23.

25. Gideon Granger to John Tod, 26 D 11, Granger MS, LC; Hugh Nelson to Charles Everette, 16 D 11, Nelson MS, LC; Jesse Franklin to William Lenoir, 12 F 12, Lenoir MS, UNC.

26. *Annals*, 12th Cong., 1st Sess., pp. 322–23.

27. Harper to Plumer, 14 Je 12, Plumer MS, LC.

28. Brant, *Madison the President*, pp. 442–47; Monroe to Governor David Mitchell, 4 Ap 12, 2 My 12, Monroe MS, Read Collection, GaU; William H. Crawford to George Mathews, 4 My 12, Crawford MS, Read Collection, GaU.

29. Ralph Isaacs to George Mathews, 2 My 12, Isaacs MS, Read Collection, GaU; William H. Crawford to Mathews, 4 My 12, Crawford MS, Read Collection, GaU; Crawford to James Monroe, 9 S 12, Monroe MS, LC. On September 9 Crawford wrote Monroe as follows: "The inconveniences which our fellow citizens of the South Eastern parts of the State suffer, from the desertion, & employment of their negroes, by the Spaniards, as soldiers, & the inducements which they hold out to the blacks to desert, together with depredations of the Indians, are so great, that I should be willing to obtain possession of [Florida] on any terms."

30. Madison, Draft of Message on Florida (not sent), 1812, Vol. 91, Madison MS, LC; James Monroe to Governor David Mitchell, 6 Jl 12, Monroe MS, Read Collection, GaU; Crawford to Mathews, 4 My 12, Crawford MS, Read Collection, GaU. For sentiment favoring the occupation of Florida in a war with England, see Crawford to Mathews, 4 My 12, Crawford MS, Read Collection, GaU; Anthony Porter to Governor David Mitchell, 8 Jl 12, Porter MS, Read Collection, GaU; Felix Grundy to Andrew Jackson, 4 D 11, Jackson MS, LC. For continuing sentiment in favor of a military occupation of Florida, see Crawford to Thomas Flournoy, 11 N 12, 26 D 12, Flournoy MS, LC; Crawford to David Bettetchell, 4 D 12, to ?, 3 Ja 13, Crawford MS, LC; Bolling Hall to Thomas Flournoy, 11 N 12, Flournoy MS, LC; Charles Tait to William Jones, 11 Ja 13, Jones MS, GaHS; Tait to David Mitchell, 26 Ja 14, Tait MS, Read Collection, GaU.

31. Madison, Draft of Message to Congress on Florida (not sent), 1812, Vol. 91, Madison MS, LC.

32. *Annals*, 12th Cong., 1st Sess., pp. 324–26. The Florida issue was revived in subsequent sessions. See *Annals*, 12th Cong., 2d Sess., p. 130, and William H. Crawford to ?, 3 Ja 13, Crawford MS, LC.

33. Monroe to George Hay, 16 O 12, George Hay to Monroe, 9 O 12, 1 N 12, Monroe MS, NYPL; Clay to Thomas Bodley, 18 D 13, Clay, *Papers*, I, 842.

34. Calhoun Speeches, 12 D 11, 14 Ja 13, 15 Ja 14, 25 F 14, *The Papers of John C. Calhoun*, ed. by Robert L. Meriwether (Columbia, S.C., 1959), I, 82, 154, 190, 229; Jonathan Roberts to Pascal Hollingsworth, 13

Ap 12, in *National Intelligencer*, 16 Ap 12 (MS draft in Roberts MS, HSP); Monroe to John Taylor, 13 Je 12, Monroe MS, LC; Clay to Thomas Bodley, 18 D 13, Clay, *Papers*, I, 842.

Chapter 7. *Antiwar Republicans*

1. William H. Crawford to John Milledge, 9 My 12, Crawford MS, LC; Porter in *Annals of Congress*, 12th Cong., 1st Sess., p. 1594; Peter B. Porter to William Eustis, 19 Ap 12, 20 Ap 12, Letters Received, War Department Branch, NA.

2. Thomas Sammons to James Lansing, 17 Ja 12, 18 My 12, Sammons MS, Ft. Johnson, NY; John Randolph to James Garnett, 21 Ap 12, Randolph-Garnett, MS, VaU; Thomas Sammons to Governor Daniel Tompkins, 18 Je 12, Tompkins MS, Box 3, Package 3, NYSL.

3. Martin Chittenden to Jonathan Hubbard, 6 Ap 12, Hubbard MS in Stevens Collection, NYSL; Samuel L. Mitchill to William Plumer, 17 Ja 12, Plumer MS, LC; Mitchill in *Annals*, 12th Cong., 1st Sess., pp. 1610, 1635, 1637, 1681.

4. Conditions on the northwestern frontier may be followed in "Thomas Worthington and the War of 1812," *Document Transcriptions of the War of 1812 in the Northwest*, ed. by Richard C. Knopf (Columbus, Ohio, 1957), III, 17–101; "The National Intelligencer Reports on the War of 1812 in the Northwest," *Document Transcriptions of the War of 1812 in the Northwest*, ed. by Richard C. Knopf (Columbus, Ohio, 1958), V, 1–100, and Register of Letters Received, War Department Branch, NA, especially addressed to Ninian Edwards, William Henry Harrison, and Charles Scott. Thomas Worthington, Notes on Speech, June, 1812, Worthington MS, RCHS. Also letters exchanged among Edward Tiffin, Return J. Meigs, and Thomas Worthington in Worthington MS, RCHS. Alec R. Gilpin, *The War of 1812 in the Old Northwest* (East Lansing, Mich., 1958), pp. 23–62, describes the Hull expedition.

5. Edward Tiffin to Thomas Worthington, 12 Ap 12, Worthington MS, RCHS; Alexander Campbell to Worthington, 17 Je 12, "Worthington and the War of 1812," p. 96.

6. *Annals*, 12th Cong., 1st Sess., pp. 266–98.

7. Thomas Worthington, Diary, 5 N 11, Worthington MS, LC; Worthington to Return J. Meigs, 8 Ja 12, Worthington MS, RCHS; Worthington, Diary, 14 Je 12, Worthington MS, LC. See also A. J. Foster, Diary, 13 My 12, 24 My 12, Foster MS, LC, for reports on Worthington's views.

8. Worthington, Diary, 16 D 11, Worthington MS, LC; Worthington to Return J. Meigs, 30 N 11, 8 Ja 12, 28 Mr 12, Worthington MS, RCHS; Worthington, Diary, 13 My 12, 14 Je 12, Worthington MS, LC.

9. Worthington to an Ohio State Representative, November, 1812, Worthington MS, RCHS. See also Worthington, Notes for Speech, June, 1812, Worthington MS, RCHS, and Alfred B. Sears, *Thomas Worthing-*

ton: Father of Ohio Statehood (Columbus, Ohio, 1958), p. 170. Contemporaries understood Worthington as opposed to the war declaration on the grounds of timing. Sears, *Worthington*, pp. 191, 193.

10. *Speech of the Hon. Josiah Bartlett at Kingston Plains, 10 September, 1812* (Portsmouth, N.H., 1812), p. 18, New Hampshire Historical Society, Concord; *Annals*, 12th Cong., 1st Sess., pp. 1635, 1680–82; Josiah Bartlett, Jr., to Ezra Bartlett, 30 My 12, 18 Je 12, Bartlett MS, LC. Bartlett also wrote to another correspondent concerning the war declaration: "I did think the measure premature & gave it my negative 'till it was adopted by both branches then on the question to postpone acting on the amendments I did oppose." Bartlett to Judge George Wingate, 18 Je 12, Dreer Collection, HSP.

11. *Annals*, 12th Cong., 1st Sess., pp. 1680–82; Richard Cutts to Madison, 8 Ap 12, Madison MS, LC; Richard Cutts to Brother, 29 Je 12, "Some Letters of Richard Cutts," *Collections and Proceedings of the Maine Historical Society*, IX (1898), 41; Dolley Madison to Mrs. Richard Cutts, 21 Mr 12, Madison-Cutts MS (microfilm), LC. On June 21, A. J. Foster, the British minister, recorded in his diary that "Cutts told me he was ruined." Foster MS, LC.

12. Richard Cutts to Madison, 8 Ap 12, Madison MS, LC; Cutts to Father, 10 N 12, to ?, 17 Je 12, "Some Letters of Richard Cutts," pp. 43, 40.

13. Peleg Tallman to ?, 4 N 40, quoted in Walter H. Sturtevant, "Peleg Tallman, Sailor of the Revolution, Master Mariner, and Member of Congress," *Collections and Proceedings of the Maine Historical Society*, X (1899), 442–45; Tallman to William King, 6 Je 12, quoted in Sturtevant, "Peleg Tallman," p. 436; Tallman to King, 6 N 11, 18 N 11, 21 N 11, King MS, Maine HS.

14. Henry Adams, *History of the United States* (New York, 1930), V, 363–64; Irving Brant, *James Madison: Secretary of State, 1800–1809* (Indianapolis, Ind., 1953), pp. 430–32; Irving Brant, *James Madison: the President, 1809–1812* (Indianapolis, Ind., 1956), pp. 269, 310; Dixon Ryan Fox, *The Decline of Aristocracy in the Politics of New York* (New York, 1919), pp. 58, 65, 164, 202; David Ellis and others, *A Short History of New York State* (Ithaca, N.Y., 1957), pp. 132–39; Samuel Smith to ?, 14 D 05, Smith MS, LC; William H. Crawford to John Milledge, 9 My 12, Crawford MS, LC. Two friendly accounts are E. Wilder Spaulding, *His Excellency George Clinton* (New York, 1938), and Dorothie Bobbé, *De Witt Clinton* (New York, 1933).

15. *Tribute to the Memory of De Witt Clinton* (Albany, N.Y., 1828); George Clinton to De Witt Clinton, 15 N 03, to Anthony Lamb, 8 Ja 09, quoted in Spaulding, *George Clinton*, pp. 243, 297; De Witt Clinton to Archibald McIntyre, 6 Ja 09, Misc. MS, NYHS; De Witt Clinton to Pierre Van Cortlandt, 7 Ap 12, Misc. MS, NYHS; De Witt Clinton journal entry, 1810, quoted in William W. Campbell, *The Life and Writings of De Witt Clinton* (New York, 1849), p. 126. See Jefferson's com-

ment while traveling in Europe in the 1780s on an observed difference in character between the citizens of the republic of Frankfort and those of the landgraviate of Hesse. Bernard Bailyn, "Boyd's Jefferson: Notes for a Sketch," *New England Quarterly*, XXXIII (1960), pp. 386–87.

16. George Clinton to De Witt Clinton, 10 Ap 08, De Witt Clinton MS, Columbia. For further reference on this point, see Roger H. Brown, "A Republic in Peril: the Crisis of 1812," (M.S. dissertation, Harvard Archives), pp. 205–7.

17. George Clinton to De Witt Clinton, 12 Ja 08, 13 F 08, 2 Mr 08, 10 Ap 08, De Witt Clinton MS, Columbia; Nicholas Gilman to Josiah Bartlett, Jr., 18 Mr 10, Bartlett MS, LC; Nicholas Gilman to George Logan, 28 Ja 12, 27 Jl 13, 31 D 13, Logan MS, HSP; De Witt Clinton journal entry, 1810, quoted in Campbell, *Life and Writings of De Witt Clinton*, p. 125; Jabez Hammond, *The History of Political Parties in the State of New York from the Ratification of the Federal Constitution to December, 1840* (Cooperstown, N.Y., 1846), I, 260, 263, 276, 285. Historian Hammand had been a Clintonian leader in Cherry Valley, New York, during the Jeffersonian period.

18. Samuel Shaw to Governor Daniel Tompkins, April, 1812, Tompkins MS, Box 1, Package 1, NYSL; Nicholas Gilman to George Logan, 28 Ja 12, Logan MS, HSP; George Clinton to John McKesson, 19 Ja 12, George Clinton MS, NYSL; Thomas B. Cooke to Governor Daniel B. Tompkins, 6 N 11, Tompkins MS, Box 7, Package 1, NYSL; *Annals*, 12th Cong., 1st Sess., pp. 86, 187–89, 267–98.

19. *Annals*, 12th Cong., 1st Sess., pp. 267–98; Nicholas Gilman to George Logan, 14 Je 12, Logan MS, HSP; Obadiah German in *Annals*, 12th Cong., 1st Sess., pp. 271–83; New York *Columbian* (a Clintonian newspaper), 8 Je 12, 17 Je 12.

20. Obadiah German in *Annals*, 12th Cong., 1st Sess., pp. 278, 282–83; Nicholas Gilman to George Logan, 27 Jl 13, Logan MS, HSP.

21. Matthias B. Tallmadge to Pierre Van Cortlandt, Jr., 10 Je 12, Van Cortlandt MS, NYPL; De Witt Clinton to Pierre Van Cortlandt, Jr., 7 Ap 12, Misc. MS, NYHS; Obadiah German in *Annals*, 12th Cong., 1st Sess., pp. 272–82.

22. German in *Annals*, 12th Cong., 1st Sess., pp. 279, 282; Edmund Genet (?) to Pierre Van Cortlandt, Jr., 15 Je 12, Van Cortlandt MS, NYPL.

23. New York *Columbian*, 4 Je 12.

24. Hugh Nelson to Charles Everette, 13 N 11, Nelson MS, LC; John Nicholas to Wilson C. Nicholas, 28 Ja 07, W. C. Nicholas MS, VaU. Present-day estimates of his career vary widely. Henry Adams, *John Randolph* (Boston, 1898); William C. Bruce, *John Randolph of Roanoke* (New York, 1922); William E. Stokes, Jr., "John Randolph: a Virginia Portrait" (M.S. dissertation, 1955, University of Virginia); Donald Mac-Phee, "The Tertium Quid Movement: a Study in Political Insurgency" (M.S. dissertation, 1959, University of California); Russell Kirk, *Ran-*

dolph of Roanoke: a Study in Conservative Thought (Chicago, 1951).

25. Randolph to Joseph H. Nicholson, 1 Ja 01, quoted in MacPhee, "Tertium Quid Movement," pp. 6–7; Randolph to Henry St. George Tucker, 21 Mr 01, Theodorus B. Meyers Collection, NYPL; Memoir of William A. Burwell, pp. 41–42, Burwell MS, LC.

26. *Annals*, 8th Cong., 1st Sess., pp. 1115, 2d Sess., pp. 1032, 1107; Randolph in *Annals*, 9th Cong., 1st Sess., p. 567; James Garnett to Constituents, 1806, in Richmond *Enquirer*, 25 Ap 06, quoted in MacPhee, "Tertium Quid Movement," pp. 127–28; MacPhee, "Tertium Quid Movement," pp. 77–116; Randolph to George Hay, 3 Ja 07 (misdated 06), Randolph MS (microfilm), UNC; Randolph to James Garnett, 27 Ap 06, Garnett-Randolph MS, VaU.

27. Randolph to James Garnett, 14 S 09, Garnett-Randolph MS, VaU; Randolph to Joseph H. Nicholson, 17 F 11, Nicholson MS, LC. For detailed references, see Brown, "Republic in Peril," pp. 213–14.

28. Randolph to Joseph Nicholson, 28 Mr 08, 15 Ag 08 (misdated 09), 13 N 08, 4 D 09, Nicholson MS, LC; Randolph to James Garnett, 10 F 11, Garnett-Randolph MS, VaU; Randolph in *Annals*, 10th Cong., 2d Sess., pp. 1338–50.

29. Randolph in *Annals*, 12th Cong., 1st Sess., pp. 441, 707, 1090, 716, 1089, 527, also 1590.

30. Randolph in *Annals*, 12th Cong., 1st Sess., pp. 441–55, 526–45, 707–16, especially 447, 533–34, 450, 543–44. Randolph to James Garnett, 12 Ja 12, 20 Ja 12, 1 F 12, 2 Ap 12, 14 Ap 12, 29 Ap 12, Garnett-Randolph MS, VaU; Randolph to Richard Randolph, 7 F 12, Randolph MS, LC; Randolph to Josiah Quincy, Jr., 11 D 13, to Francis Scott Key, 12 S 13, quoted in Bruce, *John Randolph*, I, 404, 399–400.

31. Randolph in *Annals*, 12th Cong., 1st Sess., pp. 451, 450; Randolph to Garnett, 15 F 12, 29 Ap 12, Garnett-Randolph MS, VaU; Randolph to Richard Randolph, 7 F 12, Randolph MS, LC.

32. Randolph to James Garnett, 1 F 12, 13 F 12, Garnett-Randolph MS, VaU; Randolph to Francis Scott Key, 22 My 13, quoted in Bruce, *John Randolph*, I, 389.

33. Randolph to James Garnett, 13 D 11, Garnett-Randolph MS, VaU. "Our friend Dick [Stanford] gave them an old fashioned & most admirable discourse to day. We shall stand (or rather *fall*) together."

34. Stanford in *Annals*, 12th Cong., 1st Sess., pp. 673–74, 669, 675; Stanford to George Logan, 4 Ja 12 (misdated 11), 12 Je 12, Logan MS, HSP. Also, Stanford in *Annals*, 12th Cong., 1st Sess., pp. 511–16.

Chapter 8. This Wicked, Foolish War

1. Stephen G. Kurtz, *The Presidency of John Adams: the Collapse of Federalism* (Philadelphia, 1957), is a good account of Federalism during the Adams administration. Lynn Turner, *William Plumer of New Hampshire, 1759–1850* (Chapel Hill, N.C., 1962), pp. 101–3, 122–31, describes Federalist obstructionism during the first years of the Jefferson

regime. Jefferson to Caesar Rodney, 24 F 04, to De Witt Clinton, 2 D 03, *The Writings of Thomas Jefferson*, ed. by P. L. Ford (New York, 1892–99), VIII, 296, 283. Norman Stamps, "Political Parties in Connecticut, 1789–1819" (M.S. dissertation, 1950, Yale University), pp. 162–226, describes for one state the constant division between the parties over legislation.

2. Fisher Ames to Christopher Gore, 3 O 03, *The Works of Fisher Ames*, ed. by Seth Ames (Boston, 1854), I, 323. A revealing discussion of the Federalist switch is Paul Boyer, "The Northern Federalists and the Louisiana Purchase" (M.S. honors thesis, 1960, Harvard Archives). Entry of 20 O 03, *William Plumer's Memorandum of Proceedings in the United States Senate, 1803–1807*, ed. by Everett S. Brown (New York, 1923), p. 13; Christopher Gore to Rufus King, 1 N 03, *The Life and Correspondence of Rufus King*, ed. by Charles R. King (New York, 1894–1900), IV, 320; Turner, *William Plumer*, pp. 104–13.

3. A careful, judicious exploration of the evidence on the secessionist plot is Meredith Mason Brown, "The Northern Confederacy: High-Federalist Political Attitudes and the Separatist Movement of 1803–1804" (M.S. honors thesis, 1961, Harvard Archives). Also, Turner, *William Plumer*, pp. 133–50, 345–46.

4. Josiah Quincy, Jr. to Oliver Wolcott, 5 S 03, quoted in Boyer, "Northern Federalists and Louisiana," pp. 46–52; Samuel Taggart to John Taylor, 28 F 08, "Letters of Samuel Taggart, Representative in Congress, 1803–1814," *Proceedings of the American Antiquarian Society*, XXXIII (1923), 307–8. William Plumer, while a Federalist, wrote in 1803 in reference to the Republicans and their program: "Are you so unreasonable as to expect an impure fountain will send forth sweet water!" Plumer to Edward Livermore, 13 Ja 03, quoted in Turner, *William Plumer*, p. 107.

5. Elbridge Gerry to James Madison, 19 F 06, Madison MS, LC; Timothy Pickering to Fisher Ames, 29 D 05, 2 F 06, Pickering MS, MHS; Samuel Taggart to John Taylor, 2 F 06, "Letters of Samuel Taggart," p. 176.

6. Chauncey Goodrich to John Treadwell, 26 Ja 10, Treadwell MS, CHS; John Rutledge, Jr., to Harrison Gray Otis, 29 Jl 06, Otis MS, MHS; James Bayard to Andrew Bayard, 30 Ja 06, "Papers of James A. Bayard, 1796–1815," *Annual Report of the American Historical Association for the Year 1913*, II, 164–65; Samuel Taggart to John Taylor, 2 F 06, 12 Mr 06, 20 D 06 (misdated 07), "Letters of Samuel Taggart," pp. 173–78, 189, 221.

7. Timothy Pitkin to John Treadwell, 23 Mr 09, Treadwell MS, CHS; George Cabot to John Rutledge, Jr., 15 Ag 08, Rutledge MS, UNC.

8. Timothy Pickering to Timothy Williams, 21 D 07, to John Mason, 4 Ja 09, Pickering MS, MHS; James Hillhouse to John Treadwell, 22 D 07, 23 Ja 09, Treadwell MS, CHS; Chauncey Goodrich to Oliver

Wolcott, 23 D 07, 31 D 07, Wolcott MS, V, CHS; Harrison Gray Otis to John Rutledge, 13 F 08, Rutledge MS, UNC.

9. Abraham Van Vechten to Ebenezer Foote, 28 Ag 08, Federalist MS, VaU.

10. For example, Chauncey Goodrich to John Treadwell, 26 Ja 10, 28 Ja 11, Treadwell MS, CHS.

11. James Hillhouse to John Treadwell, 4 Ja 08, Treadwell MS, CHS; Chauncey Goodrich to John Treadwell, 26 Ja 10, Treadwell MS, CHS; Chauncey Goodrich to Oliver Wolcott, Jr., 31 D 07, Wolcott MS, V, CHS. By 1812 Goodrich had added self-armed merchant convoys to the Federalist counterplan. "We ought, I think to claim of the Government a defence of our commerce against all nations, and take on ourselves the consequences, & perils that grow out of such defence whatever they may be. We ought to insist, that a free ingress, & egress into, & out of our harbours should be maintained—insults in them from foreign ships quelled, merchant ships allowed to arm & associate together & our exertions be on the water with all our means, on a defensive plan. In doing this, we ought not to deal in generals merely, but when we come to details afford to the community a conviction, that we are both sincere, & in earnest. In this way, we put the administration to the test, meet their terrapin system with a substitute, & give to the country a pledge, that we respect, and are ready to vindicate our rights against every nation." Goodrich to ?, 7 Ap 12, Goodrich MS, Yale. It is difficult to take this proposal as much more than a party device to win public confidence, as Goodrich himself implies. It is significant that Goodrich wanted Federalists to be more specific in their recommendations. Federalists had not done much constructive thinking about precise means to protect American commerce against belligerent seizures.

12. Samuel Taggart to John Taylor, 30 D 08, "Letters of Samuel Taggart," pp. 328–29; Joseph Pearson to John Steele, 26 Ja 10, 18 Ja 11, The Papers of John Steele, ed. by H. Wagstaff (Raleigh, N.C., 1924), II, 620–21, 651; Timothy Pickering to Gouverneur Morris, 12 Ja 10, Pickering MS, MHS.

13. Chauncey Goodrich to John Treadwell, 28 Ja 11, Treadwell MS, CHS; Timothy Pickering to Samuel Williams, 9 Ja 10, Pickering MS, MHS; Rufus King to John Trumbull, 24 Ap 09, quoted in Bradford Perkins, Prologue to War: England and the United States, 1805–1812 (Berkeley, Calif., 1961), pp. 218–19.

14. A. J. Foster to Marquis Wellesley, 9 N 11, Foreign Office Series 5, LXXVII (photostats), LC; Petition of Richmond Virginia Federalists to Congress, 1812, Senate Petitions, 12th Cong., Legislative Branch, NA; Harrison Gray Otis to Harrison Gray, 30 Ap 11, January, 1812, quoted in Samuel E. Morison, Harrison Gray Otis (Boston, 1913), II, 36–37.

15. Samuel Taggart to Timothy Pickering, 24 Ap 12, Pickering MS, MHS; Josiah Quincy, Jr., to Harrison Gray Otis, 26 N 11, Otis MS, MHS.

16. Josiah Quincy, Jr., to Harrison Gray Otis, 26 N 11, 8 N 11, Otis MS, MHS; James Bayard to William Wells, 12 Ja 12, "Papers of James A. Bayard," p. 188. Also, James Bayard to Caesar Rodney, 26 Ja 12, "James Asheton Bayard Letters, 1802–1814," *Bulletin of the New York Public Library*, IV (1900), pp. 233–34; William Reed to Timothy Pickering, 12 N 11, 20 Ja 12, Pickering MS, MHS; Samuel Taggart to John Taylor, 14 D 11, "Letters of Samuel Taggart," p. 370; Abijah Bigelow to Wife, 1 Ja 12, 5 Ja 12, 25 Ja 12, 9 F 12, 22 Mr 12, "Letters of Abijah Bigelow, Member of Congress, to his Wife, 1810–1815," *Proceedings of the American Antiquarian Society*, XL (1930), Part 2, 323–32.

17. Joseph Pearson to John Steele, 2 Mr 12, Steele MS, UNC; Outerbridge Horsey to Richard Bassett, 5 Ja 12, Dreer Collection, HSP; Outerbridge Horsey to Thomas Bradford, 4 F 12, Gratz Collection, HSP; Elijah Brigham to Dwight Foster, 11 F 12, Chamberlain Collection, Boston Public Library. Also, Benjamin Tallmadge to James McHenry, 29 F 12, McHenry MS, LC; Martin Chittenden to Jonathan Hubbard, 24 Ja 12, Hubbard MS, Stevens Collection, NYSL.

18. Josiah Quincy, Jr., to Harrison Gray Otis, 26 N 11, Otis MS, MHS; William Reed to Timothy Pickering, 20 Ja 12, 18 F 12, Pickering MS, MHS; Samuel Taggart to John Taylor, 14 D 11, "Letters of Samuel Taggart," p. 370; Samuel Dana to Timothy Pickering, 30 Ja 12, Pickering MS, MHS.

19. A. J. Foster to Marquis Wellesley, 2 F 12 (secret and in cipher), Foreign Office Series 5, LXXXIV (photostats), LC; Extract of letter from anonymous Federalist to Foster, 10 F 12, enclosed in Foster to Wellesley (secret), 12 Mr 12, Foreign Office Series 5, LXXXIV (photostats), LC; Alexander Hanson to F. J. Jackson, 7 Mr 12, quoted in Perkins, *Prologue to War*, pp. 352–53.

20. James Bayard to Caesar Rodney, 11 Je 12, "James Bayard Letters," p. 238; John Davenport to John Cotton Smith, 13 My 12, Smith MS, CHS. Also, William Reed to Timothy Pickering, 18 F 12, Pickering MS, MHS; Samuel Taggart to John Taylor, 20 Ja 12, "Letters of Samuel Taggart," pp. 378–79; Abijah Bigelow to Wife, 9 F 12, 22 Mr 12, "Letters of Abijah Bigelow," pp. 328–29, 331–32; Outerbridge Horsey to James Canby, 25 Mr 12, Canby MS (copies), Delaware HS.

21. Josiah Quincy, Jr., to Oliver Wolcott, Jr., 15 Ap 12, Wolcott, Jr., MS, XXIV, CHS; Samuel Taggart to John Taylor, 6 F 12, 21 Mr 12, 16 Ap 12, 26 Ap 12, "Letters of Samuel Taggart," pp. 381, 391–94; Quincy to Wolcott, 15 Ap 12, Wolcott, Jr., MS, XXIV, CHS; Elijah Brigham, Notes of Speech (no date, from internal evidence 1812–14), Brigham MS, American Antiquarian Society, Worcester; William Hunter in *Annals of Congress*, 13th Cong., 1st Sess., pp. 528–29.

The term "war hawks" was in common usage among Federalists during the session to denote presumably belligerent Republicans. Other terms were "war party," "war advocates," and "war spirits." For specific references to "war hawks" see Josiah Quincy, Jr., to Harrison Gray Otis, 26 N 11, Otis MS, MHS; William Reed to Timothy Pickering, 25 Ap 12, Pickering MS, MHS; Benjamin Tallmadge to James McHenry, 11 Ap 12, McHenry MS, LC; Samuel Taggart to John Taylor, 23 Je 12, "Letters of Samuel Taggart," p. 407.

22. Josiah Quincy, Jr., Memoirs, quoted in Edmund Quincy, *Life of Josiah Quincy of Massachusetts* (Boston, 1868), p. 259. Also, Samuel Taggart to Timothy Pickering, 11 My 12, Pickering MS, MHS.

23. Martin Chittenden to Jonathan Hubbard, 27 Je 12, Hubbard MS in Stevens Collection, NYSL.

24. Benjamin Stoddert to John Steele, 3 S 12, Steele MS, UNC; Stoddert to Robert G. Harper, 4 S 12, Harper-Pennington MS, MdHS.

25. Josiah Quincy, Jr., to Harrison Gray Otis, 8 N 11, Otis MS, MHS; Abijah Bigelow to Wife, 16 Je 12, 24 Je 12, "Letters of Abijah Bigelow," pp. 339-40; Roger Griswold to Samuel Dana, quoted in Samuel Dana to Timothy Pickering, 3 F 12, Pickering MS, MHS; also Dana to Griswold, 7 F 12, Griswold MS, Yale; Outerbridge Horsey to James Canby, 17 Je 12, Canby MS (copies), Delaware HS; James Bayard to Andrew Bayard, 11 Je 12, "Papers of James Bayard," pp. 199-200; Benjamin Tallmadge to James McHenry, 11 Ap 12, McHenry MS, LC; Clement C. Moore to Mother, 4 Je 12, Misc. MS, Museum of the City of New York; Martin Chittenden to Jonathan Hubbard, 24 My 12, Hubbard MS, Stevens Collection, NYSL; Chauncey Goodrich to ?, 7 My 12, Goodrich MS, Yale. Also, John Davenport to John Cotton Smith, 13 My 12, Smith MS, CHS; William Reed to Timothy Pickering, 25 Ap 12, Pickering MS, MHS; William R. Davie to Ernest Haywood, 8 Ap 12, Haywood MS, UNC.

26. Benjamin Tallmadge to James McHenry, 11 Ap 12, 17 Je 12, McHenry MS, LC; Joseph Pearson to John Steele, 19 Je 12, Steele MS, UNC; Leonard D. White to Daniel White (?), 21 Je 12, Daniel White MS, Essex Institute, Salem. Also, Martin Chittenden to Jonathan Hubbard, 1 Je 12, 18 Je 12, 27 Je 12, Hubbard MS, Stevens Collection, NYSL.

27. Joseph Pearson to John Steele, 19 Je 12, Steele MS, UNC; Josiah Quincy, Jr. to Harrison Gray Otis, 8 N 11, Otis MS, MHS; William Reed to Timothy Pickering, 12 N 11, Pickering MS, MHS; Elijah Brigham to Dwight Foster, 30 N 12, Chamberlain Collection, Boston Public Library; Martin Chittenden to Jonathan Hubbard, 27 Je 12, Hubbard MS, Stevens Collection, NYSL.

Chapter 9. A Long Stride Towards Permanency

1. Christopher Ellery to Madison, 24 Je 12, Madison MS, LC; Boston *Independent Chronicle*, 25 Je 12; Philadelphia *Democratic Press* in Boston *Independent Chronicle*, 29 Je 12. Hartford *Connecticut Courant* in *True American and Commercial Advertiser*, 26 Je 12; Boston *Columbian Centinel*, 24 Je 12; *American Mercury* in Philadelphia *Aurora*, 27 Je 12; *Boston Patriot*, 24 Je 12.

2. Thomas Sammons to James Lansing, 8 My 12, Sammons MS, Ft. Johnson, N.Y.; Clement C. Moore to Mother, 30 My 12, 4 Je 12, Misc. MS, Museum of the City of NY.

3. Benjamin W. Labaree, *Patriots and Partisans: the Merchants of Newburyport, 1764–1815* (Cambridge, Mass., 1962), pp. 141–42; William T. Whitney, Jr., "The Crowninshields of Salem, 1800–1808," *Essex Institute Historical Collections*, XCIV (1958), pp. 16–17, 31; William Plumer, Autobiography, quoted in Lynn Turner, *William Plumer of New Hampshire, 1759–1850* (Chapel Hill, N.C., 1962), p. 66.

4. Hamilton to Edward Carrington, 26 My 92, *The Works of Alexander Hamilton*, ed. by H. C. Lodge (New York, 1903), IX, 534–35; George Cabot to Timothy Pickering, 5 Ap 08, quoted in Henry Cabot Lodge, *Life and Letters of George Cabot* (Boston, 1878), p. 391.

5. Hamilton to Gouverneur Morris, 27 F 02, *The Basic Ideas of Alexander Hamilton*, ed. by Richard B. Morris (New York, 1957), p. 440; Charles Carroll to James McHenry, 4 N 00, quoted in Bernard C. Steiner, *The Life and Correspondence of James McHenry* (Cleveland, Ohio, 1907), pp. 473–75.

6. Stephen Higginson to Timothy Pickering, 17 Mr 04, William Plumer to John Q. Adams, 20 D 28, *Documents Relating to New-England Federalism, 1800–1815*, ed. by Henry Adams (Boston, 1877), pp. 361, 146; Harrison Gray Otis to John Rutledge, Jr., 8 Ja 09, Rutledge MS, UNC; Mrs. Henry Knox to Mrs. E. Thatcher, 20 Jl 12, Mrs. Henry Knox MS, Boston Public Library; Gerry to Henry Dearborn, 2 S 11, J. S. H. Fogg Collection, Maine HS.

7. William Plumer to John A. Harper, 2 Mr 12, Plumer MS; W. C. Nicholas to Ezekiel Bacon, 26 Je 08, Nicholas MS, LC.

8. James Renwick, *Life of De Witt Clinton* (New York, 1840), p. 70; Thomas Worthington, Diary, 3 N 11, 14 Je 12, Worthington MS, LC. The effect of fear on personal perception is well illustrated in the classic experiment described by Henry A. Murray, "The Effect of Fear upon Estimates of the Maliciousness of Other Personalities," in Chalmers L. Stacey and Manfred F. DeMartino, eds., *Understanding Human Motivation* (Cleveland, Ohio, 1958), pp. 327–42.

9. George Washington, Farewell Address, 17 S 96, *Sources of the American Republic,* ed. by Marvin Meyers, Alexander Kern, and John G. Cawelti (Chicago, 1960), p. 206; Jefferson to Thomas McKean, 24 Jl 01, to Levi Lincoln, 28 Ag 01, *The Writings of Thomas Jefferson*, ed. by P. L. Ford (New York, 1892–99), VIII, 79, 84. For a brief discussion of the eighteenth-century view of parties and factions, see David S. Lovejoy, *Rhode Island Politics and the American Revolution, 1760–1776* (Providence, R.I., 1958), p. 29.

10. John C. Calhoun to James Macbride, 17 F 12, *The Papers of John C. Calhoun*, ed. by Robert L. Meriwether (Columbia, S.C., 1959), I, 90; William Jarvis, Jr., to Henry Dearborn, 24 N 08, Chamberlain Collection, Boston Public Library; John McKim, Jr., to Henry Clay, 13 My 12,

The Papers of Henry Clay, ed. by James F. Hopkins (Lexington, Ky., 1959), I, 654; Joseph H. Nicholson to Albert Gallatin, 7 My 12, Gallatin MS, NYHS; Macon in *Annals of Congress*, 12th Cong., 1st Sess., pp. 661–62; Macon to Joseph H. Nicholson, 28 F 09, 25 Mr 12, Nicholson MS, LC; Calhoun to James Macbride, 23 Je 13, to Virgil Maxcy, 2 My 12, Calhoun, *Papers*, I, 177–78, 101; Edward Fox to Jonathan Roberts, 16 Je 12, Roberts MS, HSP.

11. John Stokely to James Monroe, 3 F 12, Misc. MS, Foreign Affairs Branch, NA; Richard Goodell to Wyllys Goodell, 7 N 11, Misc. MS, NYHS; Philadelphia *Aurora*, 2 My 12; Clement C. Moore to Mother, 30 My 12, Misc. MS, Museum of the City of NY; John Stokes to Monroe, 5 D 12, Monroe MS, LC.

12. Clay Speech, 31 D 11, Clay, *Papers*, I, 609.

13. Calhoun to James Macbride, 17 F 12, Calhoun, *Papers*, I, 90; King in *Annals*, 12th Cong., 1st Sess., p. 516.

14. Monroe to Crawford, 3 D 12, *The Writings of James Monroe*, ed. by Stanislaus M. Hamilton (New York, 1898–1903), V, 227; George Hay to Monroe, 1 N 12, Monroe MS, NYPL; W. W. Bibb to William Jones, 31 O 14, Jones MS, GaHS; Roberts to Matthew Roberts, 17 F 15, Roberts MS, HSP.

INDEX